book m
W9-BPR-337

HISTORIC COSTUME FOR THE AMATEUR THEATRE

By the same author

Designing and Painting Scenery for the Theatre

Theatrecraft

The Magic of Make-up

Melvill's Complete Guide to Amateur Dramatics

Historic Costume for The Amateur Theatre and how to make it

By

HARALD MELVILL

WITH DRAWINGS BY THE AUTHOR

Foreword by

CHRISTOPHER HASSALL

PHILADELPHIA
DUFOUR EDITIONS
1964

Printed in Great Britain by
Clarke, Doble & Brendon Ltd.,
Oakfield Press, Cattedown, Plymouth
for Dufour Editions

Library of Congress Catalog Card Number 63-14356

With love and admiration
for
MONA VIVIAN
to whom I owe my first round of applause in the theatre
and in affectionate memory
of dear Mrs Vivian

'Fashion is what one wears oneself.
What is unfashionable is what other people wear.'

OSCAR WILDE
An Ideal Husband,
ACT III

CONTENTS

LIST OF ILLUSTRATIONS

FOREWORD

Whether you're setting out to make costumes for a play, or write a story, or paint a picture, it's the same sort of problem for everyone, and I'm pretty sure we all feel the same kind of misgiving at the start. Let me explain, and begin with my own line of country, writing. I shall come to yours in a moment. Reading this fascinating book has given me a good deal to think about. Your problems are certainly tricky at times. I see that now. So are mine.

Holding a pen, and the right hand resting at the top of a blank page, one is conscious of a challenge, and of its being almost, but not quite, too late to draw back. The feeling is that one has rashly let oneself in for the performance of an impossible feat. The problem, as it seems at first, is just how to make something out of nothing. If, after reflection, the pen moves, and goes on to cover a second page, and then another, all to good purpose, the writer stands a chance of being regarded as a 'creative' artist. He has actually succeeded in making something where before there was only a tantalizing void. It isn't altogether true, of course, that he has made his finished work out of literally *nothing*, for of course his mind must have been playing with an idea of sorts, and around that idea were gathering memories and associations. He is no superman. Neither are you, dear reader, no matter how talented you may be. Each of us is no more than a solitary individual alone with his native gift and his store-house of memory, and there's a severe limit to these resources in the mind of any one person. If only we could 'tap' one another's memories, what startling masterpieces would ensue! But that can never be. My point is that in the arts, no less than in the ordinary business of life, we all have to 'make do' with what we have got. 'What an inspiration!' is the customary cry when, say, a picture is hung in a new position in the sitting-room, or the dining-room curtains are dyed pink, or the wife appears in last year's hat which surprisingly matches her new frock, or a nephew produces a poem of his own which is by no means as bad as it might have been. In all these cases someone is making the best of what is to hand, and 'inspiration' isn't the wrong word for it. Haven't they done on a very modest plane what the so-called inspired artists have achieved on the heights? The creative moment is the essential thing, no matter how humble the means and simple the end in view. Without it our daily existence, no less than the life of Art, would be humdrum indeed. I believe that the faculty which brings it about can be cultivated, and in this we *all need help*. So no one can say he has nothing to learn. *You* haven't said it, dear reader, or you wouldn't be handling this book. I've never said it either, so there's hope for us both. Certainly we must make do with what we have got. We are reconciled to that. But we're anxious to learn how to make the best of ourselves.

In setting out to enjoy these pages, you realize that in order to be creative yourself, making the surprising best of the material at hand, you must make the acquaintance of a creative, yet practical, artist, so as to let him strike sparks out of you. You will listen to him talking, study his examples, watch him tackling problems not unlike your own, and observe how he makes do with the limited resources within reach. In my own time I have been in a position to exclaim 'What an inspiration!' of something he has accomplished, and that's why I can safely claim to know what I'm talking about when the topic is Harald Melvill and the products of his imagination and his practical hands.

We first met in a café somewhere near Charing Cross. He seemed huge, beaming with zest, as if he had life and to spare. And I was soon put at my ease by his huge smile. Even more reassuring, in the light of the matter in hand, was his air of confidence. This was in no way immodest or overbearing, but simply 'large', like his bodily frame, as of a man conscious of his powers and eager to bend them to a conundrum, the trickier the better. Hugh Miller had brought us together. He was about to produce a play of mine called *The Great Endeavour* at the Theatre Royal, Drury Lane, and I had let my own somewhat ill-organized 'creative moments' run away with me to the point of composing a script which gave rise to acute and unusual problems in the department of stage-setting. Frankly, I had no idea how the thing could be made practicable. In that ideal place, described by Desmond MacCarthy as 'the theatre under one's hat,' I knew what I wanted, of course, but knew also that I was blandly asking for the moon. With puckered brow I outlined the action (it was about Captain Cook's voyage to Australia) and explained, rather cautiously, how within a matter of seconds a drawing-room in Soho Square had to become the deck of a sailing ship and soon be transformed again to a garden on the island of Mauritius, all without lowering the curtain. Melville was free to walk out. No one had chained him to his chair. By the end of our light snack, however, he had sketched out on the back of the menu a scheme which enabled the whole sequence of scenes to work smoothly, almost literally, on oiled wheels. The originality of his design made its own contribution to the drama. And thereby hangs a moral. The theatre requires more than one dramatist at any one time. An author alone is not enough. Nor is two enough. Writer and designer need a producer to complete the triumvirate; all three contributing the fruit of their own creative moments to a satisfying theatrical experience. In that respect, and on this occasion, I was lucky. The unconventional script 'worked' in practical terms, and for that the author can claim none of the credit.

When next I had occasion to take refuge in Melvill's ingenuity, I was confronting him in a different capacity, this time as a producer. I had undertaken to produce *The Zeal of Thy House* in the Chapter House at Canterbury for the Cathedral Festival. The auditorium there had a wide platform at one end with no proscenium arch, and the vast proportions of the Gothic interior seemed to make any effective scenic design almost an impossibility. For one thing, any 'set', in the ordinary sense of the term, was bound to be dwarfed to the miniature stature of a doll's house; and for another, any plan that did not conform to the Gothic idiom would seem like a scale model left behind after an illustrated lecture on the Ideal Home. The play by Dorothy Sayers was, fortunately, about the building of the cathedral nave by William of Sens, so the problem of style was not as formidable as it might have been. But once again, as at Drury Lane, the question was how to keep the action moving without the use of a curtain or black-out, and once again Melvill made a virtue of necessity. He learned the architectural idiom of the building and designed a permanent set of Gothic ruins (for the plot turned on the question of rebuilding after damage by fire) which served the drama by making use of the surroundings.

Apart from the success of the production, this had a sequel which must have been peculiarly gratifying to the designer. One day, when no performance was in progress, and the usual tourists were roaming at large around the Precincts, the promotor of the Festival happened to enter the Chapter House and come upon a visitor from overseas who was gazing at Melvill's structure with a look of grave concern. On being asked whether anything in particular was the matter, the stranger remarked in tones of hushed sympathy that he had *no* idea the cathedral had been so badly knocked about by the bombs!

Our third association in the gentle craft of stage presentation was again at Canterbury, and now I was once more the author. The piece this time was a miniature opera, *The Man from Tuscany*, with music by Antony Hopkins, and the story was set in eighteenth-century Leipzig. Here was no opportunity for Gothic! But somehow Melvill made us accept the business end of the Chapter House as the apartments occupied by J. S. Bach and his family when he was organist and choirmaster at St. Thomas's. Like poetry, scenic design can, and perhaps should, evoke rather than literally state a situation. Anyway, having an eye for essentials, Melvill managed to evoke his period and place in an overwhelmingly Gothic context. And perhaps that illustrates rather well one of the chief lessons to be learned from reading this book. The true artist often achieves his creative moment by reducing his problem to the bare essentials, and thereafter evoking in the spectator's mind his period of design in setting or costume. And so it comes about that the amateur with especially limited resources of money and materials is, after all said and done, in a peculiarly advantageous position—granted he sees it in the proper light and accepts the imaginative challenge which it offers. He does not possess the wherewithal for stating anything literally. He *must* evoke imaginatively. Melvill is in his element when the problem is 'off-centre', and the scope for a solution circumscribed. In that field of theatrical production I can think of no more stimulating guide, and I'm not in the least taken aback to discover that he has written a comprehensive work on Costume when I had prepared myself to write him a foreword on the art of scenic design. He is a man of the theatre in the fullest sense of the term. I recognize in these pages the same personality, the same artist with the adaptable and ingenious gift as I have known these several years. What I had not realized hitherto was the scope of his versatility and the merit of his English! The gift of a visual imagination with pen or brush in hand does not always accompany a talent for exposition. Moreover, Melvill's handwriting in his private correspondence seems to rush at you from the page with a fine, reckless abandon, as if that large fist of his were impatient to get back to the native territory of a sketch-book. I can picture his huge smile of amusement as he in turn imagines me discovering to my surprise that he holds the pen of a ready writer and, through his wealth of social and historical background, proceeds to plug one yawning gap after another in my knowledge. And now, since you have persevered this far, proceed, dear reader, to the heart of the matter, for I assure you there is better reading to come

CHRISTOPHER HASSALL

CANTERBURY

PREFACE

First came the fig leaves . . . and ever since father Adam and mother Eve sewed them together to make themselves aprons, their descendants have twisted and contorted their bodies at the dictates of fashion into almost every grotesque and fanciful shape, other than the one their Creator gave them!

To make a study of mankind and his habits, one must of necessity know something of the history that surrounded him, and the styles, manners and customs in which the times were dressed, because it is a truism that men and women belong as much to their clothes as their clothes and accessories belong to them. Who, for instance, can think of Joseph, and not of his many-coloured coat? Or remember Cinderella and forget her crystal slipper? And where is Lady Windermere without her fan?

In nature, the male animal has been endowed with the silkier fur, the gayer plumage, and the more attractive form, a fact that Adam was not slow to realize. And so we find him strutting down the ages—through the glories that were Greece, and the grandeur that was Rome—leading the sartorial parade with all the assured brilliance of the peacock.

From the first Norman William to the third of the Hanoverian Georges, fashions in England had been almost entirely of French and Italian origin, and it became due to one man alone—an Englishman named George Bryan ('Beau') Brummel, and the power of his influence—that such radical changes took place in the costume of his time.

In an age of smells, dirt and disease, 'Beau' Brummel (albeit somewhat of a fashion-plate himself) became the pioneer for simplicity in dress—at any rate as far as men were concerned—combined with a welcome personal cleanliness and hygiene. The stuffy wigs and ruffles, the choking restrictions of cravats and pantaloons (damped before putting on, so as to make them dry skin-tight to the leg), together with the sunset hues of the long Regency, slowly faded out, to be replaced by far more comfortable and efficient apparel, in browns, greys and blacks.

Until his fall from the royal favour in 1812, 'Beau' Brummel had become the unchallenged leader of fashion in Europe, bringing to English tailoring a supremacy that is still acknowledged in the world today.

And what of the future? In his tentative gropings after strange new colours and weird patterns, it would seem as if the modern young man is becoming a little tired of playing second fiddle to the girl-friend, and we may yet see him swinging with the pendulum of fashion, to become once more arrayed like Solomon in all his glory!

HARALD MELVILL

ST. AGNES
CORNWALL
1961

PART I

CHAPTER 1

Costume Plays and the Amateur

The reason why so few amateurs indulge in period costume productions is, of course, on account of the expense and uncertainty involved in hiring the clothes. Besides, if they are unable to attend the necessary fittings, they then become completely dependent upon the costumier and what he chooses to send them—though, naturally, he will always try to do his best.

Yet, if one suggests to these same amateurs that, instead of hiring their costumes, they should set to and *make* them for themselves, up go the eyebrows! What is there so outrageous in making, instead of hiring . . . or in contriving, in place of buying?

Far too many amateur societies lack the spirit of theatrical adventure, and instead continue to play for what they fondly hope is safety (which in the theatre, let me assure you, is about the most risky thing one can do!). 'Let's put on a nice, simple comedy,' they cry. 'Something modern and amusing,' under the mistaken impression that this will make less demands upon their talents! If only they would realize how heartily tired their long-suffering audiences are becoming of these eternal 'cup-and-saucer' dramas!

ESTABLISHING THE BASIC WARDROBE

In the good old days—before commercial TV made so many of us more interested in watching other people doing things, instead of doing them ourselves—most large families kept a 'dressing-up box', in which was stored all manner of amusing odds and ends for use in home theatricals. It is something like this—only, of course, on a larger and much more business-like scale—that should form the foundation of our basic wardrobe.

Now, please do not get me wrong! I am not trying to suggest that all one needs is a charade basket full of old clothes, from which, as if by magic, will emerge some elaborate costume production. Naturally, time and thought, patience and planning, will be required before the dawn of that exciting day. But, it *is* a miracle that *can* happen!

The ideal basic wardrobe would have to be built up gradually, all the time sticking to the policy that each costume—or part of a costume—that is made, would initially be designed with the double purpose of its present use and its future usefulness, to be altered and adapted, as necessity demanded, for some other play . . . and even, possibly, in some entirely different form.

The system, therefore, on which to work is to make and collect together a number of separate, adaptable and interchangeable *parts* of costumes (tunics, skirts, coats, trousers, breeches, petticoats, sleeves and tights), all of which can be worn in a variety of different ways compatible with different historical periods.

They would be constructed from plain, serviceable, self-coloured materials, to which decorative pattern and design would be added afterwards, in combination with such period-establishing etceteras as ruffles, collars, ribbons, laces, buttons and bows.

To give an example: take an ordinary fully-cut semicircular skirt (sometimes called a 'gored' skirt, because it is made up of several triangular panels, or 'gores') and either undo the back seam or, if you are making it, leave it unjoined. Bind the two edges, and add a strong hook and eye at the waist, with a row of smaller hooks and eyes, or press-studs, down each side, sewing them on about an inch or two apart. This shape can then be used 'closed', as a gracefully draped skirt, attached to a tight-fitting, long-sleeved upper part (late Gothic, 1350-1450; Richard II, Henry V, Joan of Arc) or worn 'open', as a shoulder cloak (early Gothic, 1200-1350; King John to Edward III and for the Chester, York and Coventry miracle plays) or, still earlier, as a draped Saxon mantle (900-1066; *King Lear* and *Macbeth*).

Still left 'open', but with two slits cut in the sides as arm-holes (with the edges bound) and a deep collar added to hang down the back, with borders of fur sewn down each side in front (wide at the top and narrowing towards the base), it becomes the full outer robe worn by nobles in Tudor times (1450-1550).

An alternative skirt-shape can be made from one rectangular piece of material, neatly gathered in at the top and joined to a waistband. If it is treated in a similar way to the 'gored' skirt, it can be worn either 'open' in front, over a decorated petticoat (1450-1550), or, with slight alterations in the arrangement, for almost any period where the underskirt is visible (1600-1700) or, if 'closed', as a complete skirt (Victorian or Edwardian).

Naturally, a basic wardrobe should contain several such shapes, in different materials and colours. A black one, for instance, if lined in red or white silk, and furnished with tie-cords, or a decorative clasp, could be worn as a thrown-back-off-the-shoulders cloak, and would be the sort of thing much favoured by the *fin de siècle* young dandies of those Naughty 'Nineties, while, with still further readjustments in style and decoration, it would find a place in almost any period, down the ages, where a cloak was worn.

STOCKING THE BASIC WARDROBE

As a beginning, every member of a drama group (and in turn, each of their friends) would be asked to contribute as much as he or she could towards the plenishing of the wardrobe. I don't mean in hard cash—though, of course, that is never to be despised!—but in 'kind'. Most people will find they can spare something, even if it is only an old blouse or a discarded skirt, a coat or a waistcoat—perhaps, with luck, a pair of faded curtains (which can be dyed) or an antiquated bedspread.

There is no need to strip the shirts off our backs, but most of us men have hidden-away scarves, ties and loud-coloured handkerchiefs (token of the festive generosity, if not the good taste, of some maiden aunt) that we would rather be seen dead than wearing. And where is the girl without a drawer full of odds and ends of ribbons and laces, all of which in deft hands could be usefully turned into such indispensable things as trimmings and decorations?

Sometimes a discreet letter in the correspondence column of a local newspaper, or a slip inserted in the programmes of the current production, appealing for 'old unwanted clothes *of character*', has been known to bring in rich rewards. In this manner the Farnworth Little (Amateur) Theatre procured a set of genuine late Victorian and early Edwardian costumes, in perfect condition (exactly right for a production of *The Importance of Being Earnest*), that greatly added to their wardrobe potential.

Of course, one must not depend upon being *given* everything one needs, and, despite the generosity of several aunts—and uncles, too—some materials will have to be bought, and here the following factors should influence the choice:

(i) Where is the performance to be given? *(a)* In a theatre, on a large, well-illumined stage? *(b)* In a small hall, with inadequate lighting? *(c)* For some special occasion only—as for a pageant, that is seldom performed more than once or twice, after which the costumes may be put away, perhaps never to be wanted again?

(ii) Is the material to be purchased intended for just one production (and for as many performances as it will run) or for future remodelling and use in some other play? If for the latter purpose, then the material must be firm-textured, and of a hard-wearing quality, in one plain, useful colour . . . and often a cheap material can be 'treated' so as to make it look rich and expensive by the addition of dye, pattern and surface decoration.

(iii) Qualities of weight and stiffness must also be taken into consideration. It is not enough only to know what happens on the *outside*; one must also be aware, in every sense of the word, of what 'goes on' *underneath*—even if it doesn't show—because all those paddings and stuffings, waddings and quiltings, rolls, hoops and frames, to say nothing of the petticoats (in the seventeenth century those worn by young girls were made of leather) will certainly have an effect upon that most important consideration, 'the correct silhouette'. Usually a stiff lining will go a long way towards suggesting the extra weight.

(iv) Other points to watch are *(a)* the ease with which a material drapes, and *(b)* the 'sheen' and 'light reflection'. Some colours, though brilliant in themselves, absorb so much light that unless they are brightly lit they appear dull and lifeless, and have the same effect on any other colours that come near them. Black crêpe, for instance, because it absorbs light, is negative, while black sateen, by reflecting light from its shiny surface, is positive.

(v) The effect of light. In any theatre or hall where the play is seen under artificial lighting, and at comparatively close range, the texture and quality of the materials bought and the careful finish employed in making the costumes must be borne in mind. Here, too, the choice of colour is very important, as colour sets the mood and atmosphere of a scene, highlighting the emotional content of the play as a whole. Drama centres our interest upon one particular group of people, and therefore each costume should be given a distinct personality of its own, which helps to define the character of the wearer (red for the 'Demon' and white for the 'Fairy'—as they say in pantomime!).

An open-air pageant, on the other hand, is concerned with a large number of persons rather than with individuals, and because the spectators are often seated at a greater distance away from the players than is customary in a theatre, their line of vision becomes wider and less centralized, so that the materials used can be of a cheaper quality, nor need the costumes be quite so painstakingly put together (though good 'line' and fit, of course, are still essential). It is better to avoid using patterned materials, or only to use them sparingly, with any surface designs as large and simple as possible, because, although they say that distance lends enchantment, it can also play merry havoc with a delicate pattern or intricate decoration, which then becomes a dead loss! It is not the elegance of the workmanship that has to register so much as the carrying effect of the over-all silhouette (which should, therefore, be slightly emphasized—at any rate with the principals—so that skirts are wider, sleeves fuller, trains longer and headdresses higher).

Under certain circumstances, an outline has even been known to determine the domestic architecture. Towards the end of Henry VIII' life, for example, the doorways and arches at Hampton Court Palace had to be widened, for fear that the bluff old King might become wedged between the jambs! Evidence of these structural alterations can still be seen in what are known as 'Wolsey's Apartments'.

For all out-of-door entertainment, the feature upon which to concentrate is strength of colour—which should be clear and uninvolved—with a preference towards the warmer, richer colours (red, orange, yellow) to help counteract the greens in the natural surroundings, and the blue (let us hope) of the sky, though in this blesséd plot of ours, one cannot always depend upon the ready co-operation of the weather clerk!

A man's social position and the trade or occupation he followed (even to the tools he was most likely to use) not only suggested his style of clothing, but often the very way in which he wore it, while a knowledge of the means and methods of transport (usually, in olden times, more indulged in by the upper classes) would indicate the style and shape of the outdoor costumes that were worn. In the fourteenth and fifteenth centuries Edward II, Richard II and Henry IV it was the custom for ladies to travel on horseback, sitting astride . . . they're still doing it! . . . and their skirts, therefore, were very wide and voluminous, so that they could be bunched up and tucked under them at the back, leaving plenty of spare material hanging down on either side to cover their legs . . . and so preserve the decencies!

This travel business presents another significant angle, because it definitely limits the choice of certain materials for the use of the costume designer, without the risk of anachronism. To give an instance: patterned silks, which were of Moslem origin (the silkworm was first introduced into Byzantium by the Emperor Justinian), were hardly known in this country until they were brought back by the Crusaders (First Crusade, A.D. 1059), so that this material would not be used in making an early Saxon costume.

THE COSTUME WORKSHOP

The wardrobe department—or 'costume workshop'—should be under the joint partnership of an enthusiastic designer and a competent cutter-needlewoman . . . and often just such persons as these will be found in a drama group, with their interests centred in the theatre, but much too modest or retiring (shy?) to undertake a 'playing' part, yet only too willing to 'act' in an executive capacity.

In the first place, the choice of a candidate for 'wardrobe mistress' might be a committee nomination, but it should at least carry some promise of permanency, because once one has been fortunate enough to find the right person, she should—as I am sure Polonius would have advised—be grappled to one's soul with hoops of steel! Nor should it be too difficult to find a staff to assist her amongst the members, or from 'friends' outside the group, who enjoy 'sewing and making things'.

When I was scenic artist for some of the Canterbury Cathedral

Festivals, the organizer (the late Miss Margaret Babington, O.B.E.) used to send out an appeal to the 'ladies of Canterbury', asking anyone who had an hour or so to spare to devote the time once or twice a week in assisting with the making of the costumes required for the plays. A special shed was erected, just off the Precincts, and there was never any lack of willing recruits to work in it. For some of the productions, the costume designs were provided by Norah Lambourne, and the highly professional standard turned out, under her guidance, by these amateur dressmakers was truly astonishing!

One morning, during the preparation period for *The Zeal of Thy House*, I had occasion to go into the hut, which appeared empty until I saw a woman sitting at the far end, busy sewing golden feathers on to a pair of angelic wings. With a muttered word of apology, I picked up the shears I had come in to collect and beat a hasty retreat. It was only later in the day that I discovered she was Dorothy L. Sayers (whose play we were doing) filling in an idle moment!

A well-equipped costume workshop should be provided with:

A *cutting-cum-work table*, about 42 inches wide (certainly not less than 36 inches) running down the centre of the room, with chairs, or forms, on either side and good working lights overhead, arranged to give the least possible shadows.

A *sewing-machine* . . . and if possible more than one . . . preferably electric.

Several pairs of scissors and at least one pair of sharp cutting shears.

Two or three packets of assorted needles, including bodkins—and don't forget a few 'spares' for the sewing-machines, and one or two carpet-needles (and thread).

An assortment of pins, including safety-pins, and a few pin-cushions to stick them into.

Cotton and thread, in black and white as well as in an assortment of colours, though it is worth noting that it is not always essential to sew materials with a matching colour—an exception, of course, being black and white. No. 60 for machines, and No. 30 for ordinary hand-sewing and tacking.

Two or three tape-measures, and at least one yard-wand, and a 4-foot or even 6-foot stick is jolly useful.

A *pair of pliers* and a wire-cutter (sometimes these can be combined).

Various pieces of chalk—tailor's chalk (green), white chalk and charcoal sticks.

Drawing-pins.

Balls of string in various thicknesses (for tie-dyeing as well as for decoration on costumes, sleeves, etc.).

Sheets of brown paper (useful for cutting out patterns).

Sheets of thin show-card for cutting stencils . . . several safety-razor blades.

A *large assortment of aniline (water) dyes*. If possible keep in tins in a dry place. If left open or near anything damp, these powders very soon get congealed.

Tin or bottle of knotting (for painting over cut stencils to make them waterproof).

A large assortment of medium-sized and small paint-brushes.

Various-sized tins (for mixing dyes).

A *fair-sized enamelled bath* for dyeing (*not* of galvanized iron).

Other essentials are *a sink* with running water, *a gas-ring* (and matches!), *buckets* and an odd *saucepan* or two for dissolving dye crystals and warming up dyes.

Ironing board—and electric iron (preferable to the old iron type!).

Dress-dummy.

Wig block (also useful for blocking and re-blocking old hats).

Lay in a stock of as many gadgets as you can for the sewing machines, and one of those hand-worked things for punching holes.

In a practical wardrobe, such as we are considering, where a number of plays are dressed during the year, it is a great time-saver to have handy a supply of 'measurement forms' (shown overleaf), giving particulars:

CHOICE OF MATERIALS

The choice of materials for making stage costumes which are to become a part of the basic wardrobe needs much careful thought and advance planning, because, despite the constant alterations and remodellings, the washing and the dry-cleaning, and the increasing demands of wear and tear, the costumes must still present the maximum of stage effectiveness at a minimum expenditure.

The most useful materials, especially where a 'stiff' outline is required (Tudor and Elizabethan), are plain, unbleached Bolton sheeting, and good quality, closely-woven hessian, and both can be bought by the yard, or in bolts (30 yards) in widths varying from 36 inches to 54 inches to 72 inches—and occasionally 96 inches.[1]

Of these two materials, hessian is the less easy to work with, owing to the comparatively loose weave (even in the best quality), which makes it almost impossible to cut a true, straight line with the scissors. One can, however, get round this difficulty by being extra careful with the measurements in the first place, and, if possible, make these with the hessian laid out flat on the floor, so that there is less risk of pulling or stretching it, and then picking up a thread with a pin-point, and drawing it out for the full length required for cutting (and this can be done either horizontally or vertically). The cutting is then done by following the 'open line' that the extracted thread has left on the

[1] Messrs. Russell and Chapple Ltd., 23 Monmouth Street, London, W.C.2, sell both Bolton sheeting and hessian, the latter either plain or in a large variety of colours.

MEASUREMENT FORM

Player's name ....
Name of the play ....
Part (or parts) to be played ....
Number of changes of costume, with particulars of acts and scenes ....
....
Height in stockinged feet ....
Chest or bust measurement ....
Waist measurement ....
Hips (round) measurement ....
Arm length (outside—arm bent) ....
(shoulder to elbow) ....
(elbow to wrist) ....
Arm length (inside—arm straight) ....
(armpit to elbow) ....
(elbow to wrist) ....
Armpit to waist ....
Above elbow (round) ....
Wrist (round) ....
Across shoulders (front) ....
(back) ....
Shoulder to waist (front) ....
(back) ....
Shoulder to floor (front) ....
(back) ....
Waist to floor (outside leg) ....
Crutch to floor (inside leg) ....
Crutch (to above knee) ....
(to below knee) ....
Waist to thigh (outside leg) ....
(to above knee) ....
(to below knee) ....
Calf (round) ....
Ankle (round) ....
Neck (round) ....
Head (round) ....
(forehead to nape of neck) ....
(ear to ear, over top) ....
Hat size ....
Glove size ....
Shoe and boot size (with particulars of broad or narrow fitting, and high or average instep) ....
Length of stockinged foot (this information is needed for tights) ....

surface of the material. This is a problem that, of course, would not arise with Bolton sheeting.

Joining of seams must be taken into consideration when cutting out, and these should always be on the optimistic side—especially with hessian—and a good inch should be allowed for the turn-in, while, to prevent any unpleasant scratching of the wearer's skin, it is better to bind or line all rough edges.

Bolton sheeting and hessian are both excellent materials for dyeing, as well as offering a good surface for hand-painted or stencilled designs in water-colours or poster paints (*not* oils, or any sort of metallic paints, put on with bronzing medium, if the pattern has to be washed out later, when using the costume for some other play).

Amongst the cheaper materials, where 'drape' and 'hang' are essential qualities, there are:

Cheesecloth. A thin white cotton fabric, with a soft, velvet-like pile, that takes dye well. When used to make actual costumes (not only as an accessory), it is wiser to make it up double, or to use it with a lining, to give it more 'body'.

Cotton crêpe; cotton voile. Both have a transparent texture, that makes them useful for veils, etc.

Pongee. A soft, unbleached kind of Chinese silk.

Ordinary flannel, and white or unbleached bath towelling material.

Materials that have a silky, shiny surface, include:

Sateen. A glossy woollen or cotton fabric, made in imitation of satin.

Satinet. A fabric that gives the nearest sheen to real silk, but unfortunately this is lost when the material is washed. However, if it is left unironed and made up with the wrong side out, it looks like light-weight wool!

Rayon.

Satin.

Silk.

Moiré. Watered silk.

Taffeta. A glossy, silky fabric.

When both weight and draping qualities are required together, one cannot do better than to buy heavy flannelette, which, if evenly stippled with dye, gives the appearance of velvet, and—for stage purposes—when it is faked in this manner, gives a better effect of depth and pile than the real thing . . . and is far less expensive!

Other materials are:

Burlap. A coarse canvas that takes to dye very easily. I have been told that it is used for making mail-bags in H.M. prisons, though—as yet—I have not had the personal opportunity of verifying this!

Rateen. A thick quilted or twilled woollen stuff.
Terry cloth. A velvet-pile cloth in which the loops have been left uncut.
Corduroy.
Velveteen.
Rayon damasks.
Furnishing velvets.
Curtain brocades and cretonnes.

Furnishing fabrics are often preferable to the more expensive and less brightly coloured dress-length materials, and wonderful bargains can be found at sale times . . . such as bundles of thin flannelette, cotton and linen sheets, towels and light-weight blankets (sometimes sold in pale, attractive colours, all of which will dye well), which a clever wardrobe mistress can turn to countless uses for a basic wardrobe.

For materials that are both stiff and light-weight, the least expensive are:

Tarlatan. A fine, transparent muslin.
Percale. A closely-woven cotton cambric.
Gingham. A kind of linen or cotton fabric, woven of dyed yarn, usually in stripes or checks.
Dimity. A strong cotton fabric, also in stripes.
Cambric.
Paper-weight cambric. A very fine, white linen material.
Glazed chintz. More expensive that the cambrics, but also longer-lasting.

Finally, there are the cloths of silver and gold, and though they may seem rather costly, they are actually cheap in proportion to the richness and beauty of the effect they produce.

Often, in the *Stage* and the *Amateur Stage*, one will find advertisements for the sale of inexpensive rolls and odd lengths of painted scenic canvas. This, as it stands is, of course, quite useless. But if the old paint is washed off with hot water until the basic canvas is revealed, it will provide excellent material for making stage costumes, and it takes very kindly to dyes and paints alike—especially if one is lucky enough to get hold of some of the pre-war canvas, which has all the appearance and quality of good, strong linen.[1] (Now, please don't say anything, but whenever I am working in a theatre, I always try and 'make' (pinch!) some of this old canvas if I see any handy, which, when it has been washed out, I use as dish cloths . . . and they last for years!)

DYEING

For dyeing the materials, one uses aniline *(water)* dyes, not the spirit dyes, and these are sold in powder form from as small a quantity as

[1] New (scenic) canvas is obtainable from Messrs. Brodie and Middleton Ltd., 79 Long Acre, London, W.C.2.

½ ounce and upwards, and are obtainable in a large variety of pure colours.[1]

Aniline dyes are not at all expensive to buy (the cheapest is 1s. an ounce, and the most expensive is 2s. 3d. an ounce), and they are very economical to use because, owing to their extreme potency, only a small quantity is needed at a time. For instance, about half a teaspoonful of the powder, if dissolved in hot water (but use when cool) will make a large jarful of rich, strong dye . . . using more or less of the water, according to the depth of colour required. Aniline dye is also soluble in cold water—if you are in a hurry—but hot water seems to bring out the full strength of the colours more clearly.

For intermediate shades, any two or more of the dyes can be mixed together, but it is better to do this after they have been liquefied rather than to mix the actual powders, which would make it very difficult to assess the colour tone required. Aniline dyes can also be added to the ordinary commercial dress-dyes to augment their colour values.

To render aniline dyes 'fast', so that they will not rub off from the materials when dry or leave stains on the wearer's skin (being an animal substance!), one should add a dissolved solution of Glauber salts to the liquid dye, in proportion of 1 ounce of the salts to 1 pint of hot water. This process will in no way effect the beauty or strength of the colours.

In their powder form, all aniline dyes look alike, so that one cannot tell one from another. It is, therefore, a good plan to keep them in separate, carefully labelled tins or boxes, and to store them in a dry place, as if they get damp the powders become sticky and unmanageable.

There are five main colours in aniline dyes, and with these, and the almost countless intermediate shades obtainable from mixing any two or more of them together, one should have a sufficiently wide range for any colour scheme.

These five main dyes are:

Meldoline. Blue.
Cadmium. Yellow.
Nigger brown. Very useful for outlining and shading in a design.
Scarlet. A beautiful, vivid colour.
Viridian. A deep green.

There is also jet black, but this is in crystals, not powder, and to get the full effect it should be boiled. It is, however, quite easy to do without black, and the nigger brown should serve all purposes where a dark colour is required. If one must have black, indian ink is a good stand-by.

[1] Messrs. Brodie and Middleton Ltd., are the best firm from whom to get these dyes, and, if asked, they will send a post-free colour chart and catalogue. This firm also supplies hessian and gauze, as well as scenic and all other types of paints.

Additional colours are:

Bismark brown	Canary yellow	Emerald green
Burnt umber	Old gold	Crimson
Raw sienna	Orange	Eosine pink
Walnut brown	Yellow-green	Magenta
Vandyke brown	Dark green	Mauve
Rich red	Ruby	Water red
Rhodamine pink	Pure blue	Royal blue
Turquoise blue	Violet	Silver grey

Dyeing can be done in several different ways, but, needless to say, *before* the material is cut and made up.

Where no definite design or pattern is aimed at, the whole piece of material to be dyed can be plunged into the dye-bath and hung up to dry, without wringing. This should give an even, all-over colour surface . . . but it is rather wasteful with the dye!

If it is not practical to dip a length of material, an alternative method is to paint on the dye with a 2-inch to 3-inch flat-bristled brush (according to the extent of the area to be covered), using quick, short brush-strokes and continually varying the direction. This will ensure a more even surface.

The correct way (and also the simplest) to apply the dye with a brush is for the material first to be stretched tightly between two points, and, if possible, with a space left open under it, because the dye will then paint on the surface more easily, and much less of it will be used (which is always a consideration) and it will take less time to dry, especially if the work can be done out of doors.

If it is not possible to stretch out the material in this manner, then it will have to be tacked down on a table or to the floor, or against a wall. But for whichever method you use, never have too much dye on the brush, and remember to put a paper lining under the material, because a certain amount of the dye will seep through.

By regulating the strength of the dye solution, this process of brush painting can give a surface of varying tone depths that is most effective under artificial lighting, lending a richness and beauty of texture to even the most commonplace materials.

Dye can also be sprayed on, using one of those little metal gadgets that are sold in art shops for spraying fixative on charcoal or pastel drawings. For spraying, the material should be pinned upright against a wall, with sheets of paper extending all round beyond the edges, to prevent any surplus dye from marking the wall.

(a) To obtain a deliberate *un*even, broken surface effect, the material should first be bunched up or twisted into a loose roll before being dipped. And it is usually better to apply (paint on) a pale, all-over colour tone to the material first, as otherwise, if it is white to begin with, the contrast when part of it is dyed, will be too glaring. These undyed

portions could, of course, be painted in subsequently with a brush, using a different colour or a darker or lighter tone of the main ground colour.

(b) To make a simple, rather unconventional pattern, the material can first be tied in knots, in different places. For example, a square might be tied in the centre and at the four corners, and then dipped in the dye. The pattern thus obtained—when the knots are undone—is, of course, quite rough and with a blurred outline, but the piece can be re-tied in other places, and then re-dipped, either in a stronger or weaker solution of the same colour or in another colour. And this tying can be repeated again and again, with most pleasing results.

(c) A design of lines or stripes (horizontal, vertical or oblique) can be made by rolling the material into a long strip, and then tying it with tapes at regular or varying intervals, in the places where you want the lines to come. The whole thing is then dipped in the dye.

(d) A slightly more elaborate pattern can be got by binding the material securely with string or tape in those places where the design is required, and then dipping the whole piece. By repeating this tying process and re-dipping in various colours, the whole surface can be covered with an uneven pattern of differently sized circles, triangles, diamond shapes, etc., and it is a quick way to apply a design to a plain material where perhaps an Eastern or barbaric effect is aimed at. Tie-dyeing, as this process is called, is, of course, most successful with soft materials.

(e) Dyeing can also be done by the 'batik' method that used to be so popular a few years ago with scarves and handkerchiefs, etc.

First, *very lightly* draw in the pattern—or, if the material is sufficiently transparent, a design can be placed underneath to show through and serve as a guide—and outline it with a combination of paraffin and beeswax, applied with a thin watercolour brush. The dyes are then painted between these lines, without any fear of them running, and in this way one can obtain a delightful variety of designs, and more pictorial than any of those described by other methods.

When completed, the whole design can be waxed over, and the material dipped in a dye solution to obtain a coloured background. To remove the wax, simply place the material, when dry, between two sheets of white paper, or clean blotting-paper, and run it over with a hot iron. If any surplus wax still clings to the surface, it can safely be removed with a little petrol. Batik usually gives a better result when applied to silky materials, but it can also be quite effectively used with cotton if the required design is not too small and niggling.

STENCILS

With any design where the same pattern is continuously repeated, the simplest and quickest thing is to use a stencil, but, owing to the liquid nature of the dyes, it is not always possible to avoid a slight blurring of the design, however much care may be taken. On the other hand, a certain unevenness of the outlines can sometimes be turned to advantage—so long as they are not too untidy—as it gives the effect of a tapestry weave.

If the material to be decorated is pinned against a wall, the dye can be sprayed through the stencil (but do not neglect to protect the adjacent areas beyond the limits of the stencil card) or it can be rubbed through, using a fairly stiff brush, with the bristles almost dry, so that a certain amount of pressure is needed to make a clear impression. The material can, of course, be tacked out flat on a table or floor, or any other hard surface, with a paper lining underneath.

All things considered, it is often more satisfactory to make these decorative patterns free-hand, first very lightly marking out the design in charcoal (use chalk on a dark material), which can easily be rubbed off afterwards. With a formal design, it can be quite useful to draw in a series of guide lines in squares or lozenges, according to the pattern required.

Quite strikingly beautiful 'period' designs, giving the semblance of rich brocades, can be produced by painting a repeat pattern with two or more poster paints on plain, undyed hessian, leaving a certain amount of the ground surface showing all round or between each of the units. After the design has been completed, one can add a very light all-over spray-stipple of pale dye—either just over the design itself, or only surrounding it—which will give a wonderful impression of depth and richness, and impart that mellowed effect of age. Some hessians can be bought with a pale golden-brown surface texture, and are excellent for this sort of thing.

If silver or gold or any other of the metallic (powder) colours are used to embellish a design, the whole effect can be completely ruined if the paint is too liquid or put on too solidly. The correct method is to 'drag' it on—that is to say, rub the paint in with a stiff, almost dry brush. This will give the pattern a slightly broken, uneven appearance (which is what one wants!) and one need not be too painstaking about the outlines.

There are three different ways in which to mix these gold, silver and other metallic colours. (i) By adding bronzing medium to the powder, and stirring it into a paste, using a saucer or tin lid for the purpose. This method is sometimes a little messy, as the medium tends to overrun the design. Also, it is not easy to wash out if one wants to alter it for some future occasion. (ii) By mixing the powder with a solution of hot size. This gives quite good results, and it can be washed out without any difficulty. (iii) By mixing the powders with an equal proportion of white hard spirit varnish and methylated spirit. Do not mix too great a quantity at a time, as both these spirits quickly evaporate, and the solution goes 'hard'. By this method, one can ensure a clean, clear outline, whether one is working free-hand or rubbing through a stencil card, and it is particularly effective when used for painting in the gold or silver details in heraldic designs, because it dries with a smooth, shiny surface. The only drawback is that once the paint is 'on' it is 'on for keeps', as I doubt if it will wash out.

To obtain the effect of 'heavy gold or silver embroidery', first fill in the outline of each design unit—perhaps a motif of heraldic lions or fleurs de lis—in nigger brown dye, and when this is dry, paint a thin line in gold or silver all round the filled-in shape. Next, draw in on the design itself a series of narrow, slightly separated lines to represent the metallic threads. These lines should be vertical, and thicker at the top, tapering off towards the base, so that more of the foundation brown colours shows between the 'threads'. This will have the effect of making the design look 'rounded' (raised) and this can further be accentuated by adding a suggestion of a 'shadow' at the base—that is to say, below the outline of the design. Do not put on the paint too evenly, and 'dragging' (as described above) will emphasize the 'embroidery' effect (*see* Fig. 1).

A large variety of ready-cut stencil cards can be bought from the art

Fig. 1. (a & b) with the design filled in with nigger-brown aniline dye, and the main outlines defined in black (viridian and nigger-brown dye will, if mixed together, approximate black . . . or Indian ink can be used with good effect); (c & d) showing the method used for applying the silver or gold paint to obtain the 'rounded' (raised) embroidery effect.

shops, but they are not always completely satisfactory, as they are apt to crack and become soggy after a few applications of the dye, tearing and falling apart. Many designers, therefore, prefer to create and cut their own stencils, using thin show-card and a sharp safety-razor blade.

The life of a stencil can, however, be greatly prolonged if both sides of it are painted over with a solution of knotting, which many of the art shops sell, ready made up in little bottles or tins . . . though it is much cheaper to take along one's own bottle and buy it by the pint, direct from the ironmonger.

Knotting dries almost as quickly as you can paint it on, and on this account (speedy evaporation) only a little at a time should be poured into the saucer, and the bottle well corked when not in use. Knotting has the special property of making a stencil waterproof, but even so, be advised and play safe, and cut out your stencils in duplicate!

Patterns and designs can be copied direct from contemporary materials in the museums—or reproductions of them—and from the costumes and hangings in the Old Master paintings of the period . . . and any little imperfections in the finished work will pass entirely unnoticed when the material has been cut out and made up, so do not let the fact that you are not a first-rate artist put you off! And as a little bit of further encouragement let me remind you that few of the patterns in the woven materials of the past were themselves completely perfect, and often it is from these very imperfections that one knows the piece to be genuine!

It is not, in any case, possible to reproduce exact replicas of the textures of the old-time (hand-woven) materials. For one thing, our present (mechanical) methods of weaving are entirely different—even if the basic principles are similar—and the colour dyes, which before the middle of the nineteenth century were non-mineral in origin, are now the result of aniline (mineral) dyeing that makes the brighter colours seem harsh and crude by comparison with the older dyed materials which were both bright and soft, thus presenting a wider and more varied colour range than anything we can manage today.

The designers of the Middle Ages were artists and craftsmen, to whom colour and design were of the first importance. The costumes they created were based upon a psychological understanding of their period, with an outward form that reflected the inner character and characteristics of the people who wore them.

With the coming of the Industrial Revolution a severe blow was struck at individualism and imaginative craftsmanship, the machine-made article quickly giving rise to the machine-made mind . . . one has only to look at the drab uniformity of the clothes worn by a roomful of working girls in a factory or mill to realize how pathetically true this is! One day the wheel may turn again, and bring us back to a fuller appreciation of beauty of colour and purpose of design. . . . Until then, the most that any modern costume-designer of period costumes can offer is the illusion of accuracy, controlled by the choice of the materials at his disposal and the manner in which he uses them.

Complete accuracy, however, is not always the first consideration with a stage costume, and often 'theatrical effectiveness' is more important . . . that is to say, how a costume 'behaves' when looked at from a distance, and what happens to its colours when it is seen under theatre lighting—a problem which will be dealt with later in this chapter.

THE IMPORTANCE OF THE RIGHT SILHOUETTE

The technique employed in designing a period costume for the theatre is closely related to the planning of a period stage setting . . . a matter of presenting the correct shapes and profiles. Each era in the past had a defining outline that lent character and personality to its costumes, and when in a play a definite historical period is combined with some well-known personage(s) within that period, this matter of presenting the right silhouette becomes even more important, because the audience must be helped to identify themselves with the period, and to recognize the character(s) wearing the costume(s).

A few simple practical examples will illustrate this argument. Draw a square with a considerably smaller square standing on the middle of its top line, with the top left corner 'cut' with a short, oblique, straight line. Flank the larger square with an upright semicircle on either side, and support this figure upon two widely separated pairs of straight lines, closed at the base, and set obliquely in an outward direction. The resultant shape, however roughly drawn, will not only suggest Henry

Fig. 2. Demonstrating the advantage of supplying an easily recognisable silhouette, as applying to Henry VIII, or any Tudor courtier.

VIII, but will also provide a typical working outline for almost any Tudor courtier's costume (*see* Fig. 2).

If the diameter of a semicircle is superimposed over the apex of a right-angled triangle and surmounted with a small circle, topped by a smaller semicircle, you have the popular conception of Cardinal Wolsey (Fig. 3). Or, again, by substituting an equilateral triangle in place of the larger semicircle, and topping that with a similar but much smaller triangle, with a small semicircle on top of that, you will suggest His Eminence Cardinal Richelieu (Fig. 4). And if a number of various-sized circles and semicircles are arranged, as in Fig. 5, even Smith Tertius should easily recognize Good Queen Bess! Many other geometrical figures will no doubt suggest themselves.

Naturally, the actual outlines presented by any of these famous characters would not be quite as 'basic' as these examples, but the point I want to establish is that by first visualizing the *skeleton* of a style (stripped of all its falderals) the designer can then begin to build up the period silhouette he requires, and adapt it to the particular needs of the play with which he is dealing.

It is very necessary to stress the importance of that word 'adapt', because everything in the theatre—scenery, performances and, naturally, the costumes—*must* be just that much larger than life. In other words, the designer who merely copies a genuine period costume, identical in every respect and detail though it may be, seldom produces an effective stage costume. No matter how beautiful it may look at close quarters, and despite the accuracy of period, shape and colour, it must also fulfil the pressing demands of *(a) suitability* (taking its proper place in the general scheme of the production), *(b) character* (indicating tragedy, comedy or farce . . . and usually the choice of colour and pattern will largely influence the former, while subtle exaggeration of any of the comic potentials in the costume itself, would take care of the humour) . . . and, lastly, *(c)* of *comfort*—because an actor must feel happy and 'at home' in his costume, as if he and his clothes belonged together (and it is the costume-designer's job to see to it that he both is and does). But the actor, too, must play his part, and just as in an 'old age' make-up half the realistic impact he achieves is due to 'thinking' himself to be the age he is supposed to be, so in a period costume he must imagine himself as the character he is portraying.

No actor can find self-expression in dialogue alone—he must have the assistance of action and gesture—and this is more than ever true with costume drama, where every motion of the head, shoulders and arms . . . especially the arms . . . is supplementary to the spoken word.

There is an old proverb that teaches us that 'Manners maketh the man'. It is equally true that, in the first place, it is his costume that helps to dictate his manners—and his mannerisms—as well as often influencing his movements and behaviour.

My advice to any amateur about to play in a period production would

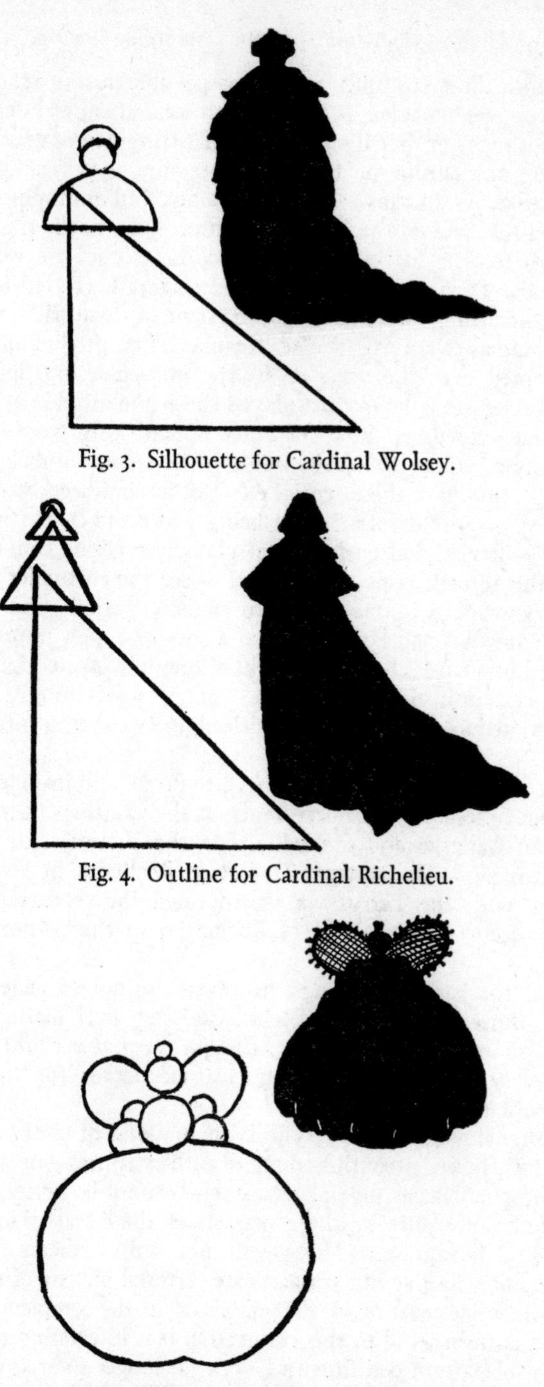

Fig. 3. Silhouette for Cardinal Wolsey.

Fig. 4. Outline for Cardinal Richelieu.

Fig. 5. Silhouette for Queen Elizabeth I.

be to get into those costumes as soon as possible *during rehearsals*, and then, if it can be managed, to continue to wear them at home until the first night is over, so that the 'business' of sitting down, getting up, and the opening and closing of doors, etc., becomes as easy and natural to perform in silks and satins as it is in a T-shirt and drain-pipes!

A period costume on the stage must never look 'new', or as if it were being worn for the first time. The romantic clothes we wore when I was with the Terrys were often the old originals, created for them in the days when things were made to last (some of them still doing valiant service as long as twenty years after the play's first production). Adapted and re-adapted over the years to fit the ever-changing figures of the actors and actresses, who in turn played those famous old parts, mended, patched and darned, as these costumes undoubtedly were, they never looked shabby. Under the stage lights, they seemed unbelievably rich and opulent, and gave the essential effect of having been 'worn' (which, by the way, is quite different from being 'worn out'.) that new clothes can never achieve. So often historical plays lose period conviction from allowing the audience (metaphorically) to see the costumier's label!

The very word 'costume' seems to suggest 'period', and while it is probably true that some people have a sort of rough impression (and often you'd be surprised to find just how rough!) of the kind of clothes worn in a certain historical period, it is not very safe to rely upon these unsubstantiated and often wholly misleading twentieth-century impressions.

Fortunately, there is seldom any need to do so, and inspiration can be drawn from contemporary sources, such as the paintings in the National and Portrait Galleries and the exhibits in the Victoria and Albert and British Museums. (The costume I wore as Rochester in *Sweet Nell of Old Drury* with the Terrys was based upon the seventeenth-century portrait of John Wilmot, Earl of Rochester, in the National Portrait Gallery.)

Many of the earlier paintings, however, are not so generally informative as those of later periods, because they deal mainly with the purely religious aspects of life . . . though on that account, of course, they are very useful in supplying costume details for the medieval morality and miracle plays.

Any designer who wishes to check on the kind of clothes they wore in the sixteenth, seventeenth and eighteenth centuries—in which many of the more popular costume plays are set—cannot bo better than study the wonderful portraits by those masters of their craft, Holbein, Van Dyke and Gainsborough. These will not only indicate the correct silhouette, but will give him an accurate sartorial picture of the times—even to the very texture of the materials used—complete in colour, design and pattern. And in this connection it is interesting to note that some forms of pattern continue in favour far longer than any other sort of decoration (for instance, the 'carrick' bend of which Henry VIII was so fond), and there are materials being made today that incorporate designs that were in common usage as long ago as the reign of Henry V (1413-1422) (*see* Fig. 6).

When a designer is considering this matter of shape and design in relation to stage costumes, he should acquaint himself fully with the general conditions of life pertaining to the particular period—and country—with which he is dealing, always bearing in mind the influence on fashion of 'suitability' and 'comfort' . . . in other words, the ease and freedom with which the wearer of the costume can move about . . . because, however pictorially effective those skin-tight pantaloons may look, the designer must ask himself that all important question, 'Are they *practical*?' There used to be an old song, 'I do not need a country seat, because I can't sit down!'

Costumes should never be treated as something separate and apart from the production as a whole, and from the start the producer, costume-designer and scenic artist must see eye to eye, so that each is

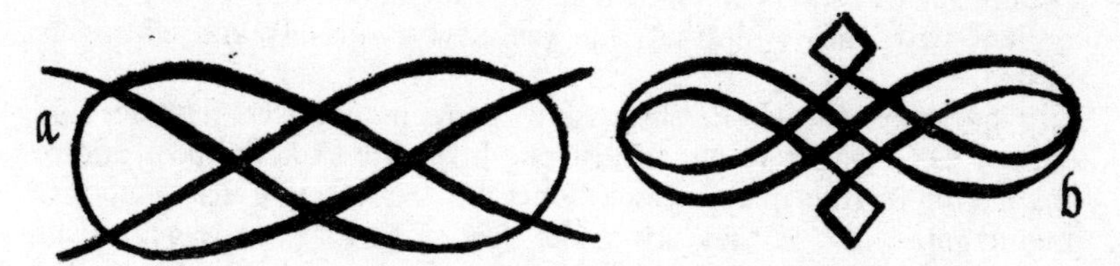

Fig. 6. (a) the Carrick Bend, a favourite costume pattern design with Henry VIII; (b) another old time pattern unit.

fully aware of, and in complete agreement with, what the others hope to achieve.

When a scenic artist works on a play, he carefully reads the script in order to understand (get to 'know') the different characters who interpret the plot . . . to find out what each of them does . . . why they do it . . . and what happens to them when they've done it! In this way—by becoming on intimate terms with them—he can more readily assess their mental reactions, and so estimate the probable colour schemes and styles of decoration with which such people would surround themselves . . . because it is an undeniable truism that the walls and furnishings of most rooms reflect the personality of the men and women who live in them.

With a costume-designer, the basic principle is the same, except that when he reads the play it is to get a clear idea of the way the author wanted each of his characters to *look*. The scenic artist's walls are the result—the effect—of behaviour as governed by mind and matter . . . whereas the designer's costumes must depict the spiritual and moral processes—in other words, the temperament of the wearers.

In some cases, of course, both scenic and costume designs are the joint work of one man (or woman), but where this is not the case, these two departments must be considered in close relation to each other (though still under the ever-watchful Big Brother eye of the producer), so that colours do not clash or a door opening is constructed so low that it will not admit a tall, feathered headdress. This is the sort of thing that sometimes is not discovered until the scene-cum-dress rehearsal, when it is almost too late to do anything about it, and in the end—after much heartburning and recrimination—it will probably be the plumes that are sacrificed, because, after all, it *is* easier to cut down a feather than it is to heighten a doorway (though any costume-designer worth his salt would sooner go to the stake than admit it!).

During the whole of the four years I worked as scenic artist at the Coliseum Theatre Repertory Company in Oldham, only *one* of the actresses took the trouble to find out what colour I was painting the next week's setting. Every Tuesday morning, regular as clockwork, she would pop in to the paint-shop (studio) before rehearsal, and take away a sample of the main colours, which I would dab on to a piece of paper for her, with the result that she was always suitably and effectively dressed.

In outlining the close relationship between producer, designer and artist, I feel I ought to put in just one little word for the poor author . . . having written plays myself. Once his 'masterpiece' has gone into production, 'that', as they say in the classics, 'is that', and as far as he is concerned his opinion is seldom consulted—certainly not to the extent that some people might imagine—and the further away from the theatre he keeps during rehearsals the better pleased everyone will be . . . unless, of course, he is producing the play himself!

LIGHTING

The request one so often overhears in shops, 'May I, please, take it to the door and see it by daylight?' is not of much use when buying materials for stage costumes, and one should always try to choose them under a strong artificial light . . . or, better still, by the nearest approach to the actual lighting colour (if this is known beforehand) in which the made-up costume will ultimately appear.

This is because stage lighting can play such unforeseen tricks, even with the most beautiful materials . . . one moment delighting you with an effect you never dreamed of and the next scaring you out of your five wits, with a result you will certainly dream about.

Generally speaking, any coloured light will enhance its own colour in a material (a blue light, for instance, picking up the blues in any costume in the blue range, with pink or amber doing the same with red).

The three light primaries are red, green and blue. Intermediate shades are obtained by the addition of any one primary to another thus: red plus green equals yellow, red plus blue equals magenta, and blue plus green equals blue-green, while if the light beams of all three primaries are superimposed in equal proportion the light they produce approximates as nearly as possible to white.

Each of the light primaries has its complementary secondary, thus: red, blue-green; green, magenta; blue, yellow.

Blue-green plus magenta equals blue if the filters are placed one in front of the other. Blue-green plus yellow equals green under the same circumstances, and yellow plus magenta, if used in the same way, equals red. If they are added in pairs as a source of light, then the result in each case would be to produce white.

Each primary and its complementary secondary, when placed in front of a lighting lantern, should produce black. For example, red and its complement, blue-green, as colour filters, would in fact filter out all the visual spectrum, the reason for this being that the red filter is minus blue-green and the blue-green filter is minus red. Looked at in another way, if you take a red filter, a blue filter and a green filter and put all three in front of a lantern, the light produced should, in theory, be black, but, in practice, it is more like a deep, dirty brown!

The three primary colours (pigments) are red, blue and yellow. When coloured light is blended with these colours in materials, blue on yellow will produce green, red with blue gives magenta, and orange can be obtained from red on yellow . . . and, of course, the other way round.

What happens is that the colour or colours common to both the pigment (or dye) and the light illuminating them is reflected, so that a magenta light on an orange dress will appear red, because red is common to both the magenta light and the orange dress (*see* Figs 7*a* and 7*b*).

The lighting scheme that amateurs usually have to accept when hiring a hall is blue (Nos. 18, 19, 32)[1] plus amber (Nos. 2, 4, 33). But this is not always a very satisfactory combination, as the ambers have a somewhat deadening effect on most other colours (in materials) except with red and orange, and under this lighting scheme pinks lose their brightness, and blues, and most greens, become grey, with magenta turning to a murky brown. Both red and green are unfortunate lighting colours on materials, and a red dress under a green light, or a green costume under a red light, will give the appearance of being brown.

A more popular colour (lighting) association—at any rate from the costume-designer's angle—is rose pink (No. 7), steel blue (No. 17) and pale straw (No. 3), which gives the best all-round results when combined with other colours (except those in the red-orange-magenta range), so that any pink in a costume would come up well, with blue showing to better advantage than under amber.

[1] These numbers refer to the Strand Electric Company's gelatine mediums, and further particulars—and sample book of colours—can be obtained from them at 29 King Street, Covent Garden, London, W.C.2 (TEMple Bar 4444).

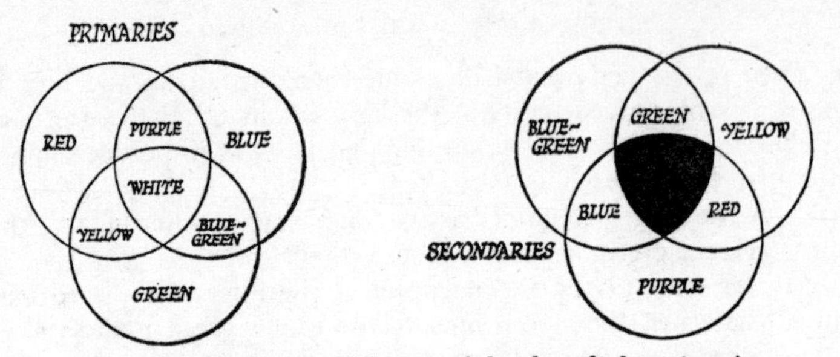

Fig. 7. (*Left*) Additive. If beams of the three light primaries, Red, Green and Blue, are superimposed in the right proportions, they produce WHITE. Intermediate shades are achieved by additions of any one of the Primaries to another thus: Red plus Green equals Yellow; Red plus Blue equals Purple; and Blue plus Green equals Blue-green. Each Primary has its complementary secondary thus: Red —Blue-green, Green—Purple, Blue—Yellow.
A beam of a primary superimposed on its complementary secondary produces WHITE. Beams of three secondaries superimposed also produce WHITE. The above is called additive colour mixing.
(*Right*) Subtractive. Quite a different result is achieved when more than one colour filter is placed in front of the *same* light source (subtractive colouring). Thus: Blue-green plus Purple in front of one lantern equals BLUE. Blue-green plus Yellow in front of one lantern equals GREEN. Yellow plus Purple in front of one lantern equals RED. Blue-green, Yellow and Purple superimposed in front of one lantern produces BLACK.

The safest lighting is with whites, under which all colours can effectively be used, provided they are bright, strong and direct in themselves. As a rule, however, white is considered too hard and harsh a light for ordinary play purposes . . . though it is often used in ballet.

There is, however, one colour that it is almost impossible to light satisfactorily *except* under white, and that is vermilion, which loses its true colour value if used with any of the ordinary lighting combinations required for other colours, so that often the only thing to be done is to substitute a clear scarlet for the vermilion, and to correspondingly tone down any other colours (materials) used with it.

All stage illumination looks better if the main sources of light are 'frosted' (light frost No. 31, heavy frost No. 29), and by thus diffusing the lighting rays one does away with the risk of hard outlines between one lighting area and the next, otherwise almost impossible to avoid.

A young British-Italian actor friend of mine named Gina Coya has patented an extremely ingenious and useful little gadget, which offers theatre lighting conditions in miniature, from which a costume-designer can quickly assess the true effect on fabrics from any lighting combination—as, for examples, a deep rose (No. 12) on a soft green velvet gown . . . or a blue-green (No. 16) on a yellow curtain—without the necessity of using the actual stage lighting-plant.

He has called his invention the Selector ColourScope, and it is supplied with two little lighting bulbs and a small dimmer-control. A wheel, fitted with sections of Strand Electric gelatine colour mediums, throws the various lighting effects upon strips of differently coloured materials, joined together to form one long (reversible) ribbon, which turns over a couple of spools. The whole thing is so compact that it can be carried in a brief-case, and Gina Coya hopes that soon no costume department will be able to do without one (*see* Fig. 7*a*).

But in the meantime, when searching the shops for costume materials, take my tip and carry with you several strips of differently coloured gelatine medium and a strong torch-lamp, with which it should be possible to get a pretty good idea of what may happen to those materials under varying lighting conditions.

Pure white as a costume material is often thought to be too glaring to look well on the stage, and an off-white sometimes gives a better effect. In the film studios, men's shirts, collars and cuffs, and any whites in the women's dresses, are sprayed over with a pale yellow ochre mixture before the 'shooting' commences.

I took a very dim view of this practice when on one occasion I 'walked on' as an extra in a cocktail party scene. I never discovered what the stuff was they used, but I do know that my dress-shirt was completely ruined, and no matter how often it was sent to be washed, the yellow never quite came out . . . and entirely my own fault, of course, for insisting on wearing my own 'props'!

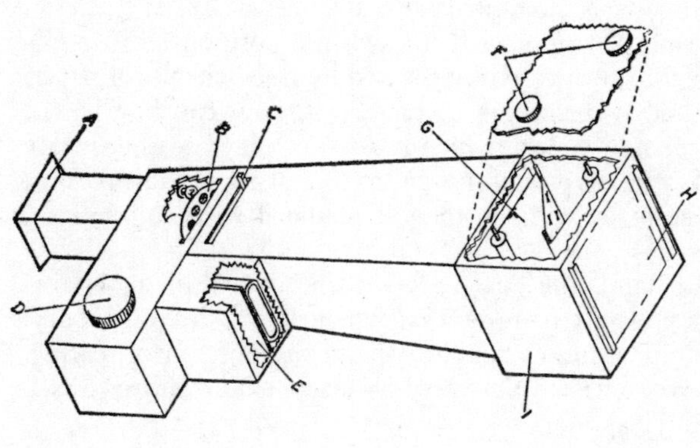

Fig. 7a. Selector ColourScope.
(a) Eye-piece;
(b) colour wheel;
(c) lever for quick release of white screen;
(d) dimmer and switch;
(e) battery compartment;
(f) knobs for colour selection;
(g) ribbon of different colours, reversible;
(h) plate covering screen;
(i) box, reversable.

CHAPTER 2

Armour and Chain Mail

A 'metal' breastplate can be made from pliable cardboard. In its first stages, it should be moulded to the figure of the player who is to wear it, and this can be done by slightly damping the cardboard and, where necessary, cutting out notches ('darts') at the top, base and sides, so as to get the right shape, and then rejoining them across with thin string.

When the correct shape has been arrived at, the whole piece of cardboard should be covered with several layers of thin, torn-up little pieces of paper (newsprint will do), with each piece pasted or glued on so that it slightly overlaps the next.

If the breastplate is to be decorated with any sort of 'raised pattern', this can be made from string or cord, tacked into position with needle and thread, and then in turn carefully covered by the little bits of paper. If the design required is something more solid, then it can first be cut out from thick cardboard or felt, which is sewn or glued to the surface and then 'papered' over. Upstanding 'bosses', or other ornaments of a similar kind, can be made with buttons or moulded with cotton-wool, soaked in paste.

It is essential to 'bind' the outer edges with some thin material—surgical bandage is probably best—so that when the whole thing is dry, tapes can be affixed for tying on the breastplate without fear of tearing. Usually the front section is all that need be made, as the wearer's back can be masked by a cloak.

When the pasted-on paper is thoroughly dry (give it a day or two if you've the time to spare), the whole surface should be painted over with some dark, brownish colour as an undercoat. When that is dry, the breastplate can be painted with aluminium paint—and to get the best effect 'dry-brush' it on, so that the undercoat partly shows through. Armour on the stage must never look brand new, as if it had just come from the smithy, or have too highly polished a surface, as it ruins the effect if it reflects the lighting!

A breastplate can also be made from a panel of felt, which, after it has been shaped as described above, must be painted over with a thick, strong solution of size, letting it thoroughly soak in. When it has become quite dry and firm, cover the whole surface with the little pieces of torn-up paper pasted on, and when that is dry put on the undercoat, and, finally, the aluminium. Any raised pattern is, of course, sewn on the surface before the size is applied.

There is yet a third way, and that is to make the shape from the smallest-mesh chicken-wire-netting, which bends easily to give the body contour. This too is covered with torn-up paper pasted on to give it a surface solidity, and when dry treated in a similar way to the cardboard and felt armour.

Naturally, armour made in this manner will not give back any 'clink or clang' when worn in a fight scene!

In Elizabethan times, with the improvement in firearms, suits of armour became less and less worn, with many a fighting man wearing no more protection than his helmet and a steel gorget or neck-guard over his doublet.

The gorget, like the breastplate, can be made from shaped felt, with an upstanding collar, and three overlapping sections for the neck and shoulder-piece. Add studs or any other sort of applied pattern—a border of twisted string, for instance, round the lower edge—before stiffening the shape with size solution. When dry, it is covered with the glued-on paper strips, and finished off as described above. Don't forget to leave an opening for putting on and taking it off, and to have this at the back is probably the best position (*see* Fig. 8).

Chain-mail is generally made the laborious way, by knitting it in coarse brown string, using a pair of large wooden needles, and following the jersey and stocking patterns for the arms and legs. It should seldom be necessary, however, to knit a complete suit of chain-mail, as it can generally be arranged for the greater part of the body to be covered by a surcoat, which can be quite long both back and front, and be painted or embroidered with decorative heraldic emblems.

When applying the aluminium paint, draw the brush very lightly over the knitting that just the tops of the 'links' are painted, with the underlying brown showing through. Be sparing with the paint, as if too much is used the whole effect can be spoiled. For a final touch of realism, just before the aluminium paint is dry lay the knitting on some hard surface—preferably stone—and smartly hammer it out flat with a mallet. Except that one naturally misses the slight 'ring' of the metal, it is almost impossible from a short distance away to detect any difference in appearance between the knitted and the genuine article!

Quite a good effect for chain-mail can also be obtained by using some of those rough-mesh floor-clothes, dyed a dark brown and then joined together and shaped to the arms and legs. These cloths can be used as well for making chain-mail hoods (which otherwise would have to be knitted) using a Balaclava helmet pattern. When the right shapes are made, the aluminium paint is applied as described above. Before putting on the leggings, it is as well to slip a pair of stout leather soles inside the feet.

Some little time ago I saw a production of *Saint Joan* at the Old Vic., and some of the chain-mail seemed to have been 'faked' by using a grey cloth with a painted pattern (or it may have been woven) of tiny squares in a darker grey, with a few added touches of black. This material was

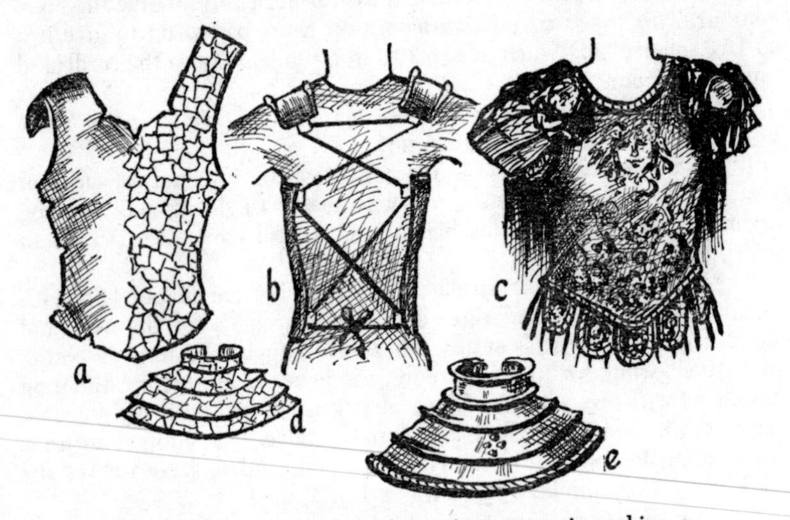

Fig. 8. (a, b & c) Showing the various stages in making a breastplate, with the 'raised pattern' built up with felt or string; (d & e) the method for making a gorget. During the reign of Elizabeth I this was sometimes worn in conjunction with a neck ruffle.

loosely bunched together on shoulders and arms, with here and there a smear of aluminium paint as a highlight. From where I was sitting in the front row of the circle, the illusion of chain-mail was complete, and it was only my usual nosiness, in wanting to see it at closer quarters, that made me examine it through my opera-glasses.

The armour (breastplates and greaves, etc.) appeared to be made of black rubber composition, similar to the rubber mats you sometimes find in bathrooms and lavatories, which is, of course, exceedingly pliable and easy to 'shape' to the body. Here, too, were smudges of aluminium paint for the highlights, and in some instances raised heraldic devices had been added on top, and then painted in with reds, blues, gold and silver. Leather straps were attached and used for fastening, and the over-all effect of metal armour was extraordinarily convincing—and not so difficult to produce!

My programme credited the armour to the work of two young ladies (I find it safer to assume that all ladies in the theatre are young!) named Phyllis Dohoo and Audrey Taylor.

The Norman 'hauberk' was a sleeveless jerkin, closely covered with either metal scales or rings, and such a garment could be reproduced by making a tunic of brown felt or suéde, and covering it with those

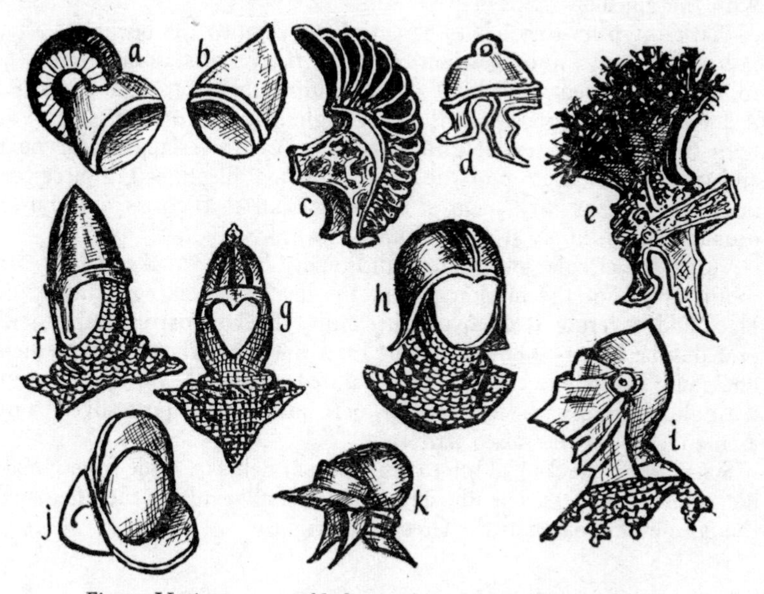

Fig. 9. Various types of helmet: (a) Assyrian; (b) Assyrian; (c) Grecian; (d) Roman Legionary; (e) Roman General; (f) Norman soldier, 1066; (g) English, early 14th century; (h) English, latter half of 15th century; (i) Italian helmet; (j) Elizabethan (late 16th century); (k) Jacobean soldier (early 17th century).

flat metal discs they sell for mending holes in pots and kettles, or by sewing on rows of flat metal washers, all of which are obtainable from any ironmonger. These will have the added advantage of giving a decided 'clink', but otherwise, as an alternative, a pretty good effect can be had by painting on these rings with aluminium, with carefully placed dashes of black here and there for the shadows.

Gauntlet gloves can be made from adding cuff-pieces to a pair of those string gloves one can buy, painting them over with brown first, and then with aluminium.

Helmets are made on the foundation of a skull cap, or one can use the crown of a bowler hat or an old felt hat with the brim cut off, with the required shape built up by glueing on pieces of torn-up paper; and remember to start with plenty of head-room, as this building-up process will tighten the cap. The front peak, ear-flaps, and the turned-down neck-guard at the back of the 'burgonet', or the turned-up, pointed front peak of the 'morion', with the flat, semicircular piece cutting vertically through the top of the crown (both these helmets are Elizabethan) or the projecting pieces of any other type of helmet can be made from buckram, firmly sewn to the foundation cap, and then made more solid with the glued-on strips of paper.

With any brim that has to be curled up, dampen the buckram (after it has been sewn into position) and roll it over something round—a rolling-pin or even a bottle, if you've nothing better to hand—and let it dry before you proceed further. Next glue on the torn-up paper, but with these helmets tear it into long strips, each overlapping the next and carried over the top of the shape, covering all projecting pieces on both surfaces, as well as over all joins, and if there is any raised ornamentation, apply it as explained above.

To fix the circular piece, one will literally have to make a tight slot in the crown of the morion and fit the piece in, holding it firmly in place and covering it all over with more glued-on paper, and it will probably be better to cut the shape from thick strawboard rather than buckram. The whole thing is then painted, first with brown and then with aluminium, with little touches here and there of pure silver paint as highlights on the raised pattern.

Some of the Greeks had huge crests to their helmets, made from metal, horsehair or feathers. The Romans, too, had similar tops to their helmets, though never as large as the Greeks (*see* Fig. 9).

CHAPTER 3

Romantic Uniform

Generally speaking, if a uniform is of some special regiment (that is to say, easily recognizable) or from another country, where accuracy may be important, it is safer to hire it. Uniforms always make a brave show on the stage (actors love wearing them!) and the outlay is well worth while. On the other hand, with a little ingenuity, it should not be too difficult a job to 'fake the effect' of an ordinary military turn-out of the early 1800s. Several uniforms are featured in Barrie's *Quality Street* (1805-15) and in *Vanity Fair*, by Thackeray (set around 1815). Also, of a later period, for *Marigold*, by L. A. Harker and F. R. Pryor (1842), and, later still, for Surtes Cook in Rudolph Besier's play, *The Barretts of Wimpole Street* (1846).

To begin with, the coat must be red, and it should have tails—and if there is nothing available of that type and colour in the wardrobe, how about dyeing a pyjama jacket to which tails have been added? The coat may possibly need a little shaping at the waist and under the arms, and, to give it the necessary weight (bulk), it should either be lined or worn over a long-sleeved pullover. Turn up the collar, and stiffen it all round by adding a strip of white felt, and two 6-inch-deep turn-back cuffs of the same material must be made for the sleeves. Line the coat-tails with white, and place a gilt button on either side of the central back-slit. The front inside edges of the jacket also need lining, so that when they are turned up and held back with a gilt button the white is visible. Sew some yellow or gold cord in a 'wavy' line round the top and bottom edges of the collar and cuffs, and add a small gold cut-out crown towards the top front of each cuff, with a gilt button fixed just below it.

Epaulettes will have to be made and added to the shoulders. These can be cut out from thick white felt, with a yellow or gold cord edging, and a gilt button sewn at the narrow end, near the neck. The wider (circular) end needs padding underneath, so that it stands out at an angle to the sloping end of the shoulder with 3-inch to 3½-inch lengths of gold metallic cord used for the hanging fringe.[1]

Six 1-inch wide parallel horizontal 'bars' of white felt, set about 1¼ inches apart, run across the chest of the coat, narrowing as they go down, with the top one 12 inches long, and the bottom one 6 inches. The front of the jacket fastens with hooks and eyes, not buttons, and

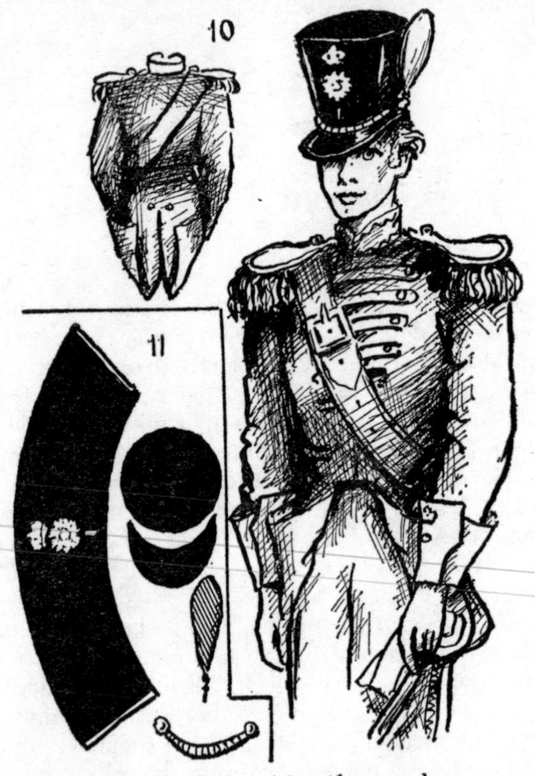

Fig. 10. 'Romantic' uniform, and
Fig. 11. Shako (diagram).

over the right shoulder, and under the epaulette and left arm, goes the baldrick (4-inch wide white felt or webbing) with a white cord edging, and a large square gilt buckle at chest level sewn to one end of it, with the other 'tongue-shaped' end passing through it. The white trousers should narrow slightly towards the instep and be 'strapped' under the black boot. 'Duck' would be the right material, but white tennis flannels would do if the ends of the legs are adjusted (*see* Fig. 10).

[1] Metallic fringe cord can be bought by the yard from those little back-street shops in Soho, of which there are several in Poland Street.

The circular hat—or 'shako'—was flat-topped and had a peak, and this will have to be made from cardboard and covered in black sateen to give the 'shine' (better than painting it with enamel, which sometimes gets scratched). It should be 8 inches or 9 inches high, and as it is slightly wider at the top than round the forehead it will have to be 'cut on the cross', in the same way as when designing a lampshade. A small gold crown goes on the front, near the top, with a round gold 2-inch-diameter 'boss', with twelve little teeth round the edge, underneath it, and the figure '1' below that. Sew a thin yellow or gold cord round the rim of the black peak, with a thicker plaited gold cord just above it, going from one side of the hat to the other across the front, and held at each end with a gilt button. On the left side of the hat is fixed a little 9-inch-high green brush-like feather tuft—*not* a cockade (*see* Fig. 11).

For musical comedies, which often take place in some fictitious Ruritanian surroundings, interest can be added to the uniforms by designing the jackets in different colours (light and dark blue, various shades of green, red or black) or wearing a white coat, with the trousers in some other colour. Of course, a completely white uniform, with a lot of gold braiding and a coloured belt and stripe down the outer seam of the trousers, can always be calculated to 'knock 'em for six' in the cheaper parts.

For countries further east, add a full knee-length skirt to the jacket, and leave it open in front to show the baggy knickerbockers (blue, red, green or black) and high red—blue or black boots, with or without gold decoration, and wear a tall, round fur hat with a cloth top and without a peak, and with a brush plume on the left side. And the further east you go, the more barbaric and colourful the uniforms can become.

For court dress uniform, worn by an ambassador, use a black tail-coat with upstanding collar, but no lapels, a lace jabot at the neck and a frill at the wrists, and with a stencil apply a 3-inch-wide formalized 'leaf' design in gold paint all round the edge of the coat, including the collar,

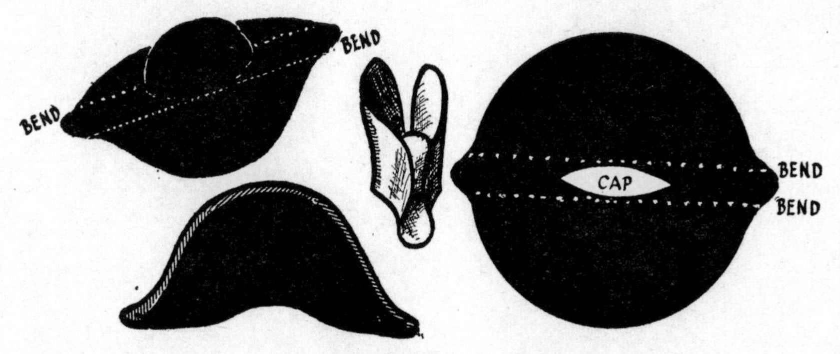

Fig. 12. Cocked hat (diagram).

cuffs, pocket-flaps and the tails. Such a coat would be worn with skin-tight white knee-breeches, white stockings (use tights), black pumps with silver buckles, white gloves and a black cocked hat, which, if it is carried under the arm, is easy enough to suggest. If, on the other hand, it has to be practical, it will have to be made from cardboard (stiff, but pliable) covered with some non-shiny material, and with an inner 'cap' —rather like a tea-cosy in shape—neatly sewn round the edge of the cut-out hole in the cardboard shape (*see* Fig. 12). It is not always necessary for a sword to be carried, but, as Surtes Cook specially refers to his when calling on Henrietta Barrett, in his case one would have to be hired.

CHAPTER 4

Stage Jewellery

Medallions, brooches and any other type of raised or rounded ornament can be built up and modelled with papier-mâché, which you can make at home by mixing flour and water together, and stirring into a paste and bringing to the boil on a gas-ring (stir all the time to prevent burning).

Small pieces of torn-up newspaper—about the size of a 2s. bit—are added and stirred in until the mixture becomes a thick, glutinous mess, which, when cool, can be modelled like clay.

Medallions, buttons, etc., should be based upon flat cut-out shapes (cardboard), but, for the sake of lightness (weight), if possible make the larger pieces hollow at the back. This can be done by lightly pressing the papier-mâché over a plasticine mould which has first been covered with a piece of damp gauze or butter muslin, so that, when dry, the relief will come away easily without sticking. It may take two or three days to dry, and, of course, the process would be quicker if the model is put into an oven (warm, but not cooking heated).

When completely dry, the pieces can be pulled away from the moulds, and then gilded, silvered or decorated in any way one wishes. 'Jewels' can be added in hollows left purposely to receive them, and one should make provision at the back for fastening to the dress, cloak or hat, or leave holes through which chains can pass for necklets and bracelets.

Alternatively, jewels can be made from plastic wood, which is light and easy to model and dries almost immediately. It can be bought in tins and tubes (Rawlplug is the best), but it is more expensive than making one's own papier-mâché. Always keep the plastic wood lid or screw-top on when not in use, as, if air gets to it, it dries up and then is completely useless.

Crowns can also be built from papier-mâché or buckram, but it is generally safer to use a wire foundation as well. When making a crown from papier-mâché, press the jewels you are going to use into the surface while it is still soft, to make a 'bed' for them, so that when the crown is dry they can be glued into position, with a little ring of thin cord round them for added decoration and to help keep them firm.

All sorts of intricate modelling can be done with string in various thicknesses, or with plastic wood, and sometimes in junk shops one can find boxes full of those old-fashioned glass lustres in squares and rounds, in blue (amethyst), red (ruby), green (emerald), amber (topaz) and crystal (diamond), each with two little holes, all ready for threading the gilt wire by means of which they can be turned into rings, pendants, or 'crown jewels'.

Dried peas, if carefully covered with cream-coloured celophane, make wonderfully realistic pearls—and, of course, if all else fails, there are always Rowntree's clear gums . . . provided you do not wear them out in the rain (pageants), which can be quite disastrous!

Individual jewels can also be made to any size required from lumps of cotton-wool soaked in size solution, which, when dry, can be painted with metallic colours or covered with the shiny outer coverings from toffees or chocolates.

For the less conventional and more 'modern' jewellery, a visit to Woolworth's store can produce astonishing results, not from the jewellery section, but from the ironmongery and other household goods counters . . . things like stair-rod sockets, parts of wireless and TV sets, ring-headed screws, and there is no end to the fascinating combinations that can be achieved with ingenuity, patience, imagination—and a length of brass wire!

For period costume decoration, the coloured metal tops from mineral water bottles make excellent buttons (pierce two holes at the sides and sew on) or studs and bosses on armour. Any confectioner who sells mineral waters on draught would gladly save these stoppers . . . if asked nicely!

Even the coloured tops of the milk bottles—blue, amber, green and silver . . . is there also a red one?—have their uses as costume decoration, and where a number of them are used together, they produce a most musically metallic symphony!

PART II

CHAPTER 5

Biblical

When one speaks of 'Biblical costume', one is usually thinking of the Hebrews, and in creating costumes for plays dealing with Old and New Testament subjects, a designer must bear in mind the influences—both cultural and domestic—of those other great and ancient civilizations (Chaldean, Canaanite, Assyrian, Babylonian, Persian, Egyptian, Greek and Roman), which, as powerful neighbours or conquering forces, so greatly affected the Jewish way of life, and consequently their costume.

The earliest form of clothing, so far as we know of it, was those skin coats (most likely sheepskin) made for Mr. and Mrs. A after that regrettable misunderstanding in the Garden. Certainly Cain and Abel wore no more, and when working in the fields probably considerably less!

Playrights have neglected exploring the dramatic potentials of the earlier Adam and Eve story, for reasons which, I suppose, we must accept as obvious, yet I remember when I was a schoolboy seeing an extremely naïve version of the 'Sixth Day Creation' (as a side-show in a fair), in which the somewhat revealing pink stockinette fleshings—loosely fastened up the back with hooks and eyes, of which one or two were missing—seemed a little crude, even to my juvenile perceptions . . . and I was much more interested in the acrobatics of the serpent!

By the days of the Flood, the known world had become largely agricultural, and cloth was being woven in wool or flax, from which a T-shaped tunic made its first appearance. Shaped like a stubby cross, it was made in one piece, with a hole in the middle for wearer's head to pass through, and it hung loosely and unfitted to the figure (knee-length for young men, and down to the ankles and caught in at the waist with a narrow girdle for women and older men).

The upper part of these tunics was roughly tacked together (thonged), with the sides left open halfway down from the waist to allow for greater freedom of action.

Furs, combined with the roughest quality hessian (sackcloth), without pattern or surface decoration, though in some instances dyed dull green or blue, rusty brown or an earthy ochre in one all-over colour, would be the materials and colours to use for the costumes. In those days, any colouring was obtained through vegetable dyes, but we have to do our best with anilines, and the cutting and putting together, as described above, should not present any problems (*see* Fig 13).

The story of Noah and his Ark has inspired several plays and sketches, of which *Noah*, by André Obey, is the best known.

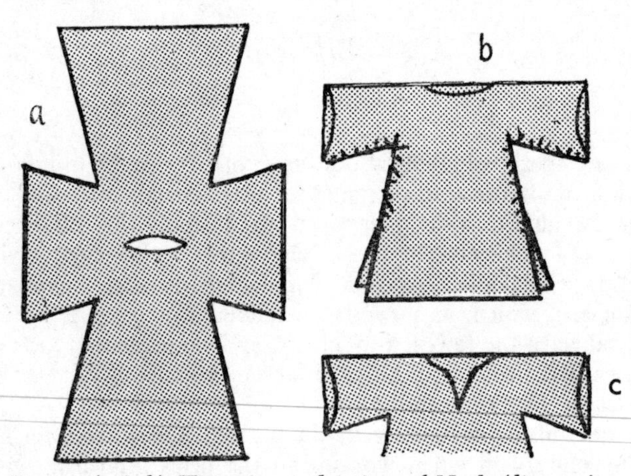

Fig. 13. (a & b) 'T' tunic, at the time of Noah (diagram); (c) alternative neck opening (later).

As time went by, a high-necked linen under-tunic with long, tight sleeves was worn by both men and women, with the top tunics of the men lengthening into robes, open down the centre, and reaching to the ankles, with a fringe round the hem. A wide, ornamented leather girdle or multicoloured woven sash went round the waist of the under-tunic, which later became correspondingly longer and provided a costume altogether more befitting the father of a family—or the dignity of the head of a tribe.

The Scriptures tell us that Abraham was born in Ur of the Chaldees, *circa* 2,500 B.C., and after a sojourn in Egypt emigrated into the land of Canaan. The costume influences, therefore, would be 'Chaldean, early-Egyptian, Assyrian and Canaanite' (and it is interesting to note that it was from the Canaanites that the Hebrews first learned the art of weaving that vertically striped terracotta and black cloth which became such a distinguishing feature of the Jewish costume).

Dramatists have found plenty of material for plays in the story of Abraham and Sarah, his wife, and *The Little Dry Thorn*, by Gordon Daviot, is one of them.

Abraham's great-grandson, Joseph, and later Moses, again connect the Hebrews with Egypt, though in the end, it was Joshua who led the Children of Israel across Jordan into the Land of Promise, with Israel dividing to the north (to fall under Assyrian domination) and Judah, the shepherd tribe, occupying the more pastoral south.

The boy David was just a shepherd lad, tending his father Jesse's flocks, when he went out alone to encounter Goliath, the Philistine's Assyrian champion, the splendour of whose armour is so vividly described by Samuel, the prophet . . . though it was, in the end, of little avail against the stone in David's sling!

The Boy David, by J. M. Barrie, deals with this episode and other adventures in David's youth before he became King. Because Elizabeth Bergner created the part in the theatre, every time the play has been reproduced since, David is performed by a woman, which to my mind is as silly as it is unconvincing, and that sort of thing is better left to pantomime. And now, I suppose, I'd better go and hide, before someone conclusively proves to me that David really *was* a woman . . . just as there are people who firmly believe that Elizabeth (not Bergner!) was a man!

Solomon (975-935 B.C.) definitely came under Assyrian influences, though his wife (would that be No. 1?), being a daughter of the Pharoah, probably continued to wear her native Egyptian dress. This custom would also apply to the Queen of Sheba, generally supposed to have been an Ethiopian, though I have yet to meet the actress with the moral courage to play her 'black'. Much as I admire the stirring acting of 'La Lollo', who appeared as Sheba in the recent film epic *Solomon and Sheba*, as far as any resemblance she bore to the Queen of the South, she might as well have been playing Snow White!

Norman Holland has written a delightful one-act episode entitled *In All His Glory*, in which the 'King of Kings, and Lord of the World', in an endeavour to amuse the 'spiritless' Queen, delivers a somewhat unconventional judgment.

Assyrian influences surround Delilah and her Philistine friends, in contrast to the simple Hebrew costume of Samson, while the tale of Ruth and Naomi, *circa* 700 B.C., with its charming glimpses into human relationships, would be played out against a more pastoral background.

In 586 B.C. Nebuchadnezzar beseiged and destroyed Jerusalem (the Babylonian captivity), and during this period came the well-known adventures of those salamanders, Shadrach, Meshach and Abed-nego . . . of Judith cutting off the head of Holofernes . . . of Tobit regaining his sight, and his son, of Tobias finding his courage—and a wife . . . and Susannah getting the better of those naughty Peeping Tom Elders!

With the famous feast of Belshazzar (the 'writing on the wall') the

Chaldean-Babylonian rule came to an end, falling to the sword of Darius, the Persian (528 B.C.). It was during his reign that Daniel was cast into the den of lions, and later there is the very actable story of King Ahasherus, and his obstinate wife, Vashti, and of Esther, the Jewess who managed to supplant her in the King's affections and so become his Queen (*circa* 480 B.C.).

In 331 B.C. Alexander the Great, in his turn, conquered the Persian Empire, with costume influences becoming Greek. His adventurous life, however, was cut short by his early death in 323 B.C.

In 164 B.C. Rome became the ruling power in Palestine, and, after a brief period of Hebrew independence under the Maccabees in 142 B.C., we come to New Testament times, with the costume reflecting a mixture of the Hebrew and Roman way of life.

THE HEBREWS

MEN

Setting aside the alien influences referred to above, the everyday dress consisted of the short, knee-length tunic, or the ankle-length, woollen, robe-like garment already described, with sometimes a loose smock, with long hanging-down points to the sleeves, worn over it. There was also a robe, open down the front and put on like a coat. This was called an *aba*, and probably Joseph's 'coat of many colours' was fashioned something like it.

The length of a tunic, by the way, had nothing to do with the rank of the wearer, and a King—as might be Saul or David—would just as likely have worn a short-skirted tunic when engaged in war, hunting or sport, while his attendants wore long ones. (David was certainly wearing an abbreviated tunic the day he danced before the Ark of the Covenant . . . and so 'amused' his wife, Michal.)

A large shawl draped over the tunic became as characteristic a feature with Eastern peoples as did the cloak with later Western civilizations. It was made from some soft, easy-to-drape material, with a fringe down one of the long sides, which became the base. To put it on, one narrow end was bunched together and thrown forwards over the left shoulder from the back. The rest of the shawl was taken across the back, brought forward under the right arm, and gathered up diagonally over the chest, and thrown back over the left shoulder, with the end hanging down the back (*see* Fig. 14).

Hebrew men usually wore their hair fairly long . . . very long if they happened to be Nazarites, who were not supposed to cut it at all. Many of them anointed their heads with costly oils, as a glossy head of hair was much admired, and all men had moustaches and beards.

The southern shepherd tribes wore white linen head-cloths, bound round with a twisted roll of the same material or by a coloured cord—

Fig. 14. (a & b) showing simple draping of early Hebrew shawl.

just as their desert ancestors had done—to protect their heads from the blazing sun and the burning sand. The northerners, on the other hand, wore conical caps, with the point falling forwards (or backwards), or a basin-shaped leather hat with a narrow, turned-down brim.

Fig. 15. Hebrew headgear: (a) the shepherd tribes of the south (Judah); (b) the pointed cap of the northerners (Israel); (c) leather hat, with brim (northern tribes); (d) domed hat of the Scribes and Pharisees.

Those famous 'double-acters', the Scribes and Pharisees, affected a stiff, round cap, worn over the head-cloth, and the more devout amongst them bound narrow strips of parchment round their foreheads and left wrists, bearing quotations from the Pentateuch (books of Moses). These phylacteries were believed to act as charms against danger and disease (*see* Fig. 15).

Both men and women generally went barefooted, or wore the simplest of sandals.

WOMEN

The dress of the Hebrew women consisted of: *(a)* A loose, short-sleeved, round-necked, ankle-length tunic, open down the front like a coat. *(b)* A rather tight, sleeveless tunic, with a V-shaped neck, reaching to the ankles and following the lines of the figure. Both of these garments were worn with a narrow girdle. *(c)* A loose tunic with long, pendent sleeves, reaching to the ground, with an ornamented sash with long, fringed ends wound round the waist. On top of this might be worn a loose, open, robe-like coat (similar to the men's *aba*), and as time went on women's clothes became more and more voluminous, until by New Testament days any suggestion of 'shape' or figure had almost entirely disappeared! (*see* Fig. 16).

All women—except those famous harlots—wore some form of head-dress over their elaborately braided hair, and upper-class ladies wore stiff little felt caps, plentifully besprinkled with sequins, with their heads and necks bound round with gauzy white veils (not unlike the twelfth-century wimples) or patterned scarves with fringed ends.

Fig. 16. Hebrew woman.

Their humbler sisters had to content themselves with the pointed cap, as described for men, or with a large shawl that covered the head and shoulders—as would be worn by the Madonna in a Nativity play.

Until recently it was still the custom for all Western women to cover their heads when entering a cathedral or church—and a protection as slight as a pocket-handkerchief . . . or even a piece of paper . . . was acceptable as fulfilling the letter of the law! I think, however, that St. Paul must have had something more substantial in mind, as the women of his day were compelled to cover their entire heads and faces with a veil, in which eye-holes were cut, which must have made them look like some weird sisterhood of the Ku-Klux-Klan!

Amongst the Hebrews, only the women wore jewellery—anklets, bangles, bracelets, rings, ear-rings . . . yes, and even rings through their noses!

Linen and wool were the main materials used, in dark tones of red, blue, brown, grey and, of course, white. Silk, though it was sometimes worn, was generally thought too sumptuous and smacking of the foreign invader!

The perpendicular red-and-black-striped cloth that became so typically a Hebrew motif was woven with either uniformly broad or alternating broad and narrow stripes, or with one broad and then several narrow stripes. Occasionally variety was obtained by wearing one robe over another, each of a different colour and pattern.

THE CHALDEAN-BABYLONIANS

MEN

The distinctive feature of the costume of this period (*circa* 2,500 B.C.) and one which Abraham would certainly have worn was a draped woollen shawl, either as his sole covering (not very 'safe' for the stage) or worn over a tunic, which would be long or short, according to what he was doing at the time.

This shawl was about 120 inches by 60 inches, with both of the longer sides fringed, and it was put on in the following manner: One corner would be held under the left arm, with the rest of the material pulled across the back and forward under the right arm, across the front (covering the legs like a petticoat) and under the left arm, again across the back, and then forward under the right arm, with the shawl then gathered together, and thrown diagonally over the left shoulder, with the end brought once more across the back, under the right arm, and finally tucked in, just in front of it.

Though the Old Masters usually depict Father Abraham with a venerable beard and a shock of grey hair, it was the custom with the early Chaldeans to shave their heads and upper lips, leaving only a fringe-like beard to their chins (*see* Fig. 17).

On their heads the Chaldeans often wore round, stiff caps, rather like our modern pill-box, or a peaked, close-fitting woollen hood. When travelling about, they carried a long staff or rod (branch of a tree), both as a protection and to help them over the rough ground, as their feet were bare and unshod.

In one of the Long Galleries in Hampton Court Palace, there is a tapestry that depicts Abraham bargaining for the Field of Ephron, as a burial place for Sarah, which offers a lot of useful information for men's costumes of this period.

Fig. 17. Father Abraham: showing the shaven head and chin-beard of the early Chaldeans.

WOMEN

The usual costume for women—and there wasn't much variety—was a fairly narrow, ungirdled ankle-length tunic with short tight sleeves, and a cape-like mantle reaching halfway to her knees, and consisting of a square piece of some soft, clinging material with fringed edges. This mantle was gathered in tight pleats round the throat, and fastened in front . . . and this is just the sort of thing that Sarah would have worn (*see* Fig. 18).

The hair was most elaborately arranged in tiers of braids and coils, each bound with lengths of gold wire or ribbon, and decorated with gilt flowers and leaves, with a forehead fringe of little golden rings. Ladies of wealth and rank wore a structure of blue and gold enamels at the backs of their heads, rather like the high combs worn by Spanish

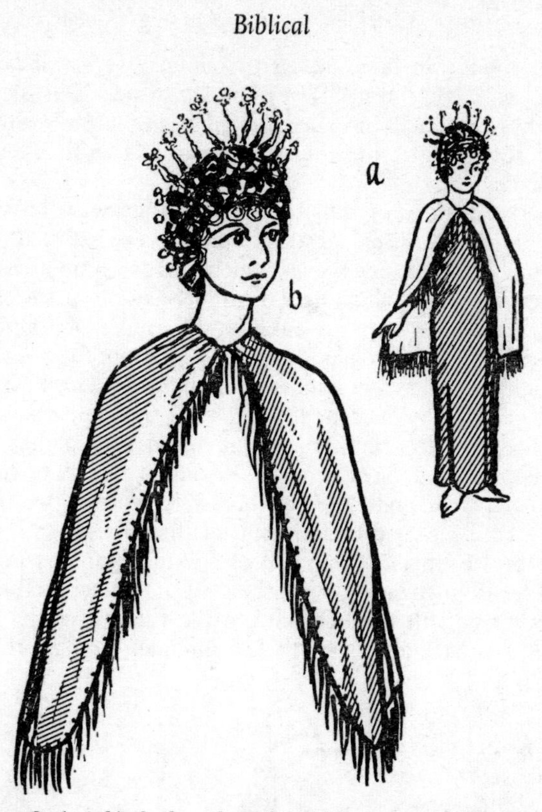

Fig. 18. (a & b) cloak and comb-headdress as worn by Sarah.

women today, but with the 'teeth' standing upright and a golden flower decorating each point (*see* Fig. 18*b*).

But though she might wear necklaces, bangles, bracelets, ear-rings and rings, madam's feet would still be bare!

THE ASSYRIAN-BABYLONIANS

MEN

By the time the Israelites had taken possession of the Promised Land (ousting the Canaanites in the process!) the Assyrians were the dominating power, with Nineveh as their military capital in the north, and Babylon the cultural capital in the south.

It was an age of great brutality and cruelty—a fighting man's world, in which there was little place for women. Yet never before in the history of the world (and not again until the Byzantine Empire, A.D. 400) had there been such splendour, or more bedizenning or bejewelling in costume, though in basic design the clothes were still quite plain: *(a)* the draped shawl by itself, *(b)* the shawl and short-sleeved tunic worn together—and *(c)* the knee- or ankle-length tunic alone, which, when worn for riding or hunting, sometimes had an inverted V cut in the front hem.

A distinctive feature of the Assyrian costume was the wide, close-fitting belt, which consisted of a strip of leather that went round the waist without being fastened, over which was worn another but much narrowed leather strap, which held the under-band in place (*see* Fig. 19).

Fighting men wore knee- or ankle-length tunics of soft chain-mail, much the same as the Crusaders wore in A.D. 1100.

In addition to the two methods for draping the shawl, as described for the Hebrews (simple) and the Chaldeans (not quite so simple) the Assyrians had another, slightly more involved system that required a somewhat larger rectangle of material—about 11 feet by 6 feet—fringed along both long sides, and folded unequally to produce two overlapping tiers, with a cord attached to both ends of this fold.

Method for wearing it: One end of the material was put over the right shoulder from the back, with the cord drawn across the chest and held at the waist with the left hand, while the rest of the shawl was taken round the back and over the left shoulder, draping the bent left

Fig. 19. Three examples of Assyrian costume: (a) the long tunic split up the front, for greater ease of movement in warfare or hunting; (b) method of draping the simple shawl; (c) method of draping the larger shawl (see also Fig. 20); (d) detail of the leather belt.

arm like an arm-sling. The folded part (top) was then taken across the front of the body, and round under the right arm, round the back again, and then coming forward past the left hip towards the right, with the remainder of the material folded underneath, and the second cord tied to the first on the right-hand side (*see* Fig. 20).

Such an arrangement with the shawl might be worn by a King, who, by virtue of his position, was also the High Priest. Yet, King or commoner—professional or amateur—it is unlikely that any man could adjust his shawl without the assistance of his 'dresser'!

It is worth noting that fringe was a most important accessory of the Assyrian costume—hems to tunics, edges for shawls, decoration on head ribbons, etc.—and the profusion with which it was employed, plus its length and thickness, and whether straight, twisted, or knotted as a tassel, all added up to define the wealth and position of the wearer.

Fig. 20. Diagrams demonstrating the draping of the larger shawl: (a) the method of holding and winding the shawl; (b) the completed arrangement; (c) the backview during process of draping.

The Assyrians had thick black hair, drawn behind the ears to hang at shoulder-length at the back and sides, with a heavy fringe across the forehead and rows of tight curls on top, bound round by a fillet (head-band) with long, fringed ends falling behind.

If suitable wigs cannot be hired, they can be made from thick black darning wool attached to a tight-fitting skull-cap (same colour as the actor's face make-up) and sewn on with a wide back-stitch, so that the wool hangs in overlapping tiers, with a parting down the centre and a heavy forehead fringe in front.

Alternatively, of course, a wig can be made from black crêpe hair (without taking out the kinky waves), and in either method, if the player wears some sort of headdress all the time (cap, hat or crown), the hair need be sewn only to the inside edge, which will save a lot of time and trouble.

All men wore moustaches curled at the ends, and long, thick curly beards cut off 'square' at the base; only eunuchs, and slaves attending on their King went clean-shaven and with their hair unbound. As the Assyrian beards looked artificial, anyway, it is quite easy to make one from black crêpe hair, shaping it to fit round the chin and jaw, and then sticking it on with white hard-spirit varnish, which is preferable to the spirit-gum bought in little bottles.

Some faces are softened by hair, and often the moustached and bearded young men one meets with in Tubes or 'buses look positively Apostolic. But not so the Assyrians! The more face-fungus they had, and the more plentiful their rings, ear-rings, bangles and armlets (in which most men would look completely 'sissy'), the more terrifying they appeared to their enemies as, like the wolf, they came down on the fold!

A hat like an inverted flower-pot (fez) with a little upstanding tab on top, or a high, stiff-crowned turban with a twisted cloth wound round the edge was the usual headdress for a King (without the thingummy for commoners). In battle, the Assyrians wore round brass or bronze helmets.

Like the Chaldeans, the Assyrians—including the King—as a rule were bare footed, but sandals or soft shoes were worn for hunting, with high leather boots, opening down the front and laced across, for battle. Shoes and sandals can be cut out from felt bedroom slippers, and then ornamented with gold paint, and the boots from thick, dark-brown (leather-colour) woollen socks, with elastic round the top edge to hold them up and the front lacing and decoration painted on. Boots can also be made from black or brown felt, seamed up the back and laced in front and attached to felt slippers.

WOMEN

The tunics worn by Assyrian women were very similar to those of the Chaldeans—long and unbelted, but with light, three-quarter-length sleeves and a high 'dog-collar' (jewelled in the case of a Queen or lady of high rank).

The shawl, however, was arranged slightly differently from the man's—rather more like an Indian *sari*—and it could be worn over either shoulder. It was 9 feet by 3 feet in size, and fringed along one long side only, which became the base.

When putting it on, one end was held in front of the hip, with the rest going round the back and forward under the opposite arm, and across the front to pass under the other arm, round the back, and forward again under the arm, being then drawn diagonally across the breast and over the shoulder, with once more round the back, and then forward to hang over the far shoulder. Try it out on a piece of paper, and you will find it isn't half as involved as it sounds!

Women wore their hair in a style very similar to the men's, gathering it into a bunch at the back to expose their ears, and with a forehead fringe bound round with a decorated fillet or crown. A small shawl or veil, besprinkled with sequins, was worn over their heads as a protection when walking in the hot sun. Their feet were bare, though on occasion they might wear sandals or soft shoes.

Wool, linen, silk and leather were the materials most in use for making the Assyrian garments, with red, green, purple, black and white for the colours, with gold and silver and jewels for ornamentation, the general effect being one of gaudy splendour rather than of good taste!

THE PERSIANS

MEN

In the year 528 B.C. the Persians conquered the ancient world and introduced a form of costume that greatly differed from the Chaldean-Babylonian-Assyrian, and this (believe it or not) was the 'coat and trousers'! Not, perhaps, quite like what we wear today, but definitely the forerunner of the late seventeenth- and early eighteenth-century garment that later developed into our modern 'two-piece'.

The main characteristic of the Persian coat was that it was no longer cut in one piece, but had separate, wrist-length sleeves that were fitted into armholes, and had a turned-back cuff, and a rectangular, turned-over collar round the neck, fastened in front with tie-ribbons.

This coat opened down the front, and reached to the ankles, and was sometimes worn draped round the shoulders like a cape, with sleeves dangling vacant and empty. I wonder how many of our gilded youth of today who sport this fashion with their teddy-bear overcoats, realize they are following in the footsteps of the Medes and Persians?

Another style of coat—which reached only to the knees and was cut away in front, with a sort of swallow-tail effect at the back, and had no collar, and was without cuffs on the long, straight sleeves—was held at the waist by a narrow belt. A similar garment to this was introduced into England during the twelth century by the knights returning from the First Crusade (while in Victorian times it became very popular as a 'dressing-wrap'!).

All Persians wore trousers, which were cut to follow the shape of the leg, gradually narrowing to the ankles, with a vertical line of braid down the outer leg, which greatly added to the 'slim' effect (*see* Fig. 21).

The Persians did not, however, entirely reject the tunic, though it differed from that of the Assyrians in length (often falling only to the knees) and in the tight, wrist-length sleeves . . . and, of course, the trousers appearing underneath.

Fig. 21. (a) A young Persian, in hood, coat (pelisse) and trousers, which were tailored to his leg, almost like tights. There was a vertical stripe of trimming down the outer seams (not visible in this drawing) which added to the slim effect; (b) a Persian woman, with draped scarf; (c, d & e) alternative types of hoods; (f) the ceremony of 'presenting the flower' (based on an old Persian painting).

Over such a garment, a King or nobleman might wear a robe, which was made in this manner; a rectangle of material (in dimension twice the height of the wearer from shoulder to floor, and with a width from finger-tip to finger-tip of the outstetched arms) was folded in half, with a hole cut for the head, and the sides seamed up to leave an armhole opening, 18 inches long on either side. A narrow belt was placed closely round the waist, and the material then drawn tightly across the back to bring the fullness to each side, and then pulled up

Fig. 22. Method of draping the robe of a Persian king.

under each arm, so that it hung over the belt in a wide swag, with the material at the front falling in a series of diagonal folds (*see* Fig. 22).

A King would probably wear sandals or soft shoes (felt) turned up over the toe, and with a slight point at the back of the heel, similar in shape to what we nowadays call 'Turkish' slippers. On the other hand, bare feet were quite frequent—with king or slave!

A rather charming custom of the ancient Persians was for a young man, when he went out for an early morning stroll, to carry a flower, which he presented—with wishes for a happy day—to the first person he might meet . . . whom (if he knew his stuff) would undoubtedly be a pretty girl . . . and I have been told the custom still prevails in Iran today!

Persian men wore their hair shorter than the Assyrians—but much more curly—and either covering or exposing their ears. The ends of their moustaches turned downwards, and their beards were longer and more pointed. Frequently, they wore no headdress, but had a twisted roll of cloth tied round their heads just above their bushy black eyebrows (crêpe hair stuck on, or the natural brows pushed the wrong way with a stick of Leichner No. 12 black grease-paint).

One form of headdress was a high, round crown-like band, trimmed along the top edge with feathers. Servants wore hoods, rather like white linen Balaclavas, that loosely encircled the face and covered the chin. There was also a stiff round hat, like a bowl—and, indeed, the crown of a bowler hat, painted white, with a small bunch of coloured ribbons hanging down at the back, would be exactly right. A hat such as this would probably be worn by a steward or upper servant (*see* Fig. 23).

Soldiers and fighting men, wore a similar hat, but made from iron (paint with a mixture of silver and black) with a chain mail Balaclava (knitted) framing the face—similar to those worn by the Crusaders.

Fig. 23. Types of Persian headdresses: (a) the fighting man's hood; (b) fillet worn when out hunting; (c) This headdress—looking like a birthday-cake, with a row of feathered candles—is not a king's crown, but the hat worn by a steward; (d) ordinary headdress—as opposed to a servant's hat; (e) turban headdress as worn by a young prince, as it might be the Shah Tahmasp. The high turban is surmounted with a long stick, known as the 'kulah', which was typical of the Safawi family. The feathers denote the wearer's princely rank.

WOMEN

The costume of the Persian women did not differ greatly from that of the Assyrians. The tunic was still long, close-fitting and unbelted, with tight sleeves and the fringed cape. One distinctive feature, however, should be noted, and that was the way in which the scarf was worn. It was a gaily-coloured strip about 12 inches to 18 inches wide and 108 inches long, fringed at both ends and down one long side. It was placed over the right shoulder from the back, so that it hung down in front of the knee. The rest of the scarf was taken across the back and forward over the left shoulder, passing diagonally over the breast and under the right arm, then across the back and forward under the left arm, turning the fringe towards the centre, with the end thrown straight back over this left shoulder to hang down behind. For stage purposes, it is generally better—and safer—to pin the folds together on the shoulders.

Hair styles were very similar to the Hebrew women, being piled high on top of their heads in elaborate braids, profusely decorated with shining ornaments, with a gauzy veil or a more solid scarf draping the head and shoulders.

Feet were usually bare, or, if shoes were worn, they were of the soft 'Turkish' variety, with the pointed, turned-up toes.

Materials and colours closely followed the Assyrian pattern, but were used with less excess—which also applies to the wearing of jewellery.

THE EGYPTIANS

MEN

The early Egyptians—perhaps more than any other of the older civilizations—exercised the influence of their culture on the ancient world. Those mighty stories of Joseph and Moses offer tremendous possibilities to the designer for contrast between the colourful Egyptian costumes and the simpler garments of the Hebrews, who, by reason of their religion and their blood, were generally isolated from open brotherhood with other nations.

By the first century B.C., however, Egypt—physically ruled by Rome, and spiritually dominated by Greece—had ceased to be one of the great powers.

Owing to the climate, most Egyptian men were very scantily dressed, though in this respect two considerations must be borne in mind: *(a)* the position (rank and importance) of the character being costumed and *(b)* his relationship to the job in which he was engaged . . . from which it will be gathered that there were but the two classes, the master and the slave, the served and the server, and there was nothing that could be done about it, unless, of course, one was lucky enough to be found floating in the bullrushes by the daughter of a Pharaoh. But, while the humblest slave, on the one hand, and the hunting Pharaoh, on the other, might both be clad in nothing more ambitious than a simple loincloth, the King's would be considerably better cut.

This scanty garment was originally merely a narrow piece of linen, wrapped round the body from the back and crossed over in front, with one end tucked into the waist and the other falling over, rather on the lines of a stock tie.

With this type of garment—on the stage—it is wise for the actor to take the precaution of wearing a jock-strap underneath. I recently saw an amateur performance of *The Firstborn* (Christopher Fry) in which the chap playing Pharoah, Junior had to fall 'dead' across the palace steps, and the flap of his white loincloth turned back, disclosing a pair of *black* bathing trunks, which completely ruined the emotion of the final curtain . . . at any rate for me, though it earned a well-deserved titter from the back seats!

Sometimes, instead of one of the ends being tucked in, it was taken backwards between the legs and fastened at the waist behind. Or the material might be stiffer, longer and fuller, and altogether more like a skirt that varied in length from just above the knees to down to the ankles, and was arranged either (shorter) with a stiff box-pleat in front or (longer) drawn tightly forwards from the back, with the material gathered in small pleats in front and tucked up into the belt, to fall in a series of graceful folds. A wedge-shaped leather tongue, or tab, hung down in front from the centre of the belt—rather like a sporran! —and it was decorated with a pattern in enamelled metal (floral or leaf design), or, if the wearer happened to be a slave, the tab would be made from cloth, with his (or her) master's name worked in hieroglyphics (*see* Fig. 24).

The Egyptians also wore the close-fitting, knee-length linen T-tunic, cut in one piece, with a round neck and short sleeves, and held at the waist by a belt. Another version, a bit longer and made of transparent gauze, was worn over a simple loincloth, while a third was designed in a soft, clinging material, with short sleeves and reaching to the ankles, with a belt round the middle.

With the long tunic, a shawl was often worn. This was a rectangular strip some 12 feet long and 3 feet 6 inches wide, and arranged in the following fashion: First, it was draped from the back to fall in front of the left shoulder, with the end just touching the instep. A belt, fastened slightly higher than the waistline, was then put right round the body and the shawl, so that the piece hanging down the back could be lifted and brought forward over the left shoulder and draped like a cloak round the left arm, and held in position in front with the unseen left hand. If desired it could, of course, be slipped back again over the shoulder, to hang behind (*see* Fig. 25).

There was also a robe, which was much fuller, and made a much more graceful garment, and which was exceedingly simply made from a rectangle of close-patterned material, in length about twice the wearer's height from shoulder to floor, with a width equal to the span of finger-tip to finger-tip of the outstretched arms.

This piece was then folded in half, and a hole cut for the head with the sides sewn up, leaving about 18 inches unjoined under the arms (these openings became the sleeves). A wide sash, coming round the hips from the back, and tied in front, with the ends hanging down, allowed the robe to be pulled tightly across the back, so that all the fullness was concentrated towards the front, which was characteristic of all Egyptian costumes where any attempt was made at draping. Sometimes this robe was worn without the sides being sewn up at all—

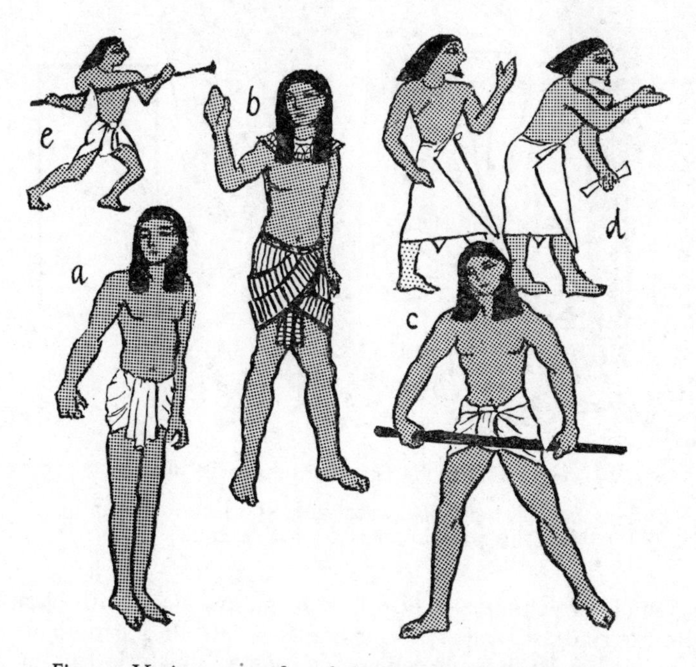

Fig. 24. Various examples of the Egyptian loin-cloth worn by men: (a & e) the simple cross-over pattern, as worn by slaves; (b) pleated loin-cloth as worn by a pharaoh—notice that the end hangs underneath, and not over, as in (a); (c) loin-cloth as worn by workers in the fields—occasionally a transparent gauzy over-tunic was worn, which covered the body, without concealing it; (d) the 'box-pleat' type of loin-cloth, as seen in Egyptian friezes.

without a sash—and with no attempt at draping. Usually, a long tight under-tunic was worn (*see* Fig. 26).

A very important adjunct of the Egyptian costume—and worn by both men and women alike—was the flat 9-inch-wide circular collar, that extended from the base of the neck to the shoulders and chest. It was made from glazed, baked clay beads—some long and narrow and others fat

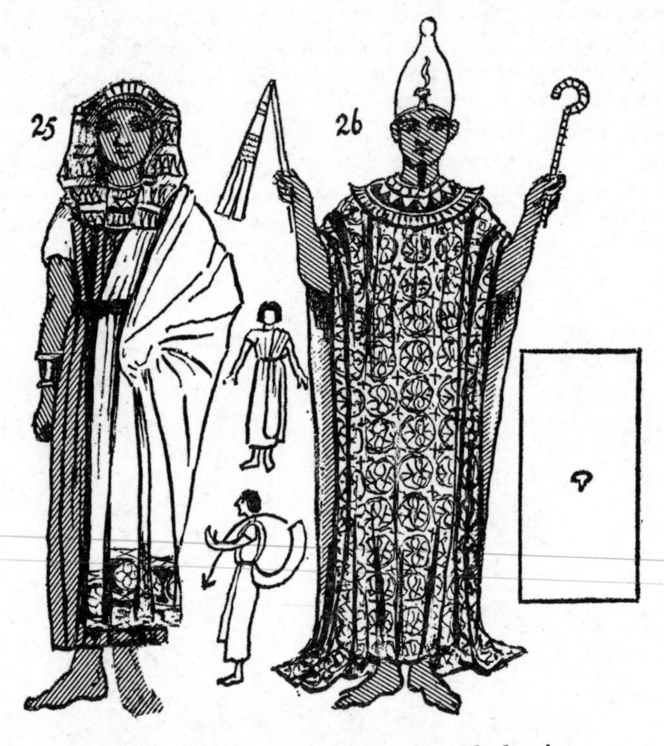

Fig. 25. The long Egyptian tunic, with shawl.

Fig. 26. Full, long robe, worn without a belt, and open up the sides. This was put on over an under-tunic.

and round—which were painted in reds, greens, blues, with black and white for contrast, and strung on flexible wire in a pattern of concentric circles. Shells and semi-precious stones and little bars of gold (bored like beads) were also used.

Such a collar, of course, looks best, and hangs with a truer feeling of the correct weight, if it is made in the right way, with the beads strung on a wire frame, as suggested above. It is, however, quite tricky, and may take a bit of time! Still, I have seen some lovely examples made by amateurs.

The collar can be cut from a circular-shaped piece of stiff linen or canvas, with an opening at the back and holes punched for lacing it together . . . and, of course, a central opening for the head! This material can then be painted with oils, or real beads can be sewn on (in which case dye the foundation as near as possible to the wearer's Egyptian skin-tone). A piece of plain white oilcloth—American cloth, I think it's called—if cut and shaped and then painted in oils, would have a definite sense of weight, and would hang well. Don't forget to bind any raw edges with white, blue or red bias-binding.

Never use glass beads or any sparkling jewels for Egyptian ornaments, which were always 'dull': gold and blue, in all its shades, including a blue with the faintest touch of green in it, were the most popular colours.

The decorated girdle, with the tongue or tab, was another important item of costume, and was made either from painted leather or embroidered material, to which sometimes metal discs were attached and worked into the pattern, which helped to weigh it down.

Flat bracelets, armlets and anklets were worn by both men and women, and these were in gold and enamels, and some of the armlets were joined together by 'bridges', one above the other, from wrist to elbow (use strips of painted elastic). The armlets can be made from empty soup, fruit or vegetable tins if they are first opened with one of the many patent can-openers that take off the top and bottom without leaving a rough edge. Anklets can be made in the same way, but the tins will have to be cut open vertically as well, and some means devised for fastening round the ankle . . . lacing seems the most practical, with holes punched along both edges. The tins should be painted in vertical parallel designs with oil paints, and jewels can be added. Occasionally these can be made from blobs of coloured sealing-wax—or clear gums!

Legs, of course, were bare, and so generally were the feet, but sandals were worn, and consisted of perfectly flat soles cut a trifle longer than the foot and ending in a point, which should be wired round the edge so that it can be turned up at the toe. A tight, wide (elastic) band, beautifully ornamented in gold and enamels, went across the instep to hold the sandals to the foot.

The Egyptians' hair was plentiful . . . and black! Not, however, woolly like the Ethiopians, nor curled like the Assyrians and Persians. There were several styles:

(a) A round, fairly tight 'bob', arranged in overlapping layers, rather like the painted heads of those wooden Dutch dolls one used to be able to buy, but without the centre parting.

(b) Similar to the above, but with the hair longer at the back and exposing the ears.

(c) A long loose 'bob', covering the ears and with a heavy fringe on the forehead. Sometimes, a simple fillet—1-inch- or 2-inch-wide ribbon—would be added and tied round the head.

(d) The hair worn long, parted in the centre, drawn back behind the ears, and hanging down at the back, with two 'rolls' in front—cut square at the ends—falling a few inches below the collar-bone at either side of the neck (*see* Fig. 27).

In the heyday of the Egyptian Empire (1600-1150 B.C.) men's hair was as often as not an undisguised wig, worn low on the forehead, and cut square at the ends, which were curled into tight little corkscrews, a few strands at a time. After 1150 B.C., when the power of Egypt was on the decline, these wigs were often dyed red and blue and other bright colours . . . probably a sign of decadence!

Sometimes these wigs were covered with a cloth 'shape', patterned in rows of vertical stripes one above the other, with horizontal lines dividing the rows. Many of the ancient sculptures and paintings on the lids of the Pharaoh's mummy cases in the British Museum show this type of headdress.

To make such a head covering, you need a piece of stiffish material, 42 inches by 36 inches with the striped design painted in first with dyes, oil colours or poster paints. A strip of webbing, or similar stiff material, is then cut 2 inches wide and long enough to go round the actor's forehead, behind his ears, and fasten at the back (hooks and eyes or press-studs). The centre of the 42 inches width is then fixed to the middle of the headband and sewn along the base in both directions.

The band should now be 'tried' round the actor's head, fastening it under the cloth, so that the loose ends at the sides fall forward. These can then be cut in a 'square' wedge in front, with the pleats sewn together to make a flat panel on each side of the neck (*see* Fig. 28). It may be necessary to insert a 'dart' at the back to give a neat, flat effect. Soft paper stuffed into the two front peaks over the fore-head should greatly help with the square shape.

Certain headdresses and ornaments were only worn by the gods and members of the blood royal, such as the *uraeus* (hooded cobra), which was attached to the crown worn by the Pharaoh, or to a metal fillet, which was tied to his head by ribbons at the back.

Fig. 27. (a, b, c & d) Four examples of Egyptian hair styles for men.

Fig. 28. Wig cover—(a) for men and (b) for women.

Ordinarily, men were clean-shaven, but occasionally—for ceremonial purposes—a thin, round, pointed beard about 6 inches long was attached to the tip of the chin, and held in position by a narrow band that followed up the line of the jaw. Such a beard could be made from black crêpe hair and attached to a thin black elastic band (*see* Fig. 29).

Fig. 29. Method of attaching Chin-beard.

WOMEN

Egyptian women wore a short-sleeved tunic very similar in style to the men's, except that it was longer—down to the calf, ankle or floor—and the high waist was confined just below the breasts by a narrow belt, with the long ends hanging down in front. This enabled the drapery to be pulled forwards from the back, so that it fell in the typically graceful, radiating folds. A cape, made from a piece of soft material, cut to three-quarters of a circle in shape, was sometimes worn over this tunic, being draped over the shoulders, with the two points tied or fastened in front and covered by the circular beaded collar (*see* Fig. 30).

The robe was also cut in a similar way to that described for men, but the method for draping it was different, so that when it was put over the head the front edges (at waist-high level) were drawn backwards and pinned behind, with the back edges tightly pulled forwards and fastened

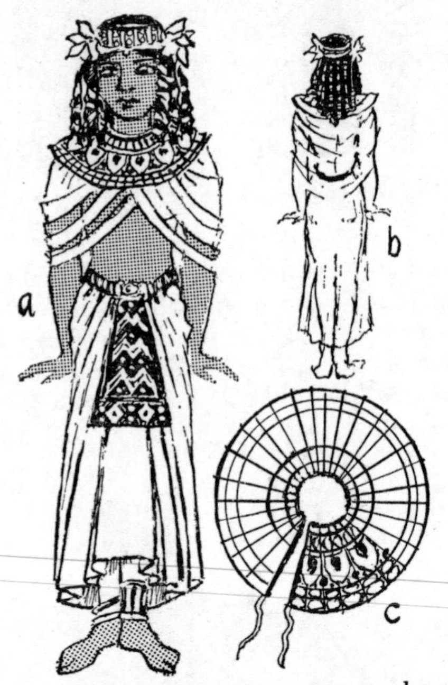

Fig. 30. (a) Egyptian woman's costume, showing the custom of bringing the fullness to the front. This diagram combines the cape and typical beaded collar, with the 'sporran' type of girdle; (b) backview; (c) detail for construction of the collar.

together over the breasts. A soft, wide girdle that came from the back between the two panels of the robe was then tied round the waist.

Women's feet were usually bare, but sandals were worn. In 1912 there was a farce at the Strand Theatre called *The Glad Eye*, which was just another description for giving the 'come hither' look, but it added a new expression to the vernacular! In the late 1920s the film-star, Mae West, gave 'the look' a new twist with her arch invitation to 'Come up and see me sometime'. In ancient Egypt the soles of some of the women's sandals had an arrangement of studs underneath that left the provocative imprint 'AKO OYOEI' in the sand . . . meaning 'Follow me'!

Female slaves were equally as scantily dressed as their opposite number, often in nothing more than an ankle-length wrap-round skirt, rather on the lines of Dorothy Lamour's famous *sarong* . . . except that in their case it came no higher than the waist (which is something Mr. Hays and his convention would never have allowed !) . . . while dancing girls were even skimpier—just ear-rings and a string of beads.

Only rarely did women cut their black hair short like the men's, and as a rule it was worn long and hung loosely over their shoulders, and down to the waist at the back. Sometimes the hair was tucked behind the ears (though more often it covered them), with the ends cut straight and arranged in ringlets or in rows of tight curls, which were ornamented with small gold discs or with gold wire or ribbons twisted in alternate spirals. Women also wore wigs of different colours, some of which were covered with the decorated cloth cases, as described above.

Often, a simple fillet (2-inch-wide ribbon) went round the head, and was tied at the back, with the ends hanging down. Or the band might be of metal ornamented with jewels, to which the *uraeus* could be added in front. Occasionally a lotus flower was placed above the fillet, with the stem lying across the top of the head—like a parting. Another characteristic head-ornament was the scent cone, filled with sweet-smelling ointment. It was about 4 inches high and 3 inches or 4 inches in diameter, and was worn balanced on top of the head, like a little crown (*see* Fig. 31).

The more elaborate headdresses were worn by the royal family, and

Fig. 31. Egyptian women's hair styles: (a) the vulture cap, symbol of Maati, the goddess of truth; (b) metal fillet, with the feathers of Isis, and the uraeus, or hooded cobra; (c) the scent-cone and lotus flower; (d) the royal feather, with ribboned fillet; (e) ornamented diadem headdress; (f) fillet, with lotus flowers.

the *uraeus* appears on the front of many a crown, with the asp motif on others. A Queen was allowed to wear the sacred feathers or plume of Isis, and Cleopatra often wore the *maati*, or vulture-wing cap. Other royal headdresses were the crowns of upper and lower Egypt, and these would have to be made from either papier-mâché or buckram mounted on a wire frame, and then painted. Thick zinc wire can be used to form the *uraeus*, or a little strip of narrow lead piping flattened out by a hammer (*see* Fig. 32).

The costuming of an Egyptian play should not prove too difficult if one bears in mind the two main essentials: *(a)* the extreme scantiness of the garments, revealing as much of the figure as possible, even when

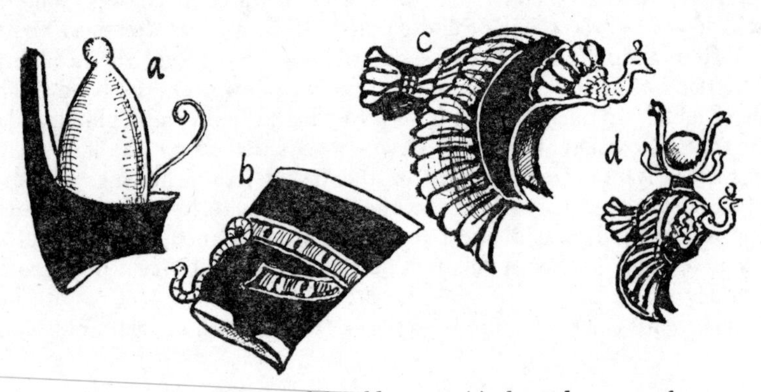

Fig. 32. Egyptian royal headdresses: (a) the red crown of Upper Egypt, and the white crown of Lower Egypt; (b) an Egyptian queen's headdress; (c & d) the 'vulture' cap of Maati, the goddess of truth—Cleopatra is often depicted wearing it.

the costume covers the wearer from neck to toe, and *(b)* that any fullness of the drapery is achieved by pulling it tightly round the body from the back, and concentrating it in front, thereby outlining the shape at the back.

Most of the clothes can be made from the simplest means, the principal material for all garments being linen—for which we can quite easily substitute cotton—and usually it was left brilliantly white, in contrast to the rich, bronzed flesh-tones, but, of course, it can also be dyed, and decorated with embroidered or appliquéd designs in bright prime colours (*see* Fig. 33).

The texture of the linen (or cotton) was either opaque or transparent as gauze, and, if the audience will stand for it, nothing should be worn underneath but full-length tights and 'fleshings' (dyed to correspond with the player's make-up), and with the material cunningly arranged

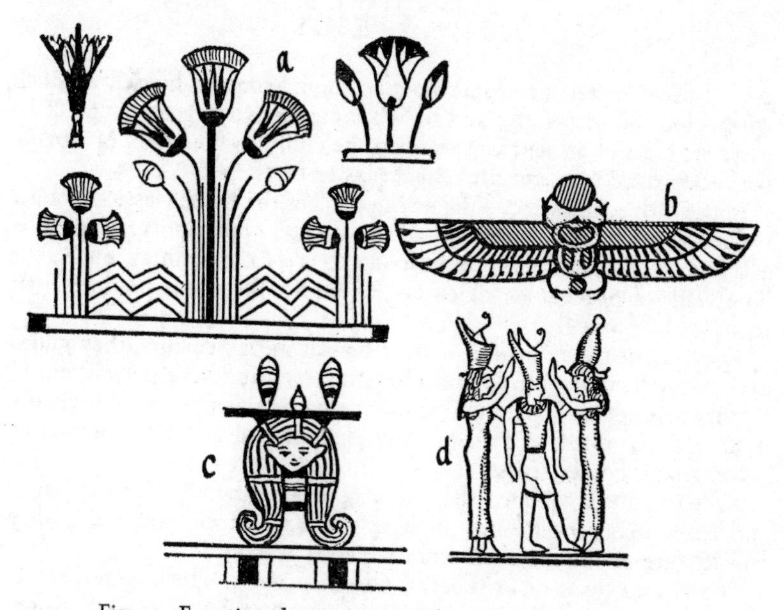

Fig. 33. Egyptian decorative motifs: (a) the lotus; (b) the scaraboeus, or sacred beetle; (c) the naos; (d) figure subject.

over the 'danger spots'! If it is essential to use thicker materials, then what is worn below is not so important, provided it is not bulgy or bumpy!

Egyptian characters can be made up in all shades of red-brown—from tan to cocoa—but the women should be less deeply coloured than the men and always paler than their female slaves.

The Egyptians used make-up quite openly, reddening their lips (though never the cheeks) and shading their eyelids with various shades of blue. The outline of the eyes was emphasized with two black lines that extended some way beyond the outer corners (*see* Fig. 34).

Fig. 34. Egyptian eye make-up.

THE GREEKS

As has been shown, a costume designer should concern himself as much with colour as with form, and he will not, therefore, get very far if he bases his ideas of ancient Greece upon the chilly testimony of black-and-white reproductions and art school plaster casts.

In the fifth century B.C.—the main period of the Greek classical dramas—Greece was a land of promise, adventure and opportunity, peopled by a warm-blooded, southern race, living in a fertile country under the blue vault of heaven. A golden age, in which there was precious little room for half-tones!

They painted the outsides of their houses in gay colours, they gilded and inlaid their furniture, and even their statues were polychromed! So that it is not surprising to learn that their garments were also vividly dyed and decorated, and all but the plainest had at least a decorative pattern or a border stripe.

As with the Egyptians, the Greek costume depended for its beauty and effect upon the manner in which it was draped, and the quality and texture of the materials from which it was made.

There were three main types of Greek garment, which were practically the same for both men (Ionian) and women (Dorian), and consisted of *(a)* the *chiton* or tunic, worn either short or long, *(b)* the *himation* or shawl, and *(c)* the *chlamys*, a cloak or mantle.

MEN

The Ionian *chiton* was worn short by the young and active, and longer by older men, and it was made from a rectangle of linen or woollen material, measuring in length from the base of the neck to the knees, or just below (about 3 feet 6 inches, which will allow for the necessary 'blousing' over the belt), with a width double the distance from finger-tip to finger-tip of the extended arms.

This rectangle was then folded in half lengthwise, and wrapped round the wearer, with the wider opening to the right, and fastened on the shoulders (pinned or sewn), with the back overlapping the front on either side of the head, leaving the neck comfortably free. There was now some loose material hanging over on each side, and this was used to form the short sleeves by being pinned together, in the typical Grecian manner, by little brooches set at 2-inch intervals down the outer arm. Sometimes a narrow-patterned border ran along the top in front of and behind the neck opening and down the outside of the sleeves, which could, of course, be sewn in preference to pinning.

A belt was added round the waist, and the *chiton* pulled up all the way round, thereby adjusting it to about mid-thigh.

Young boys, workmen and slaves often wore the short *chiton* fastened on the left shoulder only (pinned, knotted or sewn), with the right shoulder and arm free and the chest left bare.

For the longer *chiton*, of course, the length measurement would be increased, but basically the design was the same. But whichever way the *chiton* is worn on the stage, the open side on the right is usually sewn up, so that the garment can virtually be put on over the head like a shirt.

A different method, however, was employed for holding the longer garment together round the body. A long narrow cord or ribbon was folded in half, with the V loop thrown back over the shoulders from the front, and the two ends passed backwards under the arms, and linked through the V at the back. These ends are then pulled tightly, and brought forward round the waist and tied in front, with a leather belt covering the bow (*see* Fig. 35).

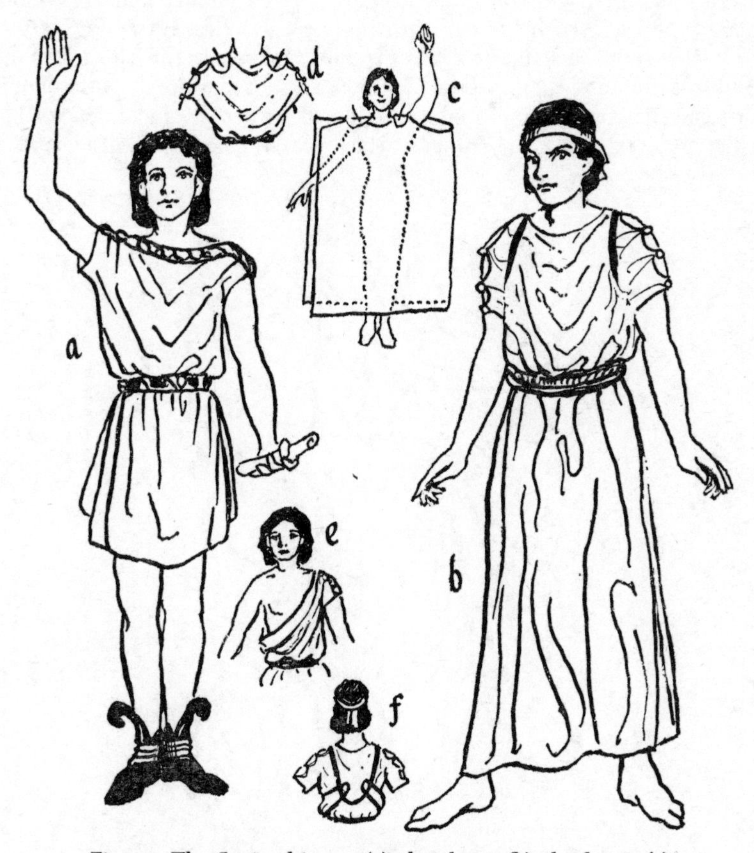

Fig. 35. The Ionic chiton: (a) the short; (b) the long; (c) diagram showing how the chiton is formed; (d) how the short sleeves are made; (e) the 'off-the-shoulder' chiton; (f) back-view of 'b', showing arrangement of girdle.

Either type of *chiton* could be made from a thin blanket, a piece of canvas or hessian (dyed) or a wide length of bath-towelling, which can be bought with a pattern of differently coloured horizontal stripes.

The *himation,* which was worn with both the long and short *chiton,* was some 9 feet to 12 feet in length, with a width equal to the distance from under-arm to ankle . . . about 4 feet 6 inches to 4 feet to 9 inches (I have estimated all these measurements from myself, but, of course, they would vary according to the height of the actor concerned).

One corner of the rectangle is held high under the left arm, and the shawl draped over the front to pass under the right arm and diagonally across the back, to come forward over the left shoulder and upper arm. The shawl is then given a 'twist' (turned back to front) as it crosses the body again towards the right arm, which it drapes rather as if it were in a sling, and continues over the right shoulder and once more across the back, with the end thrown over the left arm (*see* Fig. 36).

If the above instructions are carefully followed, the effect can be both pleasing and dignified, but I suppose only an orator, a philosopher, or some character of high rank (with lots of leisure . . . and a dependable valet!) would affect anything so elaborate and hand-impeding, and a

Fig. 36. (a) the himation; (b, c, d & e) diagram showing the four stages in draping the himation.

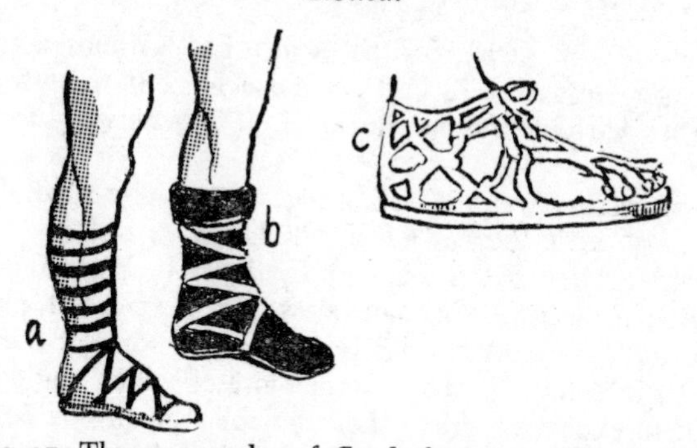

Fig. 37. Three examples of Greek footwear: (a) an early warrior—black tape and a sole! (b) Ordinary Greek footwear—a rolled-down black stocking, and white tape! (c) A more elaborate type of sandal, as seen on the feet of statues of Hermes and other of the gods.

much simpler way to wear the *himation* is just to throw one end over the left shoulder from the back, and take the rest round behind and forwards under the right arm, and then diagonally across the chest, throwing it over the left shoulder, with the end hanging down at the back, thus leaving both hands free—rather like the Hebrew shawl.

The *chlamys* was also a rectangle in shape (average dimensions, 6 feet by 3 feet 6 inches), with the two top ends fastened round the neck or held on the right shoulder with a brooch. It was often gaily patterned, and was therefore rather more popular with younger men. Some Greek statues—the Apollo Belvedere is one—seem to suggest that the *chlamys* was sometimes a man's only garment, which might prove a bit tricky on a draughty stage.

Men usually went barefooted, but on occasion sandals of the very simplest kind were worn, being little more than a thick sole, with a thong between the big and second toe, joined by another thong coming round the heel. Soft leather boots, laced up the front, were worn for hunting, some of them so close-fitting and plain that they could very easily be 'faked' with a dark sock, with a leather thong (leather football-boot laces) tied round the tops to keep them up (*see* Fig. 37).

The early Greeks wore their dark hair long and curly, either hanging down naturally round their heads or, if very long, caught up in a knot or bun at the back and decorated with gold pins!

A mourning widower would cut off his tresses and sorrowfully dedicate them to the spirit of his dear departed . . . though what she was supposed to do with them was never very certain! Charioteers and athletes at the Olympics kept their hair out of their eyes by wearing broad, flat head-bands. However, by the end of the fifth century B.C. men's hair was being cut fairly short and bound round with a simple fillet.

Generally, young men were clean-shaven, but in very early times some of them wore a stiff, little, pointed beard—but without a moustache. Older men had both a beard and a moustache, but though the beard might be worn without the moustache, a moustache was never seen on its own!

Greek men seldom went in for headgear, and protected their heads when necessary with the end of the *himation* or *chlamys*. However, there were caps, rather like those worn by the Hebrews, and a hat called a *petasos*, which was a wide-brimmed, low-crowned sun-hat, plaited from palm leaves and grasses. A curious feature is that some of them had the brims divided into four 'petals', one or more of which could be turned up or down to expose or shield the face from the sun as desired. This is curious only because we shall meet with just such a hat (but in velvet) in Henry VII's reign! There was also, of course, the winged hat of Hermes.

The Greek soldier of mythology apparently wore nothing but his *chlamys* and a helmet, but later 'battledress' consisted of a *chiton* and a leather cuirass covered with overlapping metal (bronze) scales, and bronze or brass greaves, looking exactly like metal cricket-pads!

Shields were convex, and either oval or round, with strong arm-grips on the inside, and both inside and outside were decorated. The oval shields sometimes had a sort of 'bite' cut out from the sides, that made them look like the body part of a violin. A sword-belt was worn from over right shoulder to left hip, with a short, thick and possibly curved sword. Other weapons were the javelin, the sling and the bow, with the arrows carried in a leather or basket-work quiver.

WOMEN

Until the end of the fifth century B.C. the almost universal costume for Grecian women was the Dorian *chiton* (or *peplos*) a woollen rectangle—often decorated with a border along all four sides—about 12 inches to 18 inches (sometimes more) longer than the wearer's height, and double the span of her outstretched arms in width. This was draped round her body in exactly the same way as the men's Ionian *chiton*, but with the extra length shortened to reach from shoulder to floor (or a trifle longer for 'blousing') by folding the material over all the way round at the *top*, with the two portions held together with stick-pins on either side of the neck, and with the back held tightly in a straight line and the front falling in a loose fold in what I think dressmakers call a 'cowl' or 'halter'.

A girdle was added round the waist, and the material, when it was pulled up to hang over it, was called the *kolpos*. The fold-over on the breast was an essential feature of the Dorian *chiton*, and even when the open side on the right was sewn up, as actually happened in the course of time (and as should always be done for the stage) this fold-over was usually left open (*see* Fig. 38).

As will readily be appreciated, the Dorian *chiton* allowed for a variety of different treatments, as, for instance, if the fold-over was made long enough to fall below waist-level to the hips, the girdle was often tied over it in a style known as the Minerva. Sometimes two girdles were worn, one above the other, with the *chiton* 'bloused' up over each of them, and with the hem-line of the skirt only reaching to the knees (suitable for a girl athlete or the huntress goddess, Diana).

Occasionally a long cord or ribbon was put round the neck from the back, with the two ends coming over the shoulders and crossed over the breast, and taken round the waist to the back and brought forward again, and tied in a bow in front (*see* Fig. 39).

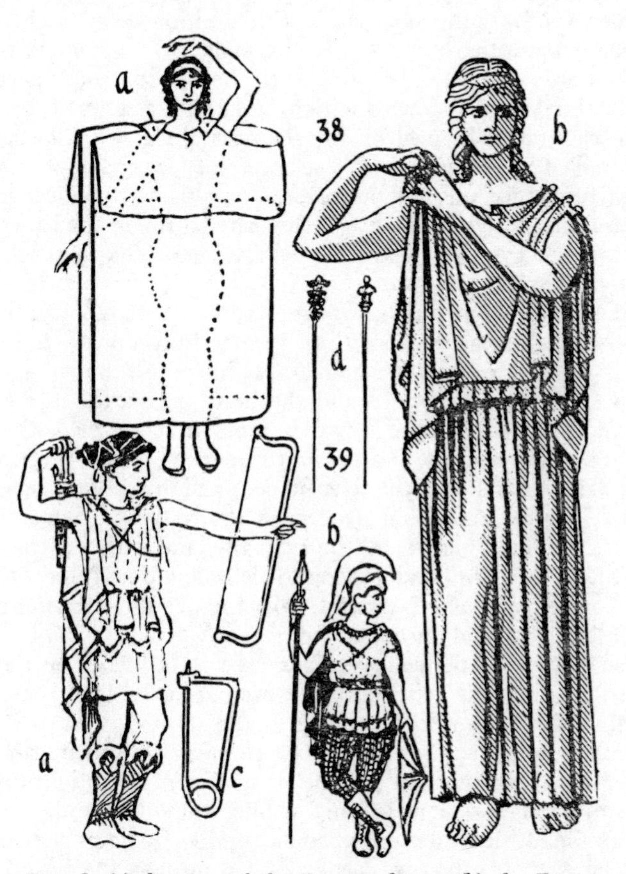

Fig. 38. (a) diagram of the Dorian chiton; (b) the Dorian chiton, with peplos and kolpos.

Fig. 39. (a) Woman athlete engaged in archery; (b) an Amazon; (c) the earliest example of a safety pin (fibula); (d) two examples of the shoulder 'stick-pins.'

The gold stick-pins referred to above for fastening the *chiton* on the shoulders were rather like Victorian hatpins with decorated heads and murderously sharp points, that stuck up towards the wearer's face. There is a legend that during one of the Athenian raids on the island state of Aegina (during a dispute for the command of the sea) only one man escaped alive, returning alone to tell of the disaster. The wives of his comrades crowded round him, each demanding where her husband was, and stabbing him with her pin until he died. As a result of this barbarous deed, the Athenians forced their womenfolk to change from the Dorian *chiton* to the Ionian, with the over-fold omitted and held at the shoulders and down the arms with buttons or brooches (*fibulae*—an extremely early example of our modern safety-pin).

Women also wore the *himation*, as described for men, but there were individual ways of putting it on. For example, *(a)* a rectangle was put round the body under the left arm, with the two top ends fastened on the right shoulder, and down the right arm, with a series of *fibulae*, or the two ends could be held by the shoulder *fibula*, with the material hanging down the front and the back and not fastened down the arm. Yet another method was to drape one end over the left shoulder to hang down in front, bringing the rest of the material round the back, under the right arm, over the breast diagonally, and draped over the left shoulder and arm.

With an extra large *himation* (about 12 feet long and 4 feet 6 inches wide), the whole head and body can be gracefully draped, thus: One corner is pinned to the right shoulder, with the rest drawn across the body in front, partly going round the head and partly covering the left shoulder and upper arm. It is then brought across the back, round the right shoulder and upper arm (which, to give the best effect, should be held akimbo) and over the left shoulder and arm. Again across the back and over the right shoulder, across the body and round the left hip, round the back and round the right hip, and with the end of the shawl held in the right hand, leaving the left hand free. These directions can, of course, be reversed, starting from the left shoulder and ending up with the right hand uncovered (*see* Fig. 40).

Women also wore the *chlamys*, fastened with a brooch on the right shoulder, draping the left side. Feet were usually bare, but gaily-coloured sandals were worn.

In the earliest periods—600-480 B.C.—women wore their hair hanging down over their shoulders in front in a series of long, tight rope-like curls, with a 2-inch-wide plain band or fillet round the head.

During the fifth century—480-400 B.C.—which came to be known as the Golden Age, their hair was generally 'put up', and the most popular and typical style was to build it out in a pointed knot at the back, which had a kind of balancing effect for the nose when seen in profile!

There were several ways in which the hair could be adorned. For example, *(a)* a diadem or coronet could be worn as an upright decoration,

Fig. 40. (a) Grecian woman, wearing the himation; (b, c, d & e) diagram showing method for draping.

over the forehead, or in reverse as a support for the piled-up hair at the back; *(b)* one, two or three tightly-wound ribbons, holding the hair closely to the head. In any of these arrangements, the temptation to unduly exaggerate the natural shape of the head must be avoided!

Both men and women alike shielded their heads from the heat of the sun with the *himation* or *chlamys*. Women also wore the sun-hat *(petasos)*, similar to the men's, but with a higher, more pointed crown, and sometimes they combined it with the *himation* (you will see girls by the seaside today wearing beach-hats over head scarves, with a very similar effect) (*see* Fig. 41).

In describing Grecian women's costume, one cannot omit mention of the Amazons, who were a warrior race of warlike females who were said to cut off their right breasts so that they could use the bow more comfortably! They dressed like men, with the short *chiton* and *chlamys*, and when they went on 'mating raids' they added a leather cuirass and leggings, wore helmets, and carried shields, javelins, bows and arrows . . . and sometimes axes (presumably in case their 'victims' showed resistance!).

One of the twelve labours of Heracles was to steal the Amazon Queen's belt. Benn Levy, in his amusing play, *The Rape of the Belt*, introduces us to the Amazonian Palace, ruled over by *two* Queens—one of whom 'falls' for Heracles and the other for his friend, Theseus.

Hippolyta, Queen of the Amazons, appears in Shakespeare's *A Midsummer-night's Dream* as the bride-to-be of Theseus, and it is a stage convention for the actress playing this part to dress it as much like an

Fig. 41. (a) the coronet worn in front, and (b) in reverse, to support the hair; (c) a ribboned headdress; (d) the petasos (sun-hat); (e) a modern girl's sun-hat, worn over a head scarf; (f) The petasos, as worn by men.

Amazon warrior as possible in the opening scene—not necessarily in full armour, but in a short *chiton*, with a leopard-skin draped over her shoulder, and greaves or high leather boots laced to her knees. During the play she also appears in a hunting scene, which gives her the opportunity to wear a Diana-like costume, carrying bow and arrows. In the final scene of the play—after her wedding to Theseus—Hippolyta is generally supposed to have accepted her future female role, and so wears the long *chiton* and *himation*. . . . Love—'tis said—will find a way.

In St. Agnes, Cornwall, a couple of summers ago, they were doing *A Midsummer-night's Dream* in our own Open-air Theatre, and I designed (and mostly made) the costumes for Hippolyta. I don't think the producer had seriously considered how this character should be dressed—

he was, in any case, much more interested in Bottom and the rustics—and when the girl who was playing the Amazon Queen strode on to the green at the dress rehearsal she looked absolutely magnificent . . . though I says it as shouldn't! She was greeted with dead silence from the other players . . . which, of course, was the greatest compliment they could have paid her!

The materials used for both men's and women's costumes must 'drape' easily and gracefully, and the clinging effect can often be helped by sewing little weights into the corners of a *chiton* or *chlamys*, and lead shot—which can be bought at any gunsmith's—is very suitable for the purpose.

As has been stated, pastel shades were not a part of the Grecian scene, and dark red, deep plum, indigo blue, violet, green, yellow, brown, black and white were the colours mostly in common use. Since, however, one cannot guarantee to buy materials in the correct colours, plus the right Grecian designs, which were mostly geometric, such as the famous Greek-key, the rosette, the dentil (tooth), wave, the guilloche (a pattern of intertwisted or interlaced bands), the laurel and water-lily (to only mention a few!), it is safer to apply both colour and decoration oneself by hand, using dyes (which will not stiffen or affect the draping qualities of the materials) and adding the designs with stencils.

All dyeing, of course, must be done before the garments are cut and made up, allowing a few inches to spare for possible shrinkage . . . especially with cotton crêpe, which gives the nearest effect to the typical crinkled folds. And do not forget to make all joins and seams run vertically, as cross-seams ruin the 'line'.

Finally, the success of a Grecian costume—just as with any other period garment—largely depends upon the actor or actress who wears it and the graciousness with which it is put on . . . and *that*, lads and lassies, is something that does not come out of a dye-bath!

THE ROMANS

Rome is said to have been founded around 753 B.C., and from its earliest history there was not much difference between the Roman and Greek costume covering the same period, and a simple form of *toga* was as often the Roman's sole garment just as his *himation* was the Greek's. But by 300 B.C. we find the Roman *tunica*—corresponding in general appearance with the Greek *chiton*—being worn under the *toga*.

The *toga* was the distinguishing mark of the Roman citizen—the badge as it were, of his nationality—and to discard it was considered an offence against the State. Only if a Roman was exiled did he lose his right to wear it.

To begin with, both men and women wore the *toga*, but later women discarded it in favour of the *palla*, which was almost identical with the Greek *himation*. If, however, a Roman matron brought censure upon her honourable estate by doing 'what she didn't oughter', she was no longer permitted to wear the *palla*, and as a punishment and a sign of her shame forced to wear the masculine *toga* . . . rather a paradox, don't you think?

From 300-30 B.C. the *toga* continued to become larger and more voluminous, but after A.D. 100 it grew narrower and more tightly wound, until in the end it was little more than a long 1-foot-wide scarf (*see* Fig. 42).

MEN

The *tunica* consisted of two separate rectangles of woollen material —either white or left in the natural colour—which were sewn up each side and along the top, leaving arm-holes and an opening for the head (no stick-pins being needed). A girdle was put round the waist, and the *tunica* pulled up all round, adjusting it to knee-length in front, though possibly a little shorter behind. Slaves, manual workers and young boys often let the *tunica* slip down from the right shoulder, leaving the chest bare, just as was the custom with the Greeks. In fact, all along the line, it was a case of when in Rome, do as the Greeks do.

A vertical purple band, about 1½ inches to 2 inches wide, passed over each shoulder and extended down the front and back of the *tunica*. It was known as the *angustus clavus*, and was looked upon as a sign of upper-class distinction with those who wore it. But later on—as so often happens when women begin to copy and adapt a masculine fashion as a form of costume decoration for themselves—this custom lost its social significance, and in time the stripes became ornamented with gold-embroidered designs . . . mostly geometric (*see* Fig. 43).

The connection, by the way, between nobility and the wearing of the purple colour (don't we all know the catch-phrase, 'Born in the purple'?) is of extremely ancient derivation. Originally it was economic in application, because the purple dye was a product of a genus of mollusc, called the *Murex*, which, owing to its rarity, naturally increased the demand . . . and the price! From the earliest times the manufacture of this dye —a deep plum, more blue than crimson—was in the hands of the Phoenicians of Tyre (hence 'Tyrian purple', a material which the Phoenician merchants of old used to trade in Cornwall in exchange for tin).

As time went by, shaped sleeves made an appearance—at first only to mid-arm, but later down to the wrist—and, in some instances, the skirt of the *tunica* was also lengthened to fall to the ankles. For a man, however, to be seen in this type of garment was looked upon as being luxuriate and effeminate . . . even with the example of Julius Caesar himself, who sometimes wore it, but then wasn't he supposed to have been 'all things to all men'? By A.D. 54-68, at a time when Nero was persecuting the Christians, the wearing of this form of *tunica* had become quite common!

In making a *tunica*, cut the front rectangle about 6 inches wider than the back one, so that when the two pieces are sewn together the front of the neck will hang forward in a loose fold, as described for the Greek *chiton*. If, in the putting together, 2 inches are allowed for the turn in at the shoulder seams, this will give the neck opening a firmer line.

A *tunica* that was reserved for the special use of emperors on triumphal occasions (such as throwing the Christians to the lions?) was the *palmata*, which was made of purple woollen material (dyed), embroidered in gold with a palm leaf design (which we can render equally well free-hand with a pot of gold paint and a brush!). But here again, in the course of time this garment lost its specialized purpose, when it was worn, first by high court officials, and later by lesser fry, with the applied decoration becoming ever more and more elaborate.

The early *toga* was roughly in the shape of a semicircle, 15 feet to 18 feet along the straight (top) edge and about 6 feet deep at the widest point. But in the theatre these dimensions would vary according to the height of the actor.

The simplest way to put on a *toga* is to drape it over the left shoulder (from the back), with the straight edge next to the body and the curve of the semicircle touching the left hand, and the lowest point just clearing the ground. The rest of the *toga* is then passed across the back, and under the right arm, at which point it is often effective to fold the material about one-third of the way down, allowing the top straight line to fall over in a loop to the front, with the curved edge down near the ankles. It is then gathered together and taken diagonally across the chest, and over the left shoulder, with the point hanging down and almost touching the ground at the back. During religious observances (sacrifices to the gods, etc.), the *toga* would be drawn up from the back of the shoulders, with the decorated edge draping the head. An Emperor, as Pontifex Maximus, would wear his *toga* in this manner if necessary (*see* Fig. 44).

A free-born citizen had a 2-inch- to 3-inch-wide purple band woven along the straight side of the *toga*, but if he happened to be suffering from a bereavement he would conceal (turn in) this stripe as a sign of his mourning . . . while if he had no stripe, he wore instead a *toga pulla*, which was grey, brown, and on some occasions black. In our times we *add* a dark band to our suits in respect for the dead.

Not only did the *toga* vary in size from period to period but by differing in colour and pattern, it distinguished between one class of wearer and another, as well as sometimes denoting the occupation for which it was worn. Care, therefore, should be taken in the choice of colour and pattern, to avoid costuming a character in a *toga* to which he has no right! For example:

(a) The *toga pura* or *virilis*, which was made from plain creamy-white wool, and when worn over his *tunica* was the everyday dress of the

Figs. 42, 43, & 44. (a) The toga praetexta, with purple border; (b) the toga pulla; (c) the toga worn over the head, for ceremonial purposes; (d) diagram of a toga; (e) the tunica, with the angustus clavus.

ordinary Roman citizen. Brutus, Cassius and Casca and the rest of the gang who murdered Caesar would be dressed like this. Caesar himself would probably wear a purple *toga* (*Julius Caesar*, Act III, Scene I).

(b) The *toga candida*, was similar to the above, but when worn by those seeking election to public office (candidates) the material was bleached or artificially whitened with chalk or fuller's earth (the Latin word *candidatus* means 'white-robed').

(c) The *toga praetexta*. This was also white, but with the addition of the purple border stripe, and it was worn by dictators, consuls, magistrates, praetors (the bodyguard established by Caesar Augustus) and by free-born boys under fourteen (and unmarried girls). After he was four-

teen, a boy was considered to be a young man, and allowed to wear the *toga virilis*. Lentulus and Metellus in Shaw's *Androcles and the Lion* would most probably wear the *toga praetexta*.

(d) The *toga picta*, which was made from purple wool embroidered with golden stars, was worn by triumphant generals—who, by the way, had to borrow it for the occasion, as such a *toga* was State property! Heavily embroidered and ornamented with gold, it was also worn by emperors—but they were allowed personal ownership! The Nero, in *Androcles and the Lion*, would wear such a *toga*.

(e) The *toga trabea*, which varied in colours according to the rank or occupation of the wearer. For instance, (i) augurs, who foretold the future, wore parti-coloured *togas* in purple and scarlet, and the Soothsayer, who warned Julius Caesar to beware the Ides of March would be dressed in this way (*Julius Caesar*, Act I, Scene 2); (ii) during the reigns of the early kings (before 500 B.C.) many *togas* were purple and white; while (iii) all-purple *togas*, worn over long white *tunicas*, were the costume of priests (Annas and Caiaphas) and those dedicated to the service of the gods.

(f) The *pallium*, which, however, was less like a *toga* than a *himation*. It was made of white wool, and was worn more by philosophers and teachers, and especially by the early Christians, in combination with the long *tunica*. It is therefore very suitable for New Testament plays, but it was not a popular garment with the ordinary Roman citizen. Yet so curious is the history of costume that by the third century A.D. the *pallium* had ousted the *toga*, replacing it as the everyday costume, with the *toga* only used occasionally as the official dress for magistrates!

This short list should cover most of the *togas* likely to be asked for, and the draping of all of them is basically the same. To recap: In front of and then back over the left shoulder, round the back, under the right arm (with the material now partly folded towards the front—though this is not arbitary), taken diagonally across the chest, and thrown back over the left shoulder.

An alternative method is: after coming under the right arm and going over the left shoulder (for the second time), to continue round the body again, and then forward across the front, and drape over the crooked left arm. Other styles, of course, will suggest themselves, and it is obvious that one person alone cannot hope to successfully drape a *toga*; he must have assistance. And, further, whatever the Romans may or may not have done, the modern actor will be well advised to put concealed safety-pins at all strategic points, such as the waist and on the left shoulder!

A useful travelling cloak, with hood attached, was called the *paenula*. It was semicircular in shape, and varied from hip to ankle length, and was made of thick woollen material (sometimes leather), and could be worn open down the front (fastened by hooks) and draped over the arms, or sewn up and put on over the head (*see* Fig. 45).

Sandals *(solea)* were worn in the house, but away from home the Roman citizen wore the *calcaeus*, which was a leather shoe with thongs wound several times round the ankle and leg and tied in front. The number and arrangement of these thongs depended upon the rank of the wearer . . . a senator, for instance, had two pairs, one set tied above the other, and his shoes were black (red for a patrician), and sometimes they were ornamented with an ivory or metal crescent on the toe-piece. Slaves were never permitted to wear the *calcaeus;* only the *solea.*

Fig. 45. (a) Roman travelling cloak with attached hood; (b) diagram for cutting cloak—without hood.

Fig. 46. examples of Roman shoes (solea) and sandals.

These *solea* were made of soft leather and laced across the instep, with a leather tongue that fell forward and covered the lacing—similar to a modern brogue shoe. The upper part of the *solea* had a cut-out design, and it can be constructed from a piece of scenic canvas, or similar material, cut out and dyed to look like leather, and then attached to a soft slipper sole of the required size. Naturally, you will buy the sole first before cutting out the upper, and the lacing can be cut in one piece with the tongue (*see* Fig. 46).

The *calcaeus* can be based upon an ordinary leather bedroom slipper (no cut-out pattern needed here). Four leather thongs (straps) each some 18 inches to 24 inches long, and about 2 inches wide where they are attached to the shoe, and then narrowing to a convenient width for binding and tying, are fixed to the sole, one on each side under the ball of the foot and under the heel. Each pair should cross over on the instep, with one bound round and tied at the ankle and the other criss-crossing up the leg.

The Roman had his hair clipped short all over his head, with the exception of a fringe of small curls on his forehead and again at the nape of his neck. At the time of the Hollywood film, *Julius Caesar*, it became the fashion in England for young men-about-town to have their hair cut in imitation of Marlon Brando, who played the part of Mark Antony. It was rather becoming.

Until about A.D. 50 men were clean-shaven, and to allow a beard to grow was another outward sign of mourning. After A.D. 50, however, a neatly trimmed beard and moustache became the mode (not unlike those worn by Edward VII and George V).

Most men went bareheaded, protecting their heads, when necessary, by drawing up the *toga* from the back. Hats and caps, however, did exist, similar to those worn by the Greeks . . . the *petasus* and the *kausia* —which was flatter in the crown—and a brimless, conical-crowned felt cap, called a *pileus*, worn by commoners and freed slaves.

Wreaths made from the real laurel and bay leaves (later imitated in gold) were given as coveted prizes, and a victorious general would be awarded the *corona triumphalis*. Julius Caesar had a special licence which allowed him to wear one always . . . perhaps to cover his baldness?

Kings and emperors wore gold coronets, high in front and narrowing towards the back. There was also a spiked golden circlet, representing the sun's rays, called the *corona radiata*, which was the insignia of divinity . . . which did nothing to deter Nero from wearing it on every possible occasion!

These wreathes, crowns, coronets, etc., can be made from buckram, cardboard or papier-mâché, and then gilded and decorated.

SOLDIERS

The Roman soldier wore a shaped-to-the-figure, decorated breastplate with a fringe of loose leather tabs, tipped and ornamented with metal, that hung from the lower edge of it to about mid-thigh. They were repeated—in a smaller, narrower size—around the tops of the short sleeves of the deep red *tunica* (a little shorter than the civilian variety) that was worn underneath the armour. A waist-length red cloak was draped over the back, with the top ends caught together and fastened with a clasp on the right shoulder, or with one end held on each shoulder.

His arms and legs were usually bare, though sometimes metal greaves and armlets were worn (similar in pattern to the Greek).

In the Roman campaigns in the north (including the invasion of Britain), leather *bracchae* (breeches), rather like our hiking shorts, but

Fig. 47. Roman Legionary—notice his 'bracchae' (breeches) of which the Roman soldier was so ashamed!

perhaps a little tighter, were issued as a concession to the colder climate. The ends of them were just visible below the hem of the short *tunica*. The legionaries, however, felt a little self-conscious and ashamed of them, and invariably took them off before returning to Rome!

Another type of armour that was, perhaps, more typical of the ordinary soldier had a metal plate that covered the chest, with below it five horizontal overlapping metal bands that encircled the body like a cuirass, each joined to the next and clasped in front with a metal boss. Four smaller vertical bands came over each shoulder—rather like shoulder straps—with the ends clamped back and front to the top horizontal band (*see* Fig. 47).

For the stage, this type of armour could be made of pliable cardboard, lined with canvas to prevent it cracking or tearing, or from imitation leather or oilcloth with a buckram backing to give it the necessary stiffness, and then painted with aluminium, with the bosses made from the metal tops of mineral water bottles.

The Roman shield was convex and rectangular in shape, and should be made from thick felt sewn to a strong wire frame, with the raised design built up with additional pieces of cut-out felt sewn into position.

The whole thing is then stiffened with a strong solution of size, and when that is thoroughly dry, covered over on *both* sides with two or three layers of the torn-up paper strips, glued on. And, finally, when that is dry, it is painted—outside as well as inside—with aluminium, with the general effect of the raised pattern heightened with highlights and shadows. And don't forget to include a strong arm-grip on the inside.

The sword was thick and short, and encased in a decorated sheath, slung from a sword belt worn diagonally from right shoulder to left hip. Helmets were of iron, and can be built up on a stiffened cap foundation. Like the Greek helmets, some of them were crested, and most of them were equipped with side-pieces that could be fastened under the chin like a strap (*see* Fig. 48).

Fig. 48. Roman general—notice the side-pieces to the helmet, which fastened under the chin (also in Fig. 47).

Soldiers wore sandals of various kinds, most of which consisted of a stout sole (some had spikes) with leather thongs crossing the instep, and winding up the lower leg.

WOMEN

The outer robe of the Roman matron—although called a *stola*—was in reality very similar to the Greek Ionian *chiton*, and was made in much the same manner, with a soft linen garment, called the *tunica interior*, worn underneath. The *stola* was pulled up under the girdle, but the over-fold on the breast and the *kolpos* at the waist were omitted.

The *stola* was made of white wool—later from linen or silk—and it hung in long, graceful folds to the feet, covering the instep. A narrow, flat band, known as the *institia*, was woven, embroidered or appliquéd round the hem.

In early Christian times, a shaped *dalmatica*, known as a *talaris*, with wide, elbow-length sleeves, was worn over a long-sleeved *tunica interior*. In cut it was much like the early Hebrew or Persian garment, with the addition of the stripes of the *angustus clavus*, but without a girdle.

Around 500 B.C., as has been stated, women had given up wearing the *toga*, replacing it with the woollen, rectangular shawl, called the *palla*. The general methods for draping it depended upon its dimensions, and in the case of a smaller size would be held on the left shoulder, with the rest of it passed round the back, under the right arm, and the two ends caught together on the left shoulder with a large round *fibula*. The larger *palla* was put on like the Greek *himation*.

Solea were worn in the house and *calcaei* out of doors, but the leather used for women's shoes was much thinner than for men, and in gayer colours, of which red and white were the more popular. The *phaecassium* was a white leather boot that covered the whole of the foot, and was tied in front with coloured cords. It was also worn by effeminate men (Spintho in *Androcles and the Lion*), and such a boot could be 'faked' by a white sock rolled down to just above the ankle, with the tie-cords added.

Initially, women imitated the Greek styles of hairdressing, but from about 50 B.C. coiffures became increasingly more and more elaborate, with the hair either braided and coiled round and round, and looking like a small bee-hive perched on top of the head, or waved and frizzed in a mass of tiny curls—not unlike the hair-style associated with Queen Alexandra and Queen Mary, and here crêpe hair, mounted on a thin wire foundation or on a hair-pad, would be the answer. A decorative band put round the head would conceal any joins between the real and the artificial. Ribbon bands were worn, anyway, by young girls and elderly, respectable matrons . . . including priestesses!

One practice indulged in by Roman ladies (?) was to blend in with their own tresses the blonde and red hair torn from the heads of conquered northern women. Nowadays, lots of girls introduce coloured streaks into their hair with the aid of peroxide of hydrogen (20v.), which gives a similar effect and is far less barbaric! For the stage, it can all be done with crêpe hair.

Wool and linen were the usual materials used in Roman garments. In later times (A.D.) silk, brought from the East, was much sought after, but, of course, it wasn't always easy to come by, and therefore was expensive . . . and correspondingly prized.

White and off-white were the predominating features in any Roman group, with here and there a *toga pulla* or *trabea* and the purple *angustus clavi* of the *tunicas* and the borders on the *togas* providing the colour contrasts.

By the second and third centuries A.D a greater variety of colours was used, and, of course, all along women had enjoyed a wider colour range —scarlet, blue, green, all shades of yellow and, of course, purple . . . though it must not be overlooked that this latter colour was restricted to the upper classes. Flame red, yellow and white were worn by brides, and all colours were rather more bright and direct than pastel, with any patterns applied in a deeper shade. Designs followed the Greek and Egyptian patterns—geometric, floral, animal and human—and in this respect often depicted mythical scenes or historical events. Motifs incorporating Christian symbols were, of course, a natural product of the times.

PART III

CHAPTER 6

Medieval

We have now seen the origin and development of the tunic as the principal feature of costume in ancient times. Now let us follow its progress as it concerns our island story.

THE SAXONS

MEN

Next to his skin, Mr. Saxon wore a plain linen shirt, such as any man might wear today, and, indeed, our modern (collar-separate) shirt is a lineal descendant. Over this shirt he wore a knee-length tunic that completely covered it, and for state occasions he would put on a full-length robe . . . unless, of course, he was a poor man, in which case he might only have the one garment!

The tunic was made of linen or wool—dyed red, green or blue, in soft dark shades, as light colours were seldom used—and the length was adjusted by being pulled through the girdle, usually allowing it to overhang a bit more on the right, giving it a lopsided effect . . . a fashion that Mrs. Saxon was not slow in imitating!

Characteristic of this tunic were the long, tight sleeves (cut in one with the body) that were worn rucked up over the wrists, so that in cold weather they could be pulled down over the hands to keep them warm (evidently the climate was no better then than now!).

The Saxon legs were covered by long, loose, trouser-like stockings, made of cloth, that reached to mid-thigh and were known as *chausses* . . . at least, that's what the Normans called them. To prevent them from wrinkling down, they were wound round with strips of coloured material or bound either just above or below the knee (below if the knee was worn bare).

I wonder if little boys of that period were as curious to know what the Saxon wore under his tunic as they are today about the Scotsman and his kilt! Did he . . . or didn't he? Well, I can tell you quite definitely that the Saxon *did*—though he was as successful at hiding his little cloth or woollen drawers as Jock is with his pants!

An indispensable feature of the Saxon man's costume was his cloak, semicircular or rectangular in shape, with the ends rounded, and varying in length to correspond with his tunic . . . from shoulder to just below the waist with a short tunic, and nearly to the ground with a full-length one. This cloak was fastened either in front or on either shoulder by the two top ends being drawn through a large, flat, open-ring brooch *(fibula)* and then knotted together. For the stage, however, this may seem a little clumsy, and the more usual procedure is to hold the cloak in position with a round, jewelled brooch-pin, leaving it loose round the neck, letting it fall into graceful folds, both back and front.

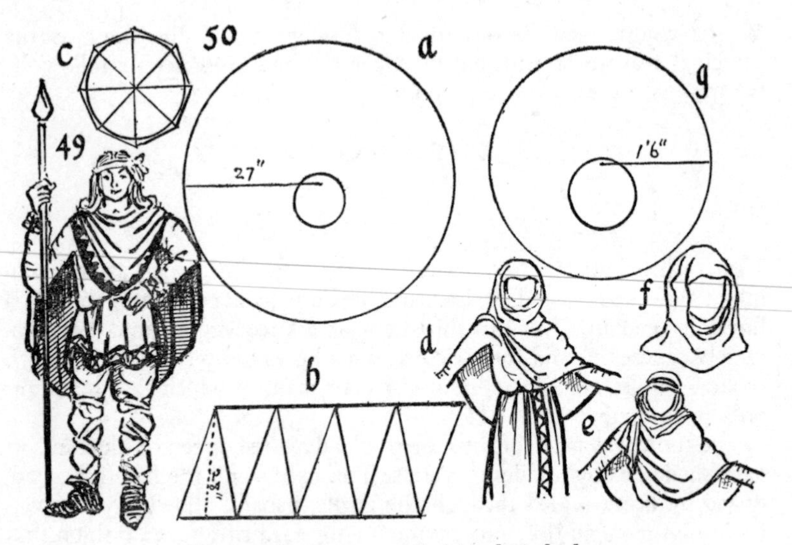

Fig. 49. The Saxon man's 'circular' cloak.

Fig. 50. (a) diagram of cloak, with hole cut out for the head—the diameter of the circle should be from about 4 feet to 4 feet 6 inches, according to the height of the wearer; (b) a quadrilateral of material, if divided into 8 triangles, which are then cut out, and placed point to point, will form a circle; (c) the height of each triangle, however, should exceed the radius of the circle by at least an inch; (d & e) the 'circular' cloak as worn by Saxon women, with either a separate 'hood', or the 'head-rail'; (f) design for the 'hood', and (g) diagram for the hood—the diameter of the circle should be from 2 feet 6 inches to 3 feet. A hole is cut out, through which the face appears.

There was also a third type of cloak or mantle which, while it can look very effective on the stage, may be a little difficult to manage without practice. This was in the shape of a complete circle, with a decorated edge, and a hole cut at about three-quarters of the diameter for the head to pass through, so that the longer portion fell down the back, with the shorter folded back across the front of the neck and draped back over the shoulders. If the actor wearing such a cloak has a great deal of arm movement (such as a *Three Musketeers*—Douglas Fairbanks, Senior—fight sequence), it is safer for these folds to be pinned or tacked into position, before he comes on, as otherwise he may find himself sadly involved! (*see* Fig. 49).

Now, I realize only too well that to provide a circular piece of cloth, with any reasonable circumference, to make a cloak of this description would entail a great deal of material (besides the waste in the cutting out). But, by cutting a quadrilateral strip of cloth into a series of 'gores', or triangular sections, and sewing them together, one can make a circular shape (with the minimum of waste). The measurements of the bases of each triangle, when added together, should equal the overall circumference of the circle required . . . and do not forget to allow sufficient material for the turn-in when the 'gores' are joined together (*see* Fig. 50).

A Saxon man seldom wore a hat. When he did (upper classes), it was made of cloth, and sometimes decorated with a very rough attempt at embroidery, and was shaped rather like the liberty caps of the French Revolutionaries. Leather or skin caps, with the hair on the outside, were worn by the lower classes.

Soft, black leather, ankle bootees of the pull-on kind adorned his feet, with occasional decoration up the front—for important people—and rough leather shoes, with instep thongs, for those of less consequence!

WOMEN

The costume of the Saxon women was equally simple. First there was a long high-necked linen chemise, over which came a full, perfectly plain tunic, that fell to the ground in graceful folds (after the Norman invasion, an embroidered band was added round the hem). It had the same closely fitting sleeves, rucked up over the wrists, as the men's . . . and for a similar reason. And, talking of sleeves, it is perhaps interesting to note that not until the seventeenth century did any woman show her uncovered arms in public . . . unless she happened to be 'one of those' (though, presumably, in the privacy of her own apartments, she might 'roll up her sleeves' when engaged in washing her smalls). When nowadays, anyone who regularly watches the TV commercials knows that it is the 'blue' that adds the whiteness to the brightness (or is it t'other way round?) it is amusing to discover that the ladies of the eleventh century added saffron to the rinsing water—not only on account of the creamy tone it imparted, but also for the fragrant smell!

Over this undergarment, the Saxon woman wore a V-necked outer tunic, reaching to her knees, with wide elbow-length sleeves, embroidered round the edges, and also round the neck opening, with the pattern continued straight down the front and round the hem. A girdle encircled her waist, through which she pulled up the outer tunic—in complimentary imitation of her lord and master.

All women who could afford them wore cloaks—either rectangular or semicircular, and held in front with a brooch. The completely circular mantle was also worn, but more usually for out of doors (*see* Fig. 51).

Fig. 51. Saxon woman's cloak.

On her head Mrs. Saxon wore what was known as a 'head-rail', that completely hid her hair and consisted of a long strip of soft silky material (upper classes) or linen (lower classes) measuring 2½ yards long and ¾-yard wide 90 inches by 27 inches). One end was passed over her head, reaching to her left shoulder, while the longer end was taken across under her chin, over her left shoulder and round the back of her neck, with the end brought back over her right shoulder to hang down in front . . . and a very becoming fashion it was, especially if she had a double chin!

Sometimes (if the neck was extra long—King Harold's lady-love was known as 'Edith with the swan neck'!) the material was passed under the chin a second time to hang down over the left shoulder.

A narrow metal (gold) circlet (a snood or band of silk for Miss Saxon) was worn round the forehead, into which a flower might be tucked. But fashions change, and with the advent of the Normans, A.D. 1066, this circlet was considered sufficient means for holding the veil in position, so that it was no longer wound round the neck, but worn to fall evenly on either side of the face, with the long ends draping the shoulders and hanging down the back, and with the hair—which was now visible—arranged in two long, braided plaits in front.

No Saxon lady was *ever* seen, indoors or out, without her head-rail . . . unless, of course, she was 'no better than she should have been'! (*see* Fig. 52).

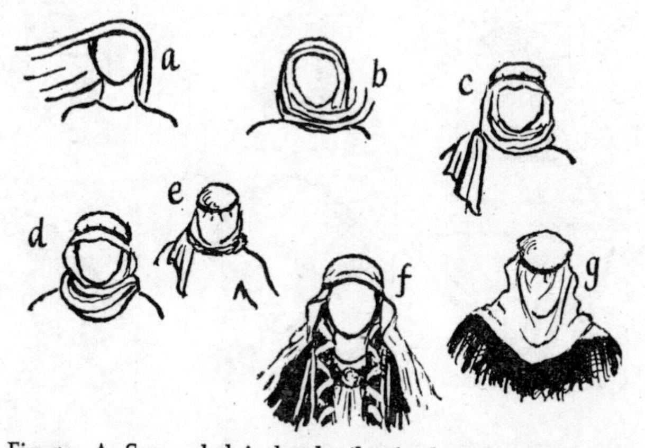

Fig. 52. A Saxon lady's head-rail: (a, b & c) show the simple method of draping; (d) with the scarf going twice round the neck, and (e) the back view; (f) shows the later style, when the hair was revealed in two long, decorated plaits; (g) the back view.

The head-rail was seldom white, and at the time of the earlier Danish invasions of our shores black was the colour most in common use.

Woollen or cloth stockings, gartered at the knee, were, naturally, never seen, and footwear was similar to that described for the men—with any kind of a heel entirely out of place . . . and period.

Now let us suppose for a moment that you have to create a Saxon man's costume . . . perhaps for a production of Shakespeare's *King Lear* (Anglo-Saxon, fifth to sixth centuries A.D.) or for one of the Arthurian legends—which, although written in the twelfth century and therefore often dressed in that more ornate period, were in actual fact dated *circa* A.D. 410 . . . and, moreover, that for some reason (perhaps economy?) you have to start from scratch!

The basic linen shirt will present no difficulty—the actor, in any case, will probably insist on wearing his B.D.V.s—and for the over tunic, what about using a man's nightshirt, dyed to the required colour? And please do not imagine that such things are no longer worn, because I know better . . . though I don't happen to wear one myself! The sleeves will have to be elongated for that typical, rucked-up effect over the wrists, but a strip cut off from all round the hem of the nightshirt should provide sufficient material for this purpose.

Plain-coloured (otherwise, dyed) pyjama trousers, worn loosely and roughly bound round with a couple of pyjama cords (dyed), will serve

Fig. 53. Headdresses that can be made from an ordinary pillow-case: (f) Henry III, 1216-72; (b) Edward I 1272-1307; (c) Edward III, 1327-77; (a & d) Edward II, 1307-27; (e) Edward IV, 1461-83.
(Note: the dotted rectangles show which way the pillow is utilised. In many cases, it would be dyed, and the 'shape' held with padding or wire.)

as leg covering, and as the girdle round the waist doesn't show any odd bit of string will do.

A plain bath-towel (again dyed) draped across back and front will make the mantle, fastened on the shoulder with a large, flat brooch (the gilded top of a potted-meat jar, with a coloured wine gum in the centre for a jewel).

A pair of black stockings, rolled down to just above the ankles (with a leather sole inserted into the foot for comfort), provide the boots, and for the Phrygian cap, what better than a cloth nightcap with the point cut off? But as the early Saxon more usually went bareheaded, a narrow strip of rolled cloth tied round his head would help to keep the hair out of his eyes!

Nor should the Saxon woman's costume present any greater difficulty. For the undergarment, use a long, fully fashioned nightdress (possibly with the addition of a couple of 'side gores'), with a short, wide-sleeved dressing-jacket, joined up the front, for the over tunic, with those tightly-rucked under-sleeves made as a pair of separate 'half-arm' pieces, with elastic at the top to hold them up above the elbows.

A long, coloured silk scarf provides the head-rail, and Woolworth's sell metal hair-bands, some of which are already decorated with artificial flowers.

A light-weight woollen blanket (dyed) would make an excellent mantle, and if a hole is cut out for the head to come through and the corners are rounded and the edge neatly bound, it is even possible to suggest the circular cloak.

Indeed, anyone given *carte blanche* in a bedroom could find all the basic materials required—sheets, pillow-cases, blankets, counterpanes and quilts—for almost any costume . . . provided there is intuition, imagination and, of course, a sewing machine!

For the uses to which, for instance, an ordinary pillow-case could be put as a headdress (*see* Fig. 53).

THE NORMANS

MEN

For some time previous to the Conquest, the upper-class Saxons had imitated the styles in France, and Norse-blooded William (who was nothing of a dandy himself . . . his interests lay more in the direction of hunting and piracy than fashion) did little to alter or influence the native costume.

There were two 'popular lines in tunics' for the young Norman to choose at this period: *(a)* one that fitted closely to his body, like a knitted pullover (called in France a *bliaut*), into which he had to be laced or sewn up along one or both of the under-arm seams every time he put it on (no buttons or hooks in the eleventh century). It was cut in one piece, with a high neck line and sleeves that were either tight from elbow to wrist (again adjusted by sewing or lacing) or worn open, showing the cuffs of the tight-sleeved undershirt.

The skirt varied in length—some wore it below the calf and others above the knee, which was sometimes left bare—and it was slit midway up the sides or at the back and occasionally in the front too, for greater comfort when horse-riding. The neck opening, cuffs and hem were ornamented with bands of embroidery, with the tunic slightly 'bloused' over the belt (so that it was not always visible) and the material of the skirt bunched over the hips at the sides.

The other tunic *(b)* was altogether more informal. About knee length and without sleeves, it hung fully and loosely from the shoulders, unjoined at the sides and held round the waist with a buckled belt. There was the usual round opening for the head to pass through, and a broad band of embroidery added about the neck and round the hem. This was worn over a loose under-tunic of linen or wool, with the typical rucked-up sleeves, with decorated cuffs (those Normans felt the cold, too!). Falling midway between the knees and the ankles, this form of tunic was very definitely the forerunner of the thirteenth-century 'surcoat' . . . about which more, anon! (*see* Fig. 54).

Under his tunic, the Norman—like the Saxon—wore short cloth or woollen drawers, with long stockings that were often specially cut and tailored to his legs! Footwear was similar to the Saxon, except that the boots were made in various colours, and not only in black.

The Norman cloak, either short or long, was fastened on the right shoulder, and his head-coverings were of the simplest . . . a small, round-topped skull-cap (a series of segments joined together to make the shape) or a conical cap with a point, and, of course, hoods, which were either separate or joined to the back of the cloaks. Some hoods were made as close-fitting as a Balaclava, so that they could be worn under a helmet (*see* Fig. 55).

The colours in general use during Norman times, though definite, were soft and not very bright, and where possible darkish tones should be used. And a point to remember is that yellow was not a popular colour, being worn mostly by Jews.

Fig. 54. Two types of Norman man's tunic: (a) the short, tight-bodied, which was often laced under each arm, and at the sides down to the waist, every time it was put on; (b) diagram for this tunic, which was cut out in one piece; (c) the longer, looser style, with (d) diagram for cutting it out—each pattern had a hole made for the head to pass through.

Fig. 55. (a) Norman cloak; (b) conical cap—worn by archers; (c) skull-cap; (d) Balaclava type hood; (e & f) the hood worn under the helmet.

WOMEN

The Norman woman was better and far more richly dressed than her Saxon cousin, and in a stage presentation this difference would naturally be stressed by the costume-designer.

Her high-necked woollen or linen tunic, with the tight sleeves (rucked-up on her wrists, with ornamented cuffs), was worn under her *bliaut*. This over-tunic, cut low at the neck to show the decorated top of the undergarment, was laced at each side so as to fit neatly to her figure, and it then flowed out freely from her hips and down to the floor with a short train.

A long, jewelled girdle passed round her waist, first from the front, and then crossing at the back to come round her hips and be loosely knotted in front, with the ends hanging down. This arrangement with the belt was very typical of the time.

A long, semicircular shoulder cloak, with embroidered edges, was fastened across the front with cords, and a small round veil covered the top of the head, flowing over the shoulders and down the back, held in place by a gold fillet round the forehead.

The Norman lady's hair was braided with ribbon into two long plaits. Her shoes and stockings were as already described (*see* Fig. 56).

Fig. 56. (a) Norman lady's costume; (b & c) diagram for cutting sleeve.

RELIGIOUS ORDERS

The monks of the Benedictine Order—which existed long before those of St. Francis or St. Dominic—wore a simple, long, white woollen, ankle-length tunic (cassock), with tight sleeves to the wrist, over which came a large, loose black gown with long, wide sleeves and a black hood attached, which hung down behind.

This outer gown was sometimes replaced by a white scapular, which was a rectangular piece of material (wool) some 15 inches by 18 inches wide, with shoulder seams and a hole through which the head could pass. It hung back and front from the shoulders like a pinafore, free and detached to within a few inches of the floor. After the fourteenth century, the entire habit became black.

The tops of the Benedictine monks' heads were 'tonsured', a custom in the Roman Church from earliest times, though in Britain before the arrival of St. Augustine (A.D. 590-604) the practice had been to shave only the front of the head, with the hair left long at the sides and back.

The friars of the Order of St. Francis (Greyfriars) wore a grey habit, which in the fifteenth century was changed to brown. A long, pointed hood fell to the waist at the back, and there was a white, knotted cord round the waist. On occasion the scapular was worn, and a short cloak for out of doors.

The Dominican friars (Blackfriars) wore a long white tunic (gown), with a white scapular. For Mass and for out of doors, a long black cloak was added, with a black hood, which had a smaller white hood inside.

The Carmelites were an order of mendicant friars, founded on Mount Carmel in the twelfth century. They wore a full white (sometimes grey) gown over the tunic, with long, wide sleeves. A cowl hood hung down at the back, and there was a girdle round the waist. The scapular was also worn, and a large white cloak, with hood, was added for out of doors.

With most of these orders, the feet were bare, but for the stage a simple, open sandal is usually worn.

Women's dress in the religious orders was very similar to the men's, the main difference being that where the monk wore a hood, the nun as a rule had a head veil, wimple or gorget.

A Benedictine nun wore a white undergarment (chemise) with a black over-tunic or gown with long, wide sleeves, and her face was swathed in a white head-rail with a black hood or a black veil covering her head and shoulders (worn over the head-rail).

The Dominican Order was founded in A.D. 1206, and a nun of this order would wear a white gown and scapular, with a black head veil worn over a white veil and *barbe*, or 'chin-cloth'.

Other orders were dressed entirely in black, except for a white head-dress, consisting of the white linen gorget and chin-cloth and head-veil (*see* Fig. 57).

No one could accuse an eleventh-century bishop of being 'under-dressed'! First, he wore a white, long-sleeved under-tunic, over which came a second white tunic, or 'alb', with an ornamented hem and a stole with fringed ends. Next there was the 'tunicle', which was a close-fitting, tunic-like vestment with a decorated hem. After that came a richly figured 'dalmatic', and a large bell-shaped 'chasuble'. Finally, he wore the *pallium*, which was a Y-shaped strip of decorated purple woollen material, conferred as a special honour on archbishops—and sometimes on bishops. On his feet were ornamented sandals, or boots reaching to his knees.

The mitre first made an appearance towards the end of the tenth century, but it was more in the shape of a cap, with the 'points' (low) at the sides and not at the front and back, as we know the mitre today. If a bishop was of royal descent, he might be allowed to wear an Anglo-Saxon crown (*see* Fig. 58).

Figs. 57 & 58. (a) A Dominican nun order founded in 1206; (b) a sister of the third order of Servites founded during the 13th century, in Florence; (c) a Franciscan—the original grey habit was changed to brown during the 15th century; (d) a Dominican; (e) a 10th century Anglo-Saxon bishop—being of 'Royal connections or descent', he wears a crown; (f) an archbishop, with mitre and carrying his cross-staff, which was usually carried by the cross-bearer; (g) the earliest form of 'mitre', which was merely a raised cap, with a band round the edge—the mitre was not 'divided' until the 10th century; (h) mitre, as worn by St. Thomas á Becket (1118-1170); (i) bishop's mitre, 12th century, in which the 'points' are still at the sides (also in Fig. h); (j) 13th century mitre, with the low 'points' back and front—the pendent bands (infulae) were probably originally tied under the chin.

THE PEASANTRY

Most villages at this time were self-providing with wool and hemp, which were woven to clothe the country folk. Over a coarse homespun, long-sleeved under-shirt, a man would wear his sack-like woollen tunic, with the sleeves a little below the elbow and a leather belt around his waist. This same sort of tunic had been worn long before the Conquest, and though m'lord might have his *bliaut* fashioned to his figure, the countryman still pulled his tunic over his head . . . as he would do for several centuries to come—and, indeed, still does today in parts of agricultural Europe and Asia.

Loose cloth trousers (sometimes of leather) covered his legs, bound round with twists of straw as a protection against thorns! He also wore a short, roughly-shaped cape (with the hem cut into 'points') round his shoulders, and a hood made from the hide of a sheep or wolf, with the wool or hair left inside as a lining.

If he were lucky, he might possess a cloak, and that, too, would be lined with sheepskin to keep out the winter cold—such cold, for instance, as the Great Frost in King John's reign, that had lasted from 11th

Figs. 59 & 60. (a) Peasant woman; (b) peasant lad working in the fields; (c) peasant woman, with her outer tunic not turned up; (d) peasant lad, with his tunic tucked through his belt, but dressed in the cloth trousers.

January until 22nd March, and 'turned the earth into iron, so that it could neither be sown nor tilled'.

But during the hot summer days, when working in the fields, he would divest himself of all but his rough cloth pants, made in the form of a knee-length skirt slit at the sides, with the longer back portion brought forward between the legs and up to his waist—rather like a baby's diaper—where both the back and the front hung down over a belt that was threaded through sockets at the sides (*see* Fig. 59).

The roughest leather shoes or skin sandals, tied with thongs, were all he could hope for . . . though, as often as not, he might have to go barefooted.

The country woman wore a long, loose, tight-sleeved gown of a similarly coarse material, reaching to her ankles and worn with a sleeveless, full-skirted, knee-length over-tunic, that sometimes had the front hem pulled tightly up and tucked through her belt, so as to hang down in a point in front.

She covered her head and shoulders with a coarse linen hood-cum-cape, with a hole cut out for her face to peep through, or she might wear a form of roughly tied head-rail (*see* Fig. 60).

Her woollen or cloth stockings were gathered below the knee, and her leather shoes (if she had any) were rather like our modern suède bootee . . . but, like the men, she more than probably went minus shoes or stockings.

SOLDIERS

Armour of any description has always presented a problem to the amateur costume-designer, and unfortunately at the time of the Conquest both Saxon and Norman soldiers alike seem to have worn a kind of tight-sleeved, knee-length, chain-mail boiler-suit, with puttee-like gaiters from knee to foot!

It would, however, be all right to wear a high-necked, knee-length, chain-mail tunic (called a 'hauberk') with wide, elbow-length sleeves, worn over a slightly longer cloth under-tunic with long sleeves, and *chausses* bound round with leather thongs as a leg-covering (*see* Fig. 61).

The hauberk of this period was a stout linen or leather tunic, on which was sewn a pattern of flat, closely-interlinking metal rings, but a similar effect can be obtained by knitting the tunic of thick brown string, using large wooden needles. But even this can be quite a lengthy job, yet the result more than justifies the effort, especially when the string is silvered over with aluminium, which gives it a wonderfully realistic appearance of steel.

Some soldiers—such as bowmen—were not dressed in chain-mail at all, but wore a sleeveless leather cuirass over a long-sleeved cloth jacket (decorated at the neck and cuffs) and wide, knee-length knickers of the same material, which were laced up on the outside seams with leather thongs. With these long *chausses* and leather shoes were worn. Such a soldier need not even wear a helmet on his head, but instead a thick woollen or felt cap, in any colour except the despised Jewish yellow (*see* Fig. 62).

A variation of the above would be to add elbow-length sleeves to the cuirass, and then cover the body part with a pattern of criss-cross 1-inch wide strips of leather, making a design of small squares, with a metal stud (brass paper-clip) placed wherever the strips cross. With this he would wear a leather hood, framing his face like a Balaclava—with or without the addition of a helmet—and either of these costumes would be easy and practical to make (*see* Fig. 63).

The eleventh century helmet was a conical shaped iron 'cap' (the crown of an old bowler hat or a papier-mâché mould made round a pudding basin) with a 'nose-guard', or 'nasal' as it was called, added in front. This partly protected the face, and was very typical of this period.

This helmet was sometimes worn over a chain-mail hood, that surrounded the face and covered the ears, neck and back of the head, with

Figs. 61, 62, 63. (a) Norman hauberk, with the overhanging 'tongues' of metal sewn on leather, or some other strong material; (b) Norman bowman—his short trousers are very wide at the knees, and are made to fasten up on the outer seams; (c) the young man who looks like the goal-keeper in an American ball game, has on a leather hauberk, with criss-cross leather strips, fastened together by metal studs. He wears a cap, to help make the helmet fit more comfortably. Underneath, he wears a long-sleved tunic, the skirt of which can just be seen between his knees.

a deepish neck-piece tucked into the top of the hauberk. This hood could be knitted from a Balaclava helmet pattern and then silvered, as described above.

The Norman shields (metal) stood as high as a man's shoulder, and had rounded tops and a pointed base—rather like a kite—and they were carried by means of a strap fitted to the inside. Some of them were roughly decorated with the warrior's personal device or emblem (*not*, however, to be confused with a coat of arms, as the heraldic system did not develop until considerably later). Saxon shields followed the Norman pattern, though occasionally the round shield, from an earlier period, might be carried into battle (*see* Fig. 64).

Either type of shield could easily be made from hardboard or stout cardboard. First cut two narrow slits, and pass through them a strip of webbing and join the ends so as to act as the carrying strap. Both sides of the shield should now be covered with canvas or hessian (glued on) neatly turned in round the edges. When dry, the whole thing should be painted brown (dye would do) and with a coat of aluminium paint, 'dragged' on with an almost dry brush, afterwards. If a design is to be used, this is added last, painting it in with dullish enamels, and without much attention to perfection of line or design, in order to give the shield that 'battle-scarred' appearance.

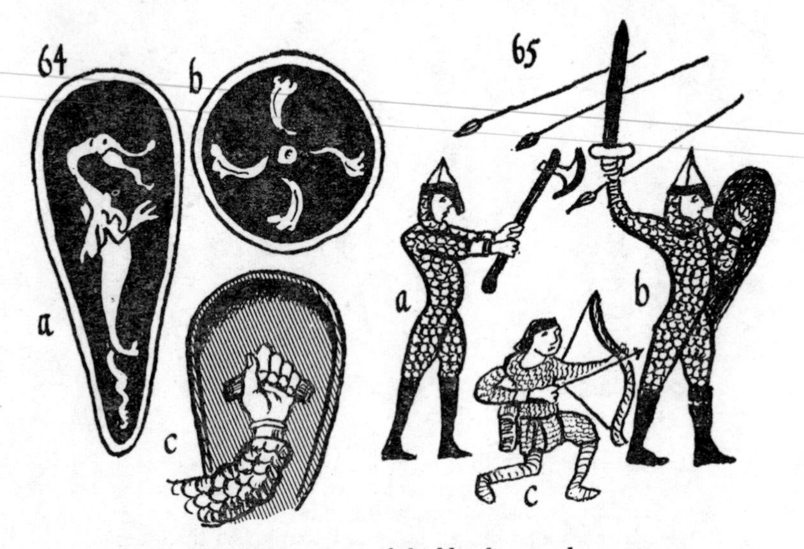

Fig. 64. (a & b) two types of shield—the round pattern was more often carried by the Saxons; (c) diagram showing 'grip' for holding the shield.

Fig. 65. (a) The two-handed axe; (b) the sword; (c) a Norman archer, with bow and arrow. All these diagrams are based on the Bayeux Tapestry.

The chief Saxon weapons were the lance and the heavy two-edged sword with T-shaped guard, either worn with a scabbard under the hauberk, with only the hilt showing above, or slung on a baldrick from the right shoulder to the left hip. The Saxons also wielded the hefty two-handed axe . . . but only the Normans used the deadly bow and arrows which won the day for them at Hastings (*see* Fig. 65).

Most of the above particulars I have gleaned from studying my copy of *The Bayeux Tapestry* (King Penguin Books, 1943).

CHAPTER 7

The Renaissance (1450-85)

With the flowering of the Renaissance, medieval influences in England rapidly died out, and the closing years of the fifteenth century became a transitionary period as far as costume was concerned, with many of the characteristics of the past overshadowed by those of the future.

From the point of view of the costume-designer, however, it is often safer to be slightly behind rather than ahead of his period.

MEN

Men now dressed in doublets, with the material arranged in an even pattern of vertical pleats, with the upper part of the body well padded, back and front. An essential feature was the upstanding collar (whaleboned or wired), which often rose halfway up the back of the head and was either tightly buttoned high under the chin or was cut away to a point in front, exposing the neck.

The sleeves were long and tight, and extended over the knuckles, so that they could be turned back as a cuff. In addition, pendant 'bag' sleeves hung from the high, padded shoulders, and often they were so long that they had to be loosely knotted together at the back to prevent them from trailing on the floor. A narrow cord went round the waist, tied in a bow behind, and usually the skirt of the tunic was so short, that it completely shocked the moralists! (*see* Fig. 66).

The belt alone would not be found sufficient for holding the pleated material in place, and besides being sewn down, it is not a bad idea to build the whole tunic upon the foundation of an ordinary waistcoat, which will serve as a lining and help to give a snug, neat fitting. The long, tight sleeves can be attached to this waistcoat, and layers of wadding inserted between it and the outer material.

Another garment distinctive of this period was called a *houppelande*.

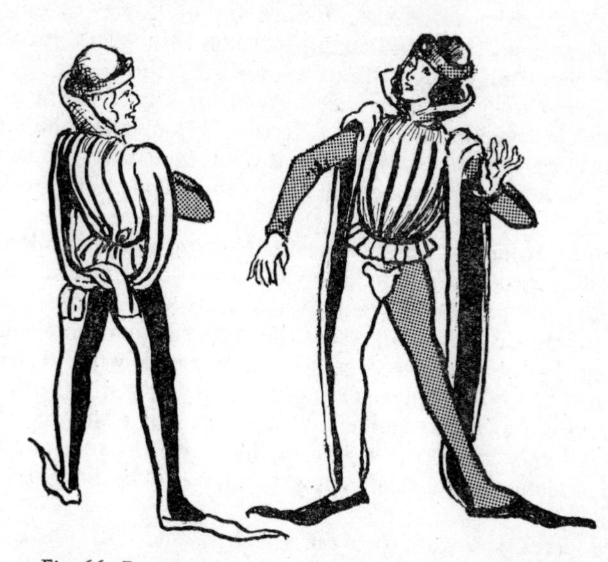

Fig. 66. Renaissance man's short tunic and 'bag' sleeves. Notice the cord at the waist tied at the back, and the long 'bag' sleeves also loosely knotted behind. See the parti-coloured tights, and the 'cod-piece' (also in Fig. 67a).

This consisted of a high-collared, girdled gown, closely fitting to the body (with those typical pleats), with long, wide, pointed, pendant sleeves, and a full skirt that reached to the ground in front, with a train at the back. To make walking easier, it was split up the centre in front from the knee downwards.

In another form, the *houppelande* was worn to only knee length—more like a tunic, and with or without a centre opening—and fitted with what were known as 'bellow sleeves', which had an ordinary wrist cuff, above which they were slit up to the shoulder, so that the wearer's arm and hand could pass through (if the hand wasn't through the cuff), with the sleeve hanging loosely down behind, rather similar to the 'bag' sleeve, but not so long (*see* Fig. 67).

A dagger in a velvet-covered sheath was slung from the waist-band, or . . . curiously enough . . . from a chain hung round the neck, with the dagger reposing on the chest!

The hems of these *houppelandes* (including the knee-slit) and the edges of the sleeves were usually scalloped (or 'dagged', as the fashion was called) or cut into a castellated or leaf-like pattern, and the whole garment (which was made from figured brocade) was lined in a contrasting colour, but for the stage only such parts as would show—the insides of the sleeves and the turn-back of the slit skirt and the reverse side of the scalloping—need concern us.

The *houppelande* can be made from a dressing-gown pattern, adapting the sleeves and collar and adding side and back 'gores' for the fullness—and don't forget the extra length for the train.

Long, heavy wool or cotton hose encased the legs of the men of this period, and as sometimes one leg differed in colour from the other, or each leg was parti-coloured, it looks as if tights would have to be used—though, believe me, it is wonderful what can be done with men's long-legged pants!

The most satisfactory way to dye the tights (for the parti-colouring) is to carefully separate the joins down the inner leg seams (use a safety razor blade), but before the dyeing is done machine a narrow line down each side of the divisions, to prevent the material from unravelling. Pin the separated pieces out as flatly as possible on a table without stretching the shape, and apply the dye sparingly with a fairly stiff brush. When dry, the seams are joined together again. Tights in one all-over colour, of course, need only be dipped, as it is hardly worth the time and trouble spent in undoing them—and, anyway, they can be bought in most colours.

A 'cod-piece' was worn between the legs, and this was a typical feature which can be seen in many of the Hampton Court Palace tapestries (*see* Fig. 66).

Ridiculously long, pointed-toed shoes, called *poulaines*, were worn with these tights, and at one period the length became so exaggerated that the tips had to be supported by chains attached round the knees! Such an extreme, however, would not be used on the stage, except for some special character part, when it might provide amusing possibilities. Ordinarily, the toe-pieces only extended some 3 inches or 4 inches, and were padded with cotton-wool to help retain the shape.

There were no heels to these shoes, of course, but often a thick wooden sole (patten) was worn under the shoe, thereby considerably adding to the wearer's height! Sometimes no shoes were worn at all, with just the long hose (tights) covering the feet, but in such a case—for the stage—a thin sole should be inserted into the foot.

Instead of shoes, socks could be worn with the parti-coloured tights, each foot of a different, contrastingly opposite colour. Or, if the tights are plain (one all-over colour), the socks can then be worn in a different colour.

Men's hair was usually dressed in what today we should call a 'page-boy' bob, either straight or curled, and with a heavy forehead fringe. Another style was to wear it closely cropped at the sides above the ears and round the back of the head, with the rest of the hair worn flat and uncurled on top, like a cap. This was a fashion that harked back to Henry V (1413-22) and those who saw Laurence Olivier in the film *Henry V* will recall that he had his hair like this.

As a rule, men went clean-shaven, but a few (who wanted to look particularly 'interesting') wore small, well-clipped chin beards with either one or two points, and a thin, turned-down moustache. Sometimes the line of the beard followed up the curve of the jaw, joining the hair. This was a style that seemed to suit dark men better than fair! Older and more important men, of course, wore longer and fuller (grey?) beards (*see* Fig. 68).

Fig. 67. (a & b). The short version of the houppelande, with the 'bellow' sleeve. Also the long style, with train and scalloped edgings.

Fig. 68. Some hair and beard styles. At the beginning of the period, men wore their hair in a natural 'bob' (not artificially curled a, d & e). But, as the period progressed, hair became much shorter, and almost as it is worn today, (b & c). Most men went clean-shaven (a, d & e). But, of course, as Henry VIII favoured the close-clipped chin beard and thin, turned down moustache, there were many men who followed his example (b & c).

There were several kinds of hat a man might wear: *(a)* a stiff, high-crowned, brimless, round felt in black or in other colours, and in shape rather like a fez, only bigger; *(b)* a conical-crowned felt hat, with a brim that was turned up at the back and sides, leaving a turned-down peak in front; or *(c)* with the brim turned up in the front only. These last two hats were often worn over a white linen or black velvet coif or hood and a scalloped shoulder cape. The opening, framing the face, was either plain or had a turned-back, scalloped surround, sometimes in a different colour. This headgear was known as a *chaperon*, and usually had a point or 'tail' that hung down at the back, called a *liripipe*, and as time went on it became longer and longer, until it touched the floor, when it was lifted up and tucked into the belt or wound loosely round the neck. Sometimes the tail was at the front, and thrown back over the top of the head, or there were two tails, one at the back and one at the front, or one on each side, or there was a sort of bag at the back, instead of a tail, or two such bags, one at each side, like elephant's ears!

Then a peculiar thing happened! The opening for the face was put round the forehead instead, and the shoulder cape was fitted with its scalloped edging arranged to hang down (or stand upright) on one side, with the *liripipe* wound tightly round the forehead, to hold the whole thing together. Naturally, each man varied the style to suit himself, and for the stage whatever final arrangement is decided upon should be sewn into position for safety's sake (as actually was done later).

To make one of these *chaperon* headdresses, cut out two ovals 3 inches or 4 inches wider in circumference than the 'round-the-head' measurement, with an 'open-fan'-shaped piece at one side of each oval, and a long 'tail', about 3 inches to 4 inches wide, on the other side. From one of these ovals cut out a hole large enough to comfortably fit over the wearer's head (put binding round the edge), and then join the two ovals together along the outer rims, including the two 'tails', but *not* the two 'fan'-shaped pieces, which should each be lined in a contrasting colour, with the lining of the one facing the lining of the other.

Put the hat on the actor's head, and bunch the two 'fan'-shaped pieces together so that they either stand upright or flop down as desired, and then bind the whole thing round the head with the tail, which, if it is first lined—on one side only—can be twisted to give a parti-coloured effect. If it is considered more convenient, this headdress can be built round a skull-cap, with the hole for the head cut out from both ovals (*see* Fig. 69).

From this form of *chaperon* there evolved what became known as the *roundel*, which was a circular, cloth-covered 'bolster', with a hole left in the middle. It was worn fitted over a skull-cap, with a bunch of scalloped trimming—lined on one side—standing upright or falling over the edge at one side, with the *liripipe* tail, now no more than just a flat strip, scalloped on both edges, and lined on one side, hanging from the other side or down the back.

To make the *roundel*, start with a ring of strong wire and pad it round with wadding until it is the required size (inside measurement to fit over a skull-cap and outside circumference about 3 inches or 4 inches wider). The ring is then neatly covered with silk or cloth, with the lined, scalloped trimming and tail added (*see* Fig. 69).

All the various hats and headdresses described in this section can

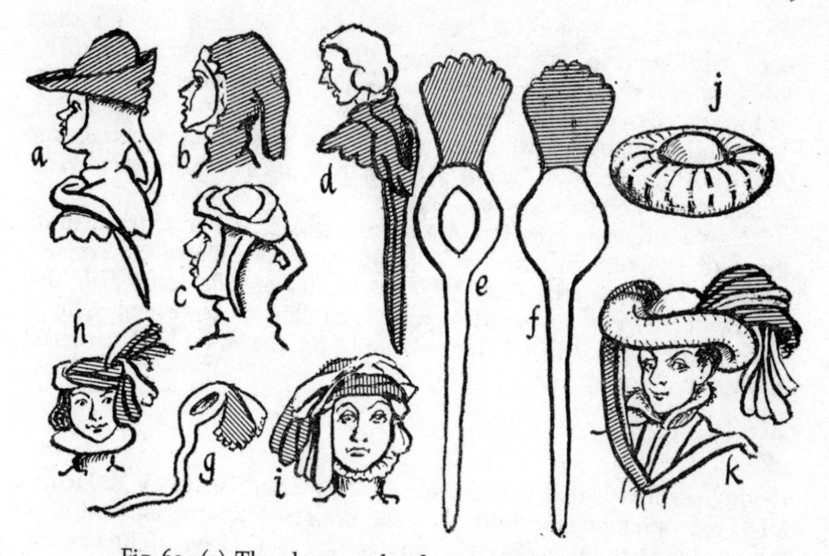

Fig. 69. (a) The chaperon hood, worn with a hat, and the long tail—liripipe—draped over the shoulders; (b) the chaperon, with a short tail—from which the liripipe developed—and the scalloped edging round the face-opening; (c) the liripipe worn wound round the head; (d) the chaperon hood pulled back from the head, to hang down behind; (e) if one is not using an actual chaperon hood to make the headdress that developed from it, the effect can be produced by cutting out two pieces of material, which are joined together as described. The under section (e) fits to the head, while (f) is the top. The 'fan' shaped sections are not joined, and if one surface of each of them is 'lined' in a different colour, this adds to the effect; (g) showing the finished headdress; (h & i) the 'upright' and 'drooping' method of arranging the 'fan' ends; (j) the 'roundel', with the foundation skull-cap—when complete, it looks rather like a motor tyre! (k) The completed 'roundel'.

have extra trimmings of fur, feathers or jewels, according to the taste (and the purse!) of the character represented.

All scalloped edging—whether for costumes or hat trimmings, and whatever the design—should always be lined to present the typical colour contrasts of the period, and to give added solidity and prevent the scallops from curling up.

In cutting, it is quite as effective to use the plain, semicircular pattern as the more involved leaf design, and usually the scalloped edge can be marked free-hand in pencil or charcoal (chalk on a dark material) and then cut out, but if you want to be very precise fold a long strip of paper into sections of about 3 inches wide by 4 inches high, and cut out a scallop shape 2½ inches wide and 3 inches high. You can then open out the strip and lay it along the edge of the material to be scalloped, drawing round the outline of each of the shapes . . . easier still would be to use a large cup as a templet.

A similar method must be employed with the lining material, but in the cutting out allow about ¼ inch to ½ inch margin round each scallop shape for the necessary 'turning in'.

To give fullness to the top of a narrow sleeve, add an extra strip of the material down the middle. To narrow a wide sleeve pattern, reduce (cut) the material from both inside and outside seams. For the 'bellow-sleeve', cut a somewhat fuller and longer sleeve and split it down the inside, with the edges bound and the lower end gathered into a plain circular cuff.

WOMEN

During the first half of the fifteenth century, from Henry IV to Henry VI (1399-1461), women wore the cote, or corset, which consisted of a full, wide skirt and a closely fitting bodice, with long, tight sleeves, which was laced up the front . . . a custom that still persists today in national peasant costumes.

The corset was followed by the surcote, which was a sleeveless garment, with a low, straight-across neck-line, and with the upper part of the 'body' cut away at the sides under the arms, until what was left was little more than the bib of an apron, back and front, to which the very full, wide skirt was attached. Through these enlarged arm-holes, which were sometimes trimmed with fur, appeared the long, tight sleeves of the cote, now worn as an under-dress.

Later still the *houppelande* came into fashion for women, and in its main characteristics it was designed very much on the same lines as for the men . . . but without the front slit in the skirt.

The most commonly worn gown in the latter half of the fifteenth century was one that fitted closely to the upper body—arranged in the typical pleats—with a low, turned-back V-shaped collar and revers that left the neck bare. The long, tight sleeves were flared at the ends to cover the fingers, or were turned back to show the lining and form a cuff.

The skirt which was exceedingly full and long, both back and front, was gathered on to the bodice, and a wide belt was worn to emphasize the high waist-line. So long, indeed, was the skirt that to move about at all it had to be held up in a big bunch over the tummy, first by one hand and then with the other, and as the lining was usually of fur or a rich satin, one may be sure m'lady was not slow in contriving opportunities for displaying it . . . one of which was to pull the material through a loop that hung at one side from the belt so that it fell in a loose cascade, showing both the lining and the under-skirt (cote).

The collar and revers, and sometimes the cuffs, were often of fur, ermine and squirrel being the favourites, with the humble rabbit way down at the bottom of the list. The amount of bosom exposed by the V neck varied, and generally the space was filled across by the upper part of the corset, and sometimes—with the extra modest—by the top of the chemise that was worn under that. On the other hand, there were some ladies who allowed the V to plunge all the way down to the waist!

The long shoulder mantle—in any of the styles already described—was still worn for most special occasions, with the circular cloak and hood for everyday use.

Women's shoes were hardly ever seen (use heelless felt slippers) and their legs *never*! There is the story of the gallant who offered the Spanish Queen a pair of stockings, only to be told—and in no uncertain fashion—that the Queen of Spain had no legs! The ladies of England, however, were more fortunate, and Chaucer, in describing the Wife of Bath, even tells us that the colour of her hose was 'a fine scarlet-red'.

Reference to this lady reminds me that although women at this period were generally depicted riding side-saddle, the Wife of Bath was none of these, but rode astride, with her legs encased in 'foot-mantles' that looked for all the world like a gigantic pair of pyjama trousers with the feet sewn up, into which the lady's legs and voluminous skirts were tucked. I think if the opportunity occurred in a play—as perhaps it might in *The Merry Wives of Windsor*, which is often costumed in this period—to allow some stout body to make an entrance wearing 'foot-mantles', which some timid young serving-man has to help her out of, instead of the threadbare worn business of pulling off top boots, a lot of slap-stick fun might be worked up. And, after all, what is *The Merry Wives of Windsor*, but a Shakespearian pantomime romp?

At the beginning of the fifteenth century, young unmarried women continued to wear their hair hanging down loosely round their shoulders, with a fillet tied round the brow. Married women pinned up their locks, and the older spinsters covered their heads, anyway! But as the century wore on, headdresses—such as turbans and small *roundels*—were worn on top of the loose, unbound hair.

In the second half of the fifteenth century *all* women wore head-coverings and, many and varied as they were, all shared three points in common: *(a)* they made her head look twice the size; *(b)* added considerably to her height, and *(c) concealed* every vestige of her hair, so that whether she had flowing tresses, like Lady Godiva, or was as bald as Yul Brynner remained her unrevealed secret!

Often the front of the natural hair-line was shaved away to emphasize the fashionable high forehead, and the eyebrows plucked to the thinnest line—or pulled out altogether. A few years ago in England plucked eyebrows were all the rage, but nowadays a more natural line is favoured.

To 'quell or vanquish' eyebrows (without pulling them out), they should be rubbed over with slightly dampened soap before the grease-paint and powder are put on. In this way they will not show from the front, especially if the area above the eyes is delicately shaded.

Naturally, few amateur actresses (who have to make 'appearances' at offices, etc., by day) will agree to shave their hair-line for the matter of a couple of performances on the stage at night. The difficulty, however, can easily be overcome by tightly binding a wide strip of white surgical bandage across the fore head and around the head, keeping it as flat and close as possible to the lower edge of the hair-line. Do not attempt to help by blocking out the hair with grease-paint, as this will come through the bandage, and be doubly careful not to get any of the face make-up along the lower edge, or the effect can be completely ruined.

The simplest of the headdresses was a tall, circular, brimless cap, with a veil thrown over it, low enough in front to partly cover the high forehead effect (a top hat with the brim removed, and worn towards the back of the head, would be exactly right!).

Lying flat in the centre of the forehead there was sometimes a semicircle of black velvet, with a hole cut out from the centre, and the top half apparently under whatever headdress was being worn. I am not sure of its origin, but it appears in several paintings of the Madonna in the French School around the period 1450-1500. This characteristic feature made a reappearance in some of the cap headdresses in Charles II's day (1660-83).

A headdress that was very typical of this period was the tall, pointed hennin, which can be made from a cone of buckram (like a dunce's hat) covered with some dark material. To begin with, it was worn fairly upright on the head, but later it slanted more towards the back, and to lessen the hard line round the face a soft piece of white material should first be placed over the head, with the front edge down to about the end of the nose. When the hennin is put on, it is folded back across the top of the forehead, and draped to hang down each side, framing the face. For an older woman—or a royal personage—use black velvet, and add a fairly wide strip of gold embroidery around the base of the cone. A long, gauzy strip—like a scarf—was often loosely wound round the cone and tacked at the tip, falling freely down behind. Don't forget the little black velvet semicircle on the forehead, and also to hide any suggestion of hair.

The most popular headdress was probably the horned wimple. First make a tight-fitting cap of buckram, with the front edge coming across the head a couple or so inches further back than the hair-line, passing behind the ears and round the nape of the neck at the back, and cover it neatly with white muslin. At either side, above the temples, and standing out at an angle of about 45°, attach (sew) two pointed 'horns' (buckram cones) similarly covered with gauzy material and then patterned on top with a criss-cross design of thin black tape, lightly tacking it where it overlaps. A narrow white elastic chin-band, to hold the wimple on, is fixed from the edge on either side. This will be found necessary, as with the additional veiling the headdress will become quite heavy.

Now take a length of gauze veiling, and fold it neatly under the chin in the centre, and take each end up the sides of the face and along the underside of each cone, and attach it to the tip, from which the veiling hangs free.

A second, fairly large square-shaped piece of gauze is folded in half, with the centre point of one edge fastened (press-stud) to the centre front edge of the cap, with just a slight overlap on the forehead, and another press-stud holding the veil at the back edge of the cap. Then take the two sides up to the top surface of the two cones, fix to the tips (another press-stud) and let the ends hang free. The purpose of the press-studs in place of sewing (which, of course, can be done if preferred) is that the veils can be removed after a performance and ironed, so that they are without creases for the next one (*see* Fig. 70).

The angle at which the two cones are fixed on the cap can be varied, either until they stand practically upright and parallel on top of the head or further back on the head, and sloping backwards. In each case the veiling is attractively draped over the cones, which can, if desired, be painted silver or gold, in which case they would not be covered with the gauze in the first place. Do not make the gold or silver solution too liquid, or it may soften the buckram and spoil the crisp shape.

There is still one other headdress that is so typical of the period that it should not be omitted, and that is the shaped *roundel.*

First, make your 'bolster', with its wire foundation, and cover it with brocade or cloth of gold or silver or ermine, and bend the sides upwards to form a U or a V in front, and a slightly wider curve at the back . . . but the angles are optional.

Then make a cap that closely fits the head and ties under the chin, completely hiding all the hair and covering the ears . . . or a round opening may be cut at each side to encircle the ear, which then, of course, is visible.

Place the shaped *roundel* on the cap so that no open spaces appear between the roll and the head, and attach it to the cap so that the point of the U or the V comes in the centre of the forehead . . . and don't forget to show as much height of forehead as possible, if necessary binding that strip of surgical bandage round the head.

A fine gauze veil with a scalloped edge can be draped across the top, falling in graceful folds behind, or a long strip of gauze may be taken under the chin and up each side of the face, and pinned at the top of each curve—slightly more towards the back—with the ends hanging down (*see* Fig. 71).

The cap should be made of metallic network—but don't let that frighten you! All you need to do is buy some of those square, flat, double-sided, glittery pot-scourers (from Woolworth's—7d. each!) and

Figs. 70, 71 & 72. (a & b) The simple and the more elaborate hennin headdress, which was first introduced at the French court by Anne of Bavaria, and later became popular in England; (c) another example of the hennin. Notice the 'ring' on the forehead (also in 'a'). This was the front of a wire netting cap—it was called a 'frontlet'—which was covered in black material (velvet, etc.) its purpose being to ease the strain and discomfort on the forehead of the wearer of these tall headdresses which were often worn at a steeply sloping angle; (d, e & f) are examples of the early 'roundel', as worn by women, 'd' with the chaperon hood, and 'e' and 'f' with a head-veil; (g, h & j) are examples of the more exaggerated form of 'roundel'; (i) is the charming and becoming 'wimple' headdress.

open them out, and neatly shape them to cover the cap, to which they are sewn. These side panels can, of course, be further ornamented with pearls and 'precious stones' (Woolie's again!).

Occasionally, with the more exaggerated styles, the opening in the centre of the *roundel* was made a bit larger than the size round the head, so that when the sides were bent upwards in the U or the V, an open space was left between them and the head, which was filled in with the same metallic net, covering the ears (or exposing them, as described above) and narrowing down to form a band under the chin. The under-cap would still be worn, and the *roundel* attached to it, back and front, as before (*see* Fig. 72).

If you've your *Alice in Wonderland* handy, you will see that the Duchess wears this type of headdress, but in Tenniel's drawings I'm surprised to notice rows of neatly curled hair! But I rather like the arrangement of the scalloped piece of material draped over the top, though I cannot help feeling that such a heavy contraption would be all the better for a chin-veil, or at any rate some elastic . . . but perhaps there is, hidden amongst all those double chins!

Clothes, for the most part, were heavy without being stiff, and the main materials used (for both men and women) were dyed wools, linen, cottons, silks and satins. Velvets, too, were in great demand, and gold-threaded brocades, and transparent tissues for veils.

Underclothes were often dyed red, and it is interesting to think that the red-flannel drawers that were such a standard joke with the late nineteenth- and early twentieth-century music hall comedy merchants were a relic from those far-off times.

Colours may be as varied and rich as desired, and the wonderful, glowing paintings that have come down to us give some idea of the wide range from which one may choose. There will be people who will tell you that this is no criterion, because the paints have mellowed and faded. That may be true—well, of course, it *is* true—but it must also be remembered that the materials of that day were far too expensive to be lightly cast aside, and often a costume descended from father to son . . . mother to daughter . . . so that the reds, blues, greens and golds became softened with time and usage, and in working out his costume plot the designer should not forget the importance of 'colour contrast', and make certain that he includes a sprinkling of blacks, browns and greys.

CHAPTER 8

Religious Drama

It must not be forgotten that *all* drama had its original roots in man's religious instincts, and in the Roman Catholic England of the early Middle Ages the traditional rites as observed at the Elevation of the Host provided the first dramatic spectacle, with the raised choir forming the stage.

Later, came the miracle and mystery plays, based upon the Bible stories—from the Creation to the Second Coming—and the lives of the saints, written and enacted by the priests for the edification and instruction of the people, and usually performed at Whitsun or the Feast of Corpus Christi.

The mystery plays of medieval times (synonymous with the still earlier miracle plays) were so called because they were performed by the guilds as part of their mysteries. In Shaw's *Saint Joan,* when Warwick calls the Executioner 'fellow', he replies, "I am not addressed as 'fellow,' my lord. I am the Master Executioner of Rouen: it is a highly skilled mystery."

Each play was really a cycle of plays, with each guild heing responsible for an episode, and the few surviving mystery plays are still known by the names of the towns where they are believed to have been acted . . . Chester, Coventry, Wakefield and York, which is the best known, and also the longest, being made up of forty-eight plays. The original manuscript of the York Cycle is in the British Museum.

There seem to be two ways in which religious drama may be presented: (i) in contemporary costume and (ii) in medieval. Naturally, the latter appealed more to the great painters by giving them fuller scope for composition and colour (besides, in many cases, being 'contemporary' with their own times). Yet the ornate surroundings with which, for instance, they trapped the simple Nativity story entirely robbed it of it original significance.

To introduce colour wherever one can is, of course, a good thing, but unless one is giving a display of *tableaux vivants*, based upon the Old Masters, it is as well to avoid any attempt at reproducing the costumes of the Middle Ages when presenting incidents from the Old Testament —or even the New Testament, for that matter.

For the Nativity story, the simpler and plainer the clothes are the better (by which I don't mean 'ugly' or shabby. After all, the only reason why the greatest event the world has ever known took place in a stable was because there was no room at the inn). This same simplicity, I think, should also apply to the Wise Men. By what roundabout means they have become the Three Kings I am not sure . . . certainly not by way of the Gospel story. As a matter of fact, only St. Matthew mentions them at all, and even he doesn't tell us how many there were! Perhaps they became 'three' because three specific gifts were mentioned!

Many beautiful colour combinations in reds, blues, greens, yellows and browns can be made with dyed hessian, which would be the most suitable material to use. Mary needs a long, plain gown, with tight, wrist-length sleeves, worn with a circular cape and hood, over a simple. white linen chaperon or coif.

Joseph would have an ankle-length gown and waist-sash, with an open robe and hood, and it might very well be patterned with the typical Hebrew stripes in terracotta and black, and there would be sandals on his feet.

But why is Joseph almost invariably represented as being so old? Surely this cannot be correct? In seeking information on this point, I was told that it was a concession to morality . . . which left me as much in the dark as before, and seems to be no acceptable reason for Mary espousing a man looking old enough to be her grandfather.

Of the adoring shepherds, two or three might have full-length gowns, others knee-length, with the shepherd lads in short tunics and shoulder capes reaching nearly to the ground, with bare legs and arms.

Since the Wise Men came from the East—which probably means a good way east of Jerusalem . . . possibly Persia? I will be generous and allow that their robes may be a bit ornamental! (Gold paint added to hessian, dyed with deep rich colours, with here and there the sombre glow of some fabulous jewel. For details of costume, see under 'Persia' in the Biblical section.) The pictorial convention is to depict one of the Wise Men as black—presumably a Moor—though Africa was to the west.

One serious request: when representing angels, please do not—repeat *not*—give them wings. Nowhere is there any Biblical authority for them, and indeed it seems that angels were seldom recognized as such, the Scriptures being full of incidents where they were 'entertained unawares'.

Neither are haloes at all necessary. These were introduced into paintings to differentiate between the saints and the sinners . . . but it is practically impossible to successfully represent a halo on the stage—without the audience being acutely conscious of the wires!

CHAPTER 9

The Tudors (1485-1547)

HENRY VII – HENRY VIII

The Renaissance was now well into its stride, and throughout the civilized world there opened up an almost unparalleled luxury and lavishness in costume, with king and commoner, courtier and peasant alike awakening to a new and lively sense of clothes-consciousness, with each country expressing its own personality in its own particular way.

Nowhere is the individuality of costume better illustrated than in the heritage of its paintings, and Holbein has bequeathed us a vivid, living portrait gallery of Tudor England under Henry VIII, as, with legs set wide apart, he bestraddles the first half of the sixteenth century—filling the frame and dominating the picture!

MEN

The high collar was now no longer worn, and the new neck line (of the under-shirt, slit down the front to allow free passage for the head and tied across with cords) was often as low as the base of the throat . . . a style that later developed into the turned-down collar so popular with Henry VIII, and later with Elizabeth I.

The sleeves of this shirt were wide and full, and both the small, tight wrist-frill and the frill round the neck were embroidered with an edging of black, blue, red or gold thread.

Next to the shirt came a doublet, which rather resembled our modern waistcoat if it was put on back to front and fastened up behind. It was cut fairly low, and straight across, with several inches of the top of the shirt showing above it. These shirts were not always white, nor necessarily made of linen, but might quite likely be of coloured silk.

The fronts of these 'stomachers', as they were called, were usually richly patterned with floral or leaf designs, outlined in gold thread. Some of them were fitted with sleeves (wrist length) and both the front and the tight sleeves were often 'slashed', with the under-shirt pulled through—or the front might be cut in a deep V, and then laced across with gold cords, with the shirt bulging through between the cords.

Next came the jerkin, with a pleated skirt down to the knees, or a little above them, with the upper part open down the front to the waist, to display the under-garment. Some of these jerkins had short, elbow-length sleeves, widely puffed at the shoulders, or they might be very full and extend down to the wrists, and both types of sleeve might be slashed. A metal belt or a sash, knotted in front, went round the waist, with a small dagger, in a velvet-covered sheath, slung from a chain hanging on the left-hand side.

Lastly came the gown, pleated in full folds at the back, and at each side in front, and worn open to show off the rich fur lining. In length, the gown was perhaps an inch or two longer (not more) than the skirt of the jerkin.

A characteristic feature of this gown was the wide fur collar, full and square at the back, broad on the shoulders, and narrowing down the front edge to the hem. Sometimes, it was sleeveless, or there might be a wide, puffed, elbow-length sleeve, trimmed with vertical bands of fur, or a wide, full-length sleeve, with a long slit starting above the elbow and ending at the wrist-cuff, through which the arm and hand could pass, with the sleeve and cuff hanging down at the back . . . like the 'bellows-sleeve' (*see* Fig. 73).

Longer gowns, reaching to the feet, were worn by statemen and scholars, such as—to choose a name at random—Sir Thomas More, whose robe would probably be of plain black velvet, rather high at the neck, and with full, wide sleeves, either slit or turned back from the wrist to form a large cuff to show the tight, wrist-length under-sleeve and the fur lining. Such a gown would also be fastened most of the way down the front.

The wearing of fur during Henry VIII's reign, carried certain conditions. For instance, no man was entitled to wear marten unless he was worth over 200 silver shillings a year. For a sable lining, he would have to be at least a viscount, while for black genet (civet cat) he would have to prove himself of royal descent!

The tops of the hose (stockings) were laced or tied to the base of the stomacher under the skirt of the jerkin, but for the stage, of course, it is simpler, and generally considered more convenient, to wear tights and braces. After 1515 close-fitting breeches—actually little more than short trunks, called 'upper-stocks'—were worn under the jerkin skirts. Some jerkins, however, were made without the pleated skirt, or opened all the way down the front like a knee-length coat, in which case the breeches were lengthened to above the knees and sometimes to just below

Fig. 73. A young man's costume. Tudor period (1515-1535).

them, with the coat held together at the waist with a button or a narrow belt.

Some of these hose ('lower stock') were still made of cloth, as in earliest times, neatly cut and shaped to the leg, but knitted stockings were now more usually worn. Occasionally, with the skirtless jerkins, both upper and lower stocks were parti-coloured, contrasting with each other as well as with the other leg (four different patterns). Garters were worn above or below the knee to keep the stockings up, as well as by way of decoration. In the three-quarter-length portraits of Henry VIII he is generally depicted wearing the Order of the Garter (below the left knee).

The typical shoe of the period was very square and flat and entirely without heels, and with 'slashings' over the toepiece. They were made of leather or velvet, and usually there was a strap crossing over the instep by which they were held on, though it was sometimes omitted.

Dark felt bedroom slippers are the best things to use here, with three slits cut in the upper toepiece, each about 1½ inches long, with coloured silk puffed through them. If the slippers are too pointed and do not give a sufficiently 'splayed' effect, you can cut out a completely new toecap from a piece of felt and sew this on, making it as wide as you please.

Black soft-leather boots (no 'slashings') reaching halfway up the calf were worn for hunting and outdoor activities, and these can be made by adding felt tops (leggings) to the slippers. The uppers should be cut in two shaped sections, with the vertical joining seams at back and front. They can then be 'laced' with silk cords or leather thongs, threaded through eyelet holes in front or on the outsides. Sometimes thick dark woollen socks, with a sole inserted, will serve the same purpose, with an elastic band round the top to prevent them from wrinkling down.

Most hats were flat-crowned and made of stiff felt, with the brim sometimes turned up all the way round and the four corners 'pinched' together to form a square shape (Henry VII). Others had the brim turned up without being 'cornered' (Henry VIII).

Some of the hats had the brims cut in petal-shape sections, one of which could be turned up or droop down, and nearly all of them were trimmed with curled ostrich feathers or/and jewelled brooches (Henry VIII went in for both at the same time). Undecorated dark felt hats or caps were worn by the ordinary citizen.

A narrow-brimmed, low-cornered velvet cap (dark red, blue or black, and sometimes green or saffron) was worn tilted to one side—generally to the right—and with a white feather plume, fastened by a jewel, decorating the front. In Holbein's portrait of young Edward VI (1547-53), which is in the Metropolitan Museum, New York, the feather it attached at the back and droops over on the left, with the cap—rather like a velvet beret in shape—decorated all the way round with a triple row of gold jewelled brooches, separated vertically by three large pearls. Painted in 1543, when the Prince was six years old, it is said to be the last of the Holbein portraits, as the artist died in the autumn of that year (*see* Fig. 74).

All men kept on their headgear—indoors and out—and never uncovered for a lady! Only in the the presence of his King—or his God—would a man go bare-headed, nor, once having taken off his hat, might he put it on again without the royal consent, and this custom held throughout medieval times and into the seventeenth century.

At the beginning of the period, hair was still often worn long (but not waved or curled), though as the sixteenth century progressed, men's hair became much shorter and almost as we wear it today.

Beards were not very fashionable—except for older men—but, of course, because Henry VIII wore a close-cut chin-beard, with a thin, turned-down moustache, there were several men who followed his example . . . just as they did with Edward VII.

A robe that is seen in many Tudor period plays is that worn by a Doge (or Duke) of Venice . . . the best known, of course, being the

Fig. 74. Examples of the hats as worn by Henry VIII and Edward VI: (a) in 1542—five years before his death—Bluff King Hal exchanged the stiff-brimmed, feather-trimmed hat, in which he is so inseparably associated in most peoples' minds, for a comfortable black velvet 'cap' . . . but, although he relinquished the feather, he retained his famous row of circular and crescent-shaped brooches . . . in fact, from all appearances, he added to the number! (c). (b) The bejewelled, feather-trimmed black velvet 'beret', as worn by Edward VI, in which Holbein painted him in 1543; (d) on other occasions, he wore a velvet 'cap', similar to his father's, but more ornately decorated with brooches and pearls. In Edward's case, the feather was fastened on the left, and a characteristic worth noticing is the four narrow gold cords, each tipped with a pearl and suspended from the edge of the cap to lie on the young Prince's forehead.

Duke in *The Merchant of Venice*. Traditionally, he wore a long, white, silk-lined cloak (no arm-holes) with a small, stiff upstanding collar, and a row of large, bobbly gold buttons all the way down the front, which, with the exception of the top two or three, were left unfastened. This cloak was usually made of some heavy material and patterned with a Venetian red-and-gold 'intertwined ribbon' design. Underneath he wore a long, white, silk, cassock-like gown with long tight sleeves. His shoes were white velvet or suède, and he wore white gloves. I have seen productions of *The Merchant of Venice,* in which the cloak only reached to about elbow length—more of a shoulder cape—with the long cassock underneath buttoned all the way down with the large gold buttons.

The Doge's cap is rather important to get right. It was made from some stiff white (patterned) material, with a high point, and rounded tip standing up at the back of the head and a broad gold band encircling the forehead. Under this a close-fitting, white linen coif was worn, tightly covering the ears, and with narrow white cords that could be tied under the chin (but which usually hung loosely down to the shoulders) at each side. A hat such as this would probably have to be shaped on a block.

There is a splendid portrait by Giovanni Bellini in the National Gallery of Loredano, seventy-fourth Doge of Venice, who was a contemporary of Henry VIII, and any actor who is cast to play the part of a Doge should most certainly go and have a look at this famous picture.

The 'Magnificoes, of greatest port' that sit with the Duke in the Trial Scene, are often dressed in scarlet gowns, with pill-box, scarlet silk caps.

A cardinal, such as Wolsey or Campeius (who 'assisted' him during the trial of Catherine of Aragon), would wear a full long, sleeveless scarlet robe, and a collared cape, reaching nearly to the waist, with both robe and cape fastened up the front with scarlet, silk-covered buttons.

Under the scarlet robe was a white vestment, patterned all over with a small brocaded design of lozenges, of which only the turn-down collar, tied with cords, would be seen at the neck, and the black-cuffed, white sleeves appearing from under the shoulder cape. The scarlet biretta—scarlet slippers—scarlet gauntlet gloves and the jewelled cross that hung on a gold chain aound his neck completed the costume.

For such ceremonies as a divorce—or a marriage—Wolsey wore an additional long-trained, scarlet outer robe, which could be buttoned up the front, but seldom was. This sleeveless garment was put on *under* the cape, and generally it needed the services of two little liveried page-boys to carry the train!

On special occasions, such as these, the Cardinal would wear the symbol of his high office, his Cardinal's hat. This was a low-crownd, wide-brimmed hat, covered with scarlet silk, with a twisted scarlet cord running horizontally across the crown and brim, with the two ends brought down at each side of the head and tied in a single cross-over knot about 9 inches below the chin. These cords had huge triangular-shaped tasselled ends, each composed of rows of smaller tassels strung together in a line, beginning with one tassel at the top, then two tassels in the next row, three in the following one, and so on, with each row widened by an additional tassel until there were five tassels in the bottom row (*see* Fig. 75).

A Cardinal's hat (Wolsey's) is emblazoned in glowing colours in one of the stained-glass windows in the Great Hall at Hampton Court Palace, and when I was painting the scenery for *The Rose Without a Thorn* at the Intimate Theatre, Palmer's Green, I was given special permission

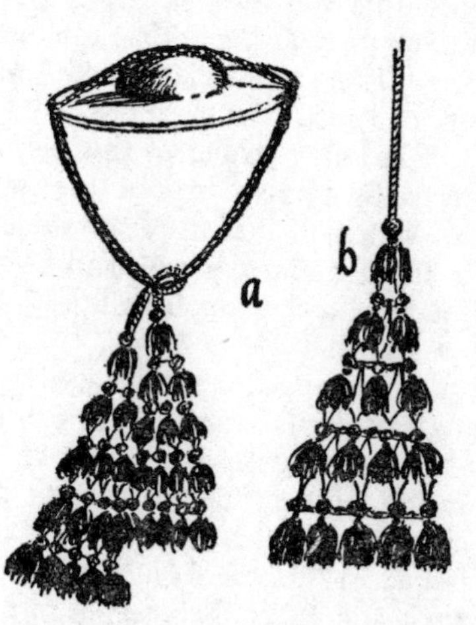

Fig. 75. (a) A cardinal's hat, with tassels; (b) detail of the tassel.

from the Office of Works to make a smaller copy of this glorious window.

When Tree played Wolsey in his production of Shakespeare's *Henry VIII* at His Majesty's Theatre in 1910, during that great speech in Act III, Scene 2, ending with those memorable words, 'Had I but serv'd my God with half the zeal I serv'd my King, He would not in mine age have left me naked to mine enemies,' Tree used to suit the action to the words, and let his great robe fall from his shoulders, and in his simple scarlet cassock he humbly knocked at the door of the Oratory, begging leave to enter. Completely un-Shakespearian, perhaps . . . but what stupendous 'theatre'!

Cranmer, who 'replaced' Wolsey in the King's favour, was a product of Henry's Reformation, and therefore he would have been discouraged from wearing the traditional vestments of Rome. Indeed, so much latitude was allowed that even the wearing of black by the clergy was no longer compulsory, provided the clothes were plain and sober in cut and colour.

Cranmer probably wore the *rochet* (a white surplice, open at the sides) over a long cassock, and a sleeveless *chimere* (a silk robe, open at the front) with white lawn sleeves sewn into the open arm-holes, and a fur tippet or stole round his neck, hanging down to well below his knees. Lastly, there would be the close-fitting cap, probably with ear-flaps, and a biretta on top. These last two were the only items of clerical dress that *had* to be black . . . although, of course, from choice, this was very often the case also with the cassock and outer robe.

The early sixteenth century was still a period for tilting and the jousts, with men in full suits of plate armour, that can hardly be simulated . . . cardboard lacking the essential clank and ring of the genuine article, so that this type of armour has to be hired.

Luckily, however, the ordinary soldier of this period fought without armour, and was protected by a heavy, padded tunic or jerkin, worn over a vest of chain-mail, of which all that need be visible is about 4 inches below the hem of the tunic, and a narrow band below the short over-sleeves. On his head he wore a chain-mail Balaclava, and a sort of pudding-basin helmet on top of that.

Peasant costume had not changed very much with the passing years, and a loose, knee-length, sleeveless tunic was worn over a full-sleeved white shirt, tight at the wrists, with a belt or a strip of twisted cloth wound round the waist. A more prosperous peasant would wear a cloth or leather jerkin in place of the tunic.

Rough-cut hose reached to the waist underneath, with cloth gaiters bound round at the ankle and under the knee, or soft leather boots half-way up the leg.

On his head and shoulders he would still wear the hood and cape *(chaperon)* or a close-fitting, round cloth cap or a wide-brimmed, felt or straw hat. Sometimes the hat was worn on top of the *chaperon*.

The making of a Tudor costume need not be anything like as elaborate and complex as the full descriptions given above. There is no necessity, for instance, to wear a complete, full-sleeved under-shirt, as the pleated neck-piece, with frilled band, centre slit and tying cords can be made as a separate sort of bib, attached to the top of the stomacher, which itself need only be cut out as a triangular panel to cover the chest, with tapes for tying it round the back.

If the jerkin has a fully pleated skirt reaching to the knees, the upper stock will not be seen, and can therefore be omitted, and if tights are worn, these will take the place of the lower stock.

Jerkins are made from patterned brocade, velvet or silk . . . and don't forget—whatever garment—that it should be padded or stiffly lined, to give the broad square typical outline.

The only complete garments, therefore, that one *must* have, are the jerkin or doublet and the outer robe (gown), and each of the differently shaped sleeves described, can be made separately, and then be tied or press-studded into the arm-holes, and one pair of sleeves, frilled at the wrist and with the upper half overlapping the lower will suggest the double sleeves.

'Slashing' can be done either by cutting the material (binding the raw edges with narrow, decorated braid) with small sections of white (representing the shirt) sewn underneath and pulled through the slits, or the 'slashes' can simply be appliquéd on top of the sleeve or stomacher or jerkin or tights, and edged round with braid. This latter method is preferable if the sleeves—or any of the other 'slashed' garments—are likely to be used again for some other type of costume. 'Slashes' on felt slippers can be outlined in gold paint. Pearls and precious stones can be sewn on wherever seems effective, and usually there was a jewel at either end of a 'slash'.

In *Twelfth Night* the clown, Feste, when addressing Orsino, says, 'Now the melancholy god protect thee, and the tailor make thy doublet of changeable taffeta, for thy mind is a very opal'—and the notes in my Shakespear describe 'changeable taffeta' as 'shot silk'. And, by the way, Englishmen, when travelling abroad, were advised to wear taffeta as a lining to their doublets . . . as a precaution against 'creepy-crawlies'!

WOMEN

During the first ten years of the period—covering Henry VII's reign—there was little change in women's costumes, and the V neck, the long, tight sleeves, and the high waists were still the fashion, with wide, full skirts, equally long all the way round, held up in front, not only as a device for showing the rich lining and decorative underskirt, but also from sheer necessity, as any sort of progressive movement would otherwise have been impossible.

There were, however, a few developments. For instance, the long, tight sleeves might be decorated (down the *back*) with a series of small 'slashes'—with a rather larger one at the bend of the elbow—through which the chemise or shift (the feminine equivalent of a man's shirt) was puffed. Or the sleeve itself might be shortened into a half-sleeve (elbow length) worn over a full, long under-sleeve . . . and remember, no bare arms!

To prevent the long train from dragging on the ground, it was sometimes caught up and fastened to the back of the waist-belt by a button or a jewelled brooch, providing yet another opportunity for displaying the lining and giving an effect that was not unlike the early bustle of 1870.

After 1510 there was a decided trend in women's fashions towards the broader masculine styles. For one thing, the *décolletée* became more square, with an upward curve over the bosom, lower at the corners, and narrowing towards the shoulders of the bodice. Except for some special occasion—such as posing for her portrait to Hans Holbein—the whole or part of this opening was filled in by the chemise, which was embroidered with a patterned border in black silk, and as likely as not might in addition be edged with precious stones. In fact, any excuse was as good as another for wearing jewellery, singly or *en masse,* and large gold brooches, with sparkling drops, pinned to the front of the dress were very popular. In Holbein's portrait of Jane Seymour in the Imperial Museum, Vienna, she is depicted wearing just such an ornament.

Jewelled chains were wound twice round the neck, once close up, with the end of the second loop tucked out of sight in the front of the dress and a pendant hanging from the top loop. This arrangement was very typical of the prevailing fashion, and appears in nearly all the famous portraits of the time. Catherine of Aragon, of course, had a large jewelled cross . . . so did Anne of Cleves, but very much smaller. Anne Boleyn wore a pendant shaped like the capital letter B, from which two large pearl drops depended. Legend has it that from her birth her long, slender throat was encircled by a different kind of 'ring', rather like a china figure that has had the head stuck on, which was rather significant in view of what happened to her on Tower Hill that fine sunny morning in 1536.

Dresses now became shorter, although they still trailed to the floor, with a train at the back. At first the whole costume was made in one piece, with the skirt closed all the way round, though the upper part might be slit in front and then laced across a stomacher (just as with the men's doublets). But by 1530 exactly the reverse became the fashion, with the skirt—which by this time was cut separately from the top and joined at the waist—opening from the waist downwards in an inverted V to disclose the richly decorated under-skirt, with the bodice slit at the *back,* and tightly laced to stretch the material smoothly over the breast. The full, wide 'bell' shape that resulted was obtained by both the under- and over-skirts being gathered in heavy pleats . . . no one seems to have thought of using 'hoops' until Elizabeth's reign!

Sleeves were tight from the shoulder to just above the elbow, after which they widened out to be caught in again at wrist with a frilled cuff. After the skirts were split down the front, the long sleeves were often part of the under-dress, the wider sleeve of the upper gown coming on top, and the broad open cuff turned back to the elbow in a heavy fold, displaying the rich silk or fur lining.

Many of the sleeves were only tied into the arm-holes, or pinned in with jewelled brooches, allowing the under-chemise to puff through between these 'bridges'. These 'ties' were thin silk cords with metal tips—very much like our modern silk shoe-laces, which could, in fact, be used—decorated with tiny floral and other shapes (which could be made from a blob of solder or plastic wood) attached to the ends.

This fashion for separate sleeves has its practical use from the costume designer's angle, as it provides the opportunity for using a variety of different sleeves with the same 'body'.

The unmarried girl still wore her hair long and parted in the centre, and drawn back over her ears, to hang down her back in loose coils or in plaits. A wide-mesh, silk net cap (sometimes called a Juliet cap by modern milliners) was worn rather far back on the head—or, alternatively, well forward to just above the eyebrows, with a single drop jewel hanging between them. This was a fashion borrowed from Italy, where women were not very impressed by the heavy, all-enveloping headdresses of the Germans and English. The eyebrows, by the way, were now less often plucked and followed a more natural line. From Holbein's portrait of Catherine Howard in the National Portrait Gallery, she appears to have had quite well-defined eyebrows.

This loose, unbound hair was also a special characteristic of the bride —as a testimony to her virtue, just as in England today a girl is decked out in virginal white. It is recorded that when Henry VIII married Catherine of Aragon in 1509, she wore a white satin dress, with her long black hair falling about her shoulders. In her case, however, this carried tremendous political significance, because Catherine, who had been married to Henry's elder brother, Arthur (who had died five months later) had always steadfastly maintained that her first marriage had never been consummated. It was not until eighteen years later when Henry began to be troubled by qualms of conscience (in the comely shape of Anne Boleyn) that divorce proceedings were begun against poor Catherine.

The headdress you will see on either of the four queens in any ordinary pack of playing cards was almost certainly originally designed from the one worn by Henry VIII's mother, Elizabeth of York, and known as the 'gable' (no, nothing to do with Clark!).

This late fifteenth-century headdress was made from a large piece of black velvet or silk, placed over the head and hanging down at the back over the shoulders. The front line over the forehead was stiffened in the centre with wire, and bent so that the material stood up in a high point like the sloping roof of a house, with the two 'outer walls' falling on each side of the face nearly as far as the belt of the high-waisted gown, with a little of the hair—neatly parted in the middle—showing under the pointed 'gable'.

A 1-inch-wide strip of white or coloured (gold) material was sewn to the front edge of the velvet, hanging down over the forehead like a 'thickening piece', and continuing down each side to within 6 inches of the ends, where it stopped short. There was no trimming round the back, but a second strip of similarly coloured material, narrow in the middle and widening out to 3 inches towards the ends, was placed over the head about 4 inches behind the 'gable' point, with the ends hanging down on either side. It was sewn to a panel of black velvet, of which about ½ inch showed all the way round as a border, and both this strip and the front edging were ornamented with a design in precious stones. There is a good portrait of Elizabeth of York in the National Portrait Gallery wearing just such a headdress.

One other headdress worn by older women in the late fifteenth century should be described, and that is the 'pleated *barbe*'. This consisted of a tight-fitting white linen cap, straight across the forehead and just tipping the eyebrows, and framing the face at the sides. Over this was draped a stiffened white linen 'gable' piece, jutting well forward in front and reaching the shoulders at the sides and back and completely hiding all the hair. The *barbe* was a white, pleated linen piece, shaped

Fig. 76. The 'gable' headdress, as worn by Elizabeth of York (Henry VII's wife). Also the 'barbe': (a) as worn by ladies of 'quality', with the chin covered, and (b) with the band worn under the chin, a style affected by ladies of lesser discrimination! (c) Diagram of the under-cap.

rather like a bib, that was pinned at the sides and fastened at the back, so that it extended over the breast in a curve, with the top edge coming just below the lower lip . . . very uncomfortable on a warm day, and rather like a starched linen vizor in appearance. *Romeo and Juliet* is sometimes dressed in this period, and such a headdress would be excellent fun for the Nurse (*see* Fig. 76).

In considering women's headdresses during the first half of the sixteenth century, it is an irresistible temptation to place them upon the heads of Henry VIII's six wives, and to view them from that vantage-point!

The displaying of her uncovered raven locks at her wedding having served its purpose, Catherine of Aragon thereafter took the greatest pains to completely conceal her hair . . . though she permitted some of her women to show a little of theirs! Many years later, Anne Boleyn (but newly home from the gaieties of the French Court) became one of Catherine's ladies, and it is said that it was by her hair that she first attracted Henry to her other charms!

Catherine's well-known 'pedimental' headdress (also seen in many of the other Holbein portraits) was a development of the 'gable', but not so high-pointed in front and with a much wider angle to the slopes of the 'roof', with the sides slightly curving in towards the cheeks and then out again at the chin, thus giving an outline more like a haystack than a house.

This headdress was known as the 'kennel', and was built on a shaped wire frame forming the 3-inch-wide roof, and extending down each side of the face as far as the bottom line of the chin, with a 1-inch-deep, outlining 'thickening piece'. This frame was covered with rich gold-coloured velvet, patterned brocade or cloth of gold, with each side-piece continuing down as a doubled 3-inch-wide strip, long enough to be folded back upon itself in a loose loop, with the two ends pinned at a point on the top of the head behind the roof-piece.

A close-fitting white linen cap covered the head, with the front line coming about an inch or so back from the hair-line. This cap also had two 3-inch-wide, doubled linen flaps, one at each side of the face down as far as the shoulders. These flaps should either be starched or have a thin wire frame inside, so that the ends can be bent upwards over the shoulders and outwards in a gentle curve.

The thickening piece referred to above is also covered with the same material as the rest of the frame, with the ends of the side-pieces extending down beyond the end of the frame and sewn to the edge of the linen cap flaps, but stopping short just before the upward curve begins. This strip should be sewn with a pattern of pearls and precious stones.

Before putting on either cap or headdress, tightly bind a 6-inch-wide strip of vertically striped velvet or silk round the head, coming from the back of the neck, with the ends crossing over the centre of the forehead (the right over the left, turban-wise) and arranged as far back on the head as possible, without showing any hair. To make use of a bandage here, as has been suggested elsewhere, would be entirely wrong. This inner strip enables the kennel to be placed at the very top of the head, which is just where it should be worn, and with Catherine it was black, but Jane Seymour, who wore a similar headdress, used gold.

The hair and the back of the head were concealed by a long, rectangular black velvet bag, that was attached to the thick edge of the kennel frame, rather like the blunted end of a *chaperon*. The lower left-hand corner was then crossed at the back of the head and pinned on the right, making an outstanding point on the left side, with the other end of the bag draped either to fall over or behind the right shoulder (*see* Fig. 77*a*). In some instances, a black veil was worn instead of the velvet bag.

The headdress chosen by Anne Boleyn when she became Queen was a far more attractive affair than the kennel. This was the crescent, or horseshoe, which stood at a slanting-backwards angle about midway across the head, so that she showed several inches of her smoothly brushed dark auburn hair, parted in the centre and drawn down tightly over her ears at the sides. The back was covered either with a short black velvet bag or a dark veil hanging nearly to the waist and attached to the lower edge of the crescent from the back.

The crescent was about 4 inches wide at the broadest part (centre) and narrowing down to the points, that were fastened at the back of the neck under the veil.

It was usually covered with some rich dark material—such as velvet, brocade or satin—with a close row of pearls (that almost certainly were genuine in those days) sewn to both the inner and outer rims of the crescent, and often there was a white or cloth-of-gold fluting added as a facing next to the hair.

In making this headdress, it is better to start with a wire frame as a foundation, over which the covering material is tightly stitched, to both the back and the front—though stiff buckram or even thick carboard could be used! The pearls, of course, come from Messrs. Woolworth. What would the costume department do without them? (*see* Fig. 77*b*).

Holbein's famous portrait of Jane Seymour shows her wearing a type of kennel headdress almost identical with Catherine's, but with just those little differences that stress the similarity. For instance, the inner linen side-flaps are much shorter, scarcely reaching the level of her mouth, and the turned-back loop of the outer material has an additional white strip on the further side, and is altogether much tighter and closer-lying to her head (*see* Fig. 77*c*).

The skirt of her deep red velvet dress is divided down the front, and worn over a silver-brocaded under-petticoat, with the large red net over-sleeves turned back at the elbow to show the silver-patterned under-sleeves, with their delicate lace wrist frills, and the wide slashing down the back held together with jewelled brooches.

The top edge of her chemise is sewn with a design of the same jewels (pearls and onyx, mounted in gold) that adorn her headdress and waist-belt, and are repeated in the typical double-row necklace and pendant.

Jane was one of Queen Anne Boleyn's Ladies-in-Waiting, and who can say where—or from whom—she learnt the trick that first caught Henry's roving eye? But it is 'thus the whirligig of time brings in his revenges'!

Quite one of the most picturesque headdresses came from Germany, and it was in one of them that Holbein painted Anne of Cleves . . . that controversial portrait that caused all the bother! As a rule, Holbein did no more than present his sitters at their best and most attractive aspect, and only in this one case can history bring the charge of flattery against him. Even so, he was not held entirely to blame, as the picture had been commissioned by Thomas Cromwell, whose private political aspirations led him to hope Henry VIII would marry Anne. This the King did—he could find no way out of it—and Cromwell paid the price of the portrait with his head!

Studying the headdress in a reproduction of this picture—of which the original is now in the Louvre—one sees that first of all there was a close-fitting linen cap, put on as far towards the back of the head as possible, without showing any of the hair, and held by a narrow chin-strap. Over this a wide strip of gold-embroidered material was tightly bound round the head and fastened at the back, with just a suggestion of the white under-cap visible over the middle of the forehead.

The attractive feature, however, was a stiffened, transparent muslin bonnet, the front edge of which jutted out straight across the forehead, with wide curves over the temples, and the long pieces at each side of the face fastened to the chin-strap, with the ends bent outwards, parallel with the shoulders. In making such a headdress, a thin steel wire would probably have to be used to retain the right shape.

Finally, a wider stiffened (by lining) gold-embroidered strip, with a gold tasselled fringe on the left end, was laid over the crown of the head and joined at the back like a hood, with the hanging-down pieces at the sides folded back upon themselves at chin level and the ends pinned on top. The fringe then hung, decorating the left side of the head (*see* Fig. 77*d*).

Holbein painted Anne of Cleves in a voluminous, high-necked, red-cloth garment, trimmed with bands of gold and studded with jewels. It is a dress, however, that reflects the Low Church modesty of the Principality of Cleves, with any suggestion of 'figure' completely overwhelmed by the excessive folds and pleats of the costume, barely showing more of Anne than her folded hands and her face with its 'half-asleep' expression.

In 1540 Catherine Howard (who was a cousin of the ill-fated Anne Boleyn) attracted Henry's attention . . . and it wasn't very long before she became his fifth wife.

Her headdress was similar to Anne Boleyn's, except that it stood more upright and was placed still further back upon her head, so that she showed quite an amount of her dark brown hair, which was parted in the centre and smoothly brushed in a curve round her face, covering her ears.

The crescent was covered in white velvet, trimmed round the outer edge with little bars of gold ornamentation. There was also a thin gold line of pattern just above the lower edge, with a pleated cloth of gold ruching touching the hair. A long black veil hung down her back, hiding the rest of her head. Catherine, too, wore a narrow white chin-strap, that held the headdress from slipping over the back of her head.

Holbein painted her in a tight black satin gown, with a high, wide, open collar, lined with white silk. A huge jewelled medallion is pinned at the front of her dress. Henry called her his 'Rose without a thorn' . . . but, unfortunately—in one so young—her bloom was decidedly full-blown (*see* Fig. 77*e*).

Four years before he died in 1547 at the age of fifty-six Henry married his sixth wife, Katherine Parr, the thirty-four-year-old widow of Lord Latimer.

Kate Parr's headdress was shaped more like a horseshoe than a crescent, with straight blunt ends coming down rather low on each side of her face. It was worn fairly far back, and held with narrow white tapes that tied in a bow under her chin. Her hair was completely hidden by a broad piece of white cambric, tightly wound round her head, and over this she wore a small, close-fitting white linen cap, with a little triangular flap, sewn round the edge with tiny seed pearls, with the point resting on her lower cheek at either side.

The headdress itself was covered with silk, matching the colour of her dress, with pearls sewn all round the top and lower edges, and a long, transparent black veil attached to the back, reaching to her waist in the centre, with the ends falling in a sweep over her shoulders to the floor (*see* Fig. 77*f*).

Her dress followed the prevailing fashion already described, with the characteristic neckline, the wide, slashed sleeves and the long dress trimmed with fur. A feature worth noting, however, was the white under-sleeves, that fell in two long points inside the wide outer-sleeves, and were caught at the wrist with a frill, edged with a pattern in black thread.

The materials used for making costumes for this period should be as rich and heavy as possible—silks, satins, taffetas and velvet (or its substitute). Woollens and fine cloth were also popular, with coarse homespun for the country folk, who wove and dyed the fabrics themselves, so that the colours would be limited.

The great fault that the amateur costumier so often makes is in not suggesting sufficient 'bulk' in the clothes, as weight and richness were the keynote of the period—an effect that can usually be attained by the addition of a stiff lining and under-padding.

Tudor colours were generally deep and dark—black velvet being particularly popular—with the white linen of coifs, veils and neck and wrist frills providing the necessary colour contrast. Other colours were magenta, deep reds and blues, greens and gold.

It is said that when poor Catherine of Aragon died at Kimbolton in 1536, Henry and Anne dressed themselves from head to toe in bright yellow to mark the occasion. But 1536 was also the year in which Anne Boleyn was beheaded . . . and Henry then dressed himself entirely in white . . . and married Jane Seymour the same day!

Fig. 77. The headdresses of the six courageous ladies who married Henry VIII: (a) Catherine of Aragon, in a modified 'gable'; (b) Anne Boleyn, in what was known as a 'French' hood; (c) Jane Seymour, in another version of the 'gable'; (d) Anne of Cleves, with her Flemish headdress; (e) Catherine Howard, in another style 'French' hood; (f) Katherine Parr, with 'French' hood, and under-cap, hiding her hair completely; (g) diagram for the 'gable' headdress; (h) diagram of the 'French hood; (i) diagram of the Flemish headdress; (j) back-view of the 'French' hood and veil.

EDWARD VI (1547–53)

Henry VIII was succeeded by his son, Edward VI, who was only nine year old when Archbishop Cranmer placed the royal crown of England upon his head. When he was sixteen, Edward died of consumption, despite the prophecy of the Milanese astrologer, Girolamo Cardano, that he would live well into middle age!

One can hardly expect to find many costume changes during so short a reign, which, to all intents and purposes, was merely a continuation of his father's. It is important, however, as being a transition period in men's clothes, which became much plainer (less ornament) with the skirts of the doublets and jerkins shortened and more tightly shaped to the body. The collar, too, became narrower, and the sleeves no longer as widely puffed, and fitting more closely to the arms.

Edward is principally remembered as the founder of a chain of grammar schools, and the famous Blue Coat School uniform as worn by the boys today is practically identical with that worn by the ordinary citizen *circa* 1550, except that the modern knickerbocker has replaced the shorter trunks, and that some of the younger men at that time wore the present long skirt of the robe cut short to the knee.

Some years ago, Viola Tree—the actress daughter of Sir Herbert Tree—startled the West End of London, by appearing in a play called *The Choice* at Wyndham's Theatre wearing an exact replica of the Blue Coat School uniform. But, contrary to expectations, the fashion (for women) did not catch on.

'BLOODY' MARY (1553–8)

It is not difficult to picture Mary Tudor as she must have looked on that August evening, 1553, as, mounted side-saddle upon a white palfrey, she rode into London to claim her father's throne, clad in a deep violet velvet gown, with tight under-sleeves and the typically wide, fur-lined outer-sleeve turned back in a large cuff to the elbow.

Her bell-shaped skirt was split down the front to display the grey and violet brocaded under-skirt, patterned with a design of intertwining leaves, a motif that was repeated on the wrist-length under-sleeves.

The high, upstanding collar of her gown was spread out in a fan at either side, with her chin framed by a tight inner collar (part of the under-dress) lined with fine stiffened white lace, and with a small opening just below her throat. A collar like this was certainly a change from the bare-bosom days of Henry VIII, who had never been averse to seeing as much of his women as fashion would allow!

The shoulders of Mary's gown were cut long and low, with the armhole seams coming 2 inches or 3 inches down the upper arm, making a distinct line where the sleeves had been fitted in. The 'gored' waist of the long, padded bodice tapered to a point in front, which was accentuated by a jewelled girdle, hanging down to her knees, with a richly jewelled ball (pomander) at the end.

On her breast glittered an enormous square-cut diamond, set hanging inside a circle of gold filigree work, with a long, pendant pearl suspended beneath. This was probably the famous 'Mirror of Naples' that had once belonged to Louis XII, and later came into the possession of Henry VIII, who gave it to Catherine of Aragon.

It would be a fascinating 'prop' to make, using a square-cut crystal lustre (junk-shop!) wired to swing loosely inside a brass curtain-ring, which could be decorated with a design of little flowers, etc., made from plastic wood and then gilded. Finally, a single 'pearl' drop ear-ring is attached underneath . . . and there you have it!

Mary's headdress was much less stiff and elaborate than the gable structure worn by her sainted mother, and consisted of a black velvet cap with a little forehead peak in front, and with the long side pieces (wired) framing her face. A shallow 'crescent', covered in cloth of gold, rose at the back of her head, with a straight strip of black velvet hanging down behind. This cap was worn rather far back, so as to show her hair, with its noticeably wide centre parting. Like the rest of Henry's children, her hair was red, and Mary dressed it tightly smoothed across the forehead, and then puffed out over the temples. Gold-mounted jewels outlined the edges of the cap, and these were repeated round her neck (between the two collars) and at her wrists, and almost every finger wore a ring. Yet the overall effect was plain and sober—as became so devout a daughter of Rome (*see* Fig. 78).

The welcoming cheering that had gladdened Mary's heart a year ago was now turned to sullen mutterings as the streets of London began to fill with King Philip's Spaniards, and, naturally, these 'dark-skinned foreigners' brought new fashions with them, the most important of which—in view of the future—was the neck ruffle. Small and neat at first, it was later to develop in size out of all proportion. Then, too, there was the high-crowned Spanish hat, a stiff black velvet 'bag', worn slightly tilted to one side and pleated into a hard, narrow brim, turned down back and front and curled up at the sides. Another hat had a wider brim round a tall, hard felt crown, with a small feather plume sticking out backwards at the top! A gold cord encircled the base, and was held in front with a sparkling jewel.

Men in Edward's reign had been clean-shaven . . . perhaps out of compliment to the boy King . . . but now, under the Spanish influence, there were more moustaches (perhaps *moustachios* would better describe the straight, thin ends) and short, neatly clipped beards, coming to a point or ending in a fork.

Shoes were again made of leather, and more nearly followed the shape of the foot (that is to say, narrower and more pointed), but slashings on the toe-pieces were still occasionally to be seen.

Fig. 78. Headdress and collar of Queen Mary I: (a) detail of the famous 'Mirror of Naples' jewel; (b) a square-cut crystal chandelier lustre, as suggested for the centre 'diamond', to be suspended in a brass curtain-ring (c) that has been decorated with a floral design, made from plastic wood, and then gilded (d).

A Spanish innovation was the top-boot, that came to just below the knee and was held up by a strap that went over the knee in front and was fastened at the back . . . but they must have had very knobbly knees for the boots to have stayed up!

Changes in costume are, however, inevitable, no matter how much one may disapprove of the people who cause them, and so during Mary's reign the stiff, square-broad-shouldered silhouette—so long associated with her father—with its flat hat and wide, splayed feet, was gradually transformed into the slim, upright figure with its short doublet, long leg and millstone ruff of the Elizabethans.

Of plays dealing with this period, there are not many. Lord Tennyson wrote one called simply *Queen Mary*, which is included in his collected works . . . but it is hardly ever performed. I once saw it given by an amateur group on a tiny stage, and found its sad, tragic story of smouldering frustration strangely interesting. With the right players for Mary and Philip (as was the case when I saw it), it can be very well worth putting on—and I recommend it to anyone ambitious enough to give it a trial.

Mary also has a leading part in *The Young Elizabeth*, by Jennette Dowling and Francis Letton. When this play was produced in London (with Mary Morris as Elizabeth), Mary was superbly portrayed by Peggy Thorpe-Bates, who looked exactly like the picture of the 'bloody' Queen painted by Antonis Mor in 1553 and which is now in the Prado Museum, Madrid.

ELIZABETH I (1558 – 1603)

In the year 1558 the tide of the Renaissance was already on the turn in Italy, but in England during the long reign of Elizabeth—and, later, under James I—it had yet to reach full flood.

With the defeat of Philip of Spain's Invincible Armada in 1588, England ceased to be 'an island off the coast of Europe', and became a sea-power to be reckoned with . . . which, thanks to the mariners of England, is still our proud boast today.

The use of gorgeous materials, with jewels as a means of lavish decoration, continued as the basis of men's and women's costumes, and one cannot help wondering sometimes what became of all the wealth which *el Draqué* and his merchant venturers filched from the Spaniards to pour into Elizabeth's coffers!

Slashing and the pulling through of the under materials, although still in evidence, now became of far less importance by comparison with the newer fashion for flat surface decoration by the application of braid, lace and embroidery—in black, white and coloured silks, or metallic threads—combined with pearls and other precious stones . . . to such an extent, that very few spaces were left unadorned.

Now, admittedly, to embroider stage costumes in this manner by hand would be too difficult and lengthy a job, but, fortunately for us, the effect can usually quite easily be 'faked' by painting the delicate patterns directly on to the materials in oils—used fairly dry—or with metallic paints. In the case of a long run, however, one must be prepared to occasionally retouch those areas which may become exposed to much rubbing or hard wear (such as elbows, backs of shoulders, etc.).

Trimmings for the ordinary costumes can be made from coloured cotton tapes, which will be less expensive than using ribbons, and yet be equally as effective when seen from a distance, and one can obtain some very pleasant contrasts from combining two or more different colours together. Galloon, soutache, gold, silver and metallic braids can then be used for the more elaborate dresses . . . nor can one be too extravagant (within the limits of one's purse) with the purchase of 'precious' stones, imitation pearls, and coloured beads!

Colour schemes used in costumes for this period appear to have consisted of two shades, of which one was often black—e.g. red and black; gold or silver and black; and, of course, black and white. Watchet (a pale blue) and white, as a costume colour-contrast, became more popular under the Stuarts. As a rule, however, the contrast provided by white was more often introduced in the starched neck ruffles and sleeve cuffs, unless—as occasionally happened—the starch itself was coloured . . . red, blue, purple, green or yellow.

In 1564 a Dutch housewife—a certain Mistress van der Plasse—discovered the secret of starching cambric, with which she cornered the market, charging £5 a time for showing people the art of cutting, pleating and 'pinching' . . . with another £1 for telling them how to mix the starch!

Ruffles and ruffs were a distinctive characteristic of the Elizabethan period, and remained in fashion until towards the end of the reign of James I (1625). Besides being expensive, many of them were extremely cumbersome and uncomfortable to wear, and therefore the soft, turn-over collar continued to vie with them for popular favour . . . and in the end survived them!

A simple narrow ruffle was attached to the shirt neck-band so that it appeared above the stand-up collar of the doublet, and it was either left open in front or tied across with tasselled cords. Such a ruffle is very easy to make, and all that is required is a strip of fine white linen about twice round-the-neck measurement and from 4 inches to 6 inches wide. Fold this strip in half down its length, and then, placing the two open edges together, tightly gather them with a strong running thread until the strip has been reduced to the required length to fit comfortably round the neck. For stage purposes it can then be sewn directly to the inside of the doublet collar, so that it stands up and frames the face. A similar method is used for making the wrist ruffles (*see* Fig. 79).

Fig. 79. Examples of neck and wrist ruffles, and cuffs.

It is an advantage to lightly starch the material before beginning work, and if wide tacking stitches are used for sewing on the ruffle it can easily be removed for cleaning purposes, and with this in view it is always as well to have a duplicate handy. But do not worry unnecessarily if some of the healthy tan make-up comes off on the ruffle, because this will not be noticeable under stage lighting, and with reasonable care a ruffle (or a turn-over collar) can usually be worn for six performances, with a matinée thrown in!

A ruff is quite a different proposition from a ruffle, and it is made as a separate item and worn as a tightly closed ring, fastened at the back. The ordinary medium-sized ruff is generally made with a radius width of from 4 inches to 6 inches, with about a 3-inch depth. Where a greater depth is required, one ruff can often be worn above another. The construction of a ruff is a little more complicated than a ruffle, but it should not prove too difficult!

First you must make a separate, white linen collar-band long enough to fit comfortably round the neck, including an overlap at the back for fastening with hooks and eyes or press-studs. If the finished ruff is to be 3 inches deep and the band is made 4 inches wide, this will allow an extra 1 inch at the base that can be tucked inside the collar of the doublet to ensure that the ruff remains neatly in position and doesn't swivel round! Or the band can be made the same width as the ruff if four hooks are sewn along the bottom edge, with corresponding eyes attached to the top of the doublet collar.

The best material to use for a ruff is lightly starched muslin, organdie or tarlatan (the latter being the easiest to work with) and, according to whether you want a tightly compressed 'Rembrandt'-style ruff or one with looser folds, you will require I yard to 2 yards, 36 inches wide.

Pin down the material, flatly and smoothly stretched on a table, and *very* lightly draw three *thin* charcoal lines, each 9 inches apart, and then carefully cut along them with a really sharp safety-razor blade (more accurate than scissors). This should leave you with four 9-inch by 36-inch (or 72-inch) strips, which are sewn together to form one long panel. Fold this in half along its length so that you have a doubled, 4½-inch wide strip, and turn in that extra ½ inch and sew it down, and then firmly press.

Now comes the tricky bit! This panel must be neatly and evenly pleated, each pleat 4 inches long, with a depth equal to the width of the collar-band (3 inches?)—and please do *not* attempt this pleating 'by eye', or the result will inevitably be ragged and untidy, but use a thin wooden or cardboard gauge, so that the depth of each pleat *exactly* equals its neighbours. Press each separate pleat as you go along.

Measure out the neck-band into four equal sections, putting a tiny, faint mark at top and bottom as a guide and fasten it together, and stand it upright in a circle and, with the sewn-down edge inwards, arrange the pleated strip round it, with the opening to the back. Each 36 inches

—or 72 inches—of the pleating should fill one of the four marked divisions on the collar-band.

With small dressmaking pins, which can be bought by the boxful, fix the top of each pleat to the neck-band, each equally spaced and as near the next one as possible. Carefully turn the collar over, and repeat the pinning along the bottom edge, being very careful to keep the pleats perfectly upright and not sloping.

When you are satisfied with the effect, neatly oversew each pleat—top and bottom—to the neck-band, and withdraw the pins. To keep the symmetrical, millstone shape, sew a long, running thread through the top and bottom outer edges of each pleat. This will not be visible from a slight distance. Lastly, add three small press-studs to the inner edges of the two end pleats—top, bottom and centre—for holding the ruff closed together at the back, after it has been put on.

This is just the plain, straightforward ruff, but sometimes a thin, white piping cord or a strip of metallic braid or even a narrow trimming of starched lace (white, coloured . . . or black, for mourning) can be sewn along the outer edges of the pleats, and, of course, this is done immediately after the material has first been folded in half.

Very typical of the period was the charming 'figure 8' pleating, and this effect is obtained by firmly holding the sewn-down ends of the gathered pleats in the left hand—or maybe an assistant will oblige—and then, starting from one end, sew the first and second pleat together at a point ½ inch to 1 inch down from the top, and the second and third pleat at an equal distance up from the bottom . . . and so on, repeating the process to the end of the strip, which is then arranged round the upstanding collar-band, as described above (*see* Fig. 80).

To open the pleats at top and bottom (to form the '8'), slightly dampen the material with a soft paint-brush, and then twist a warm curling-iron into each curve. The edges of these pleats can also be decorated with piping or lace, or with a gold, silver or coloured metallic edging painted on with a thin brush, keeping the colour fairly dry, and, of course, being careful to avoid making blots! And, if I may offer a suggestion (?), it is that before embarking upon a first attempt with one of these ruffs, have a rehearsal with a stiffish piece of packing paper.

The fashion for wearing a circular 'figure 8' ruff with a high-collared dress was very popular with Elizabethan women, who sometimes left the collar open in front. It was also worn with the low-cut bodice, which was still square in shape, with the upward curve in front, as it had been in Henry's reign. Sometimes, however, the bosom was filled in up to the base of the neck with some soft material, such as pleated *crêpe de Chine* or fine muslin, and this 'insert' was called a 'partlet', and occasionally there was an inverted V left open in the centre front from just above the line of the bodice to the throat, showing the bare skin underneath.

Fig. 80. Example of a 'figure 8' ruff: (a) the neckband; (b) diagram for cutting the material (in 36-inch or 72-inch lengths by 9 inches); (c) method of folding (pleating) the joined strips; (d) the pleated strip arranged equally round the neckband; (e) the strip pleated again, for the 'figure 8' ruff; (f) method of joining each separate pleat to the next, to form the attractive 'figure 8'.

The largest ruffs of all came in around 1580, and they often had a radius measurement of anything up to 9 inches, though they were seldom deeper than 1 inch or 2 inches. They were worn almost exclusively by men—and dandies at that—and on account of the wide circumference they required a shoulder support at the back, which was called an 'underpropper', which tipped up the ruff from behind, forming an attractive surround for the head. The method for making these cart-wheels would be the same as that already described, though with even greater care being used to keep the pleats equal and level (*see* Fig. 81).

In addition to these circular ruffs, there were several upstanding types (for women) which outlined the back and sides of some of the low-cut bodices. They were made either from starched linen—edged with lace and pleated like a fan—or stretched out flat, though still retaining the semicircular shape, and each requiring a support on the shoulders from a wire frame (*see* Fig. 81).

Some of these flat ruffs were extremely large, and one is at once reminded of the double and trefoil structures so closely associated with Queen Elizabeth I. These would be made of the finest lace or organdie stretched tightly upon a wire framework having fan-like supporting struts, and made from strong milliner's wire, bound round with ribbon or tape. The surface of these ruffs was often oversewn with a design in jewels, and a wired border worked into a lace-like pattern, with more jewels round the outer edge.

The base would have to be shaped to fit snugly round the shoulders, with the ends of the wire support coming over the shoulders in front and held in position by tape loops fitting over buttons attached to the dress, with a similar button and loop at the back. In the case of an extremely large or heavy ruff of this kind, an underpropper was worn as well.

In the famous 'Ditchley' portrait (National Portrait Gallery—artist unknown), painted in 1592 to commemorate one of those many occasions when 'Queen Elizabeth slept here,' she is depicted wearing a large two-wing ruff, fitted round the back of her shoulders, with an inner pleated ruffle of the finest starched lace. It is a splendid portrait from a costume designer's point of view, and well worth studying by anyone who contemplates creating costumes for this period.

There was another flat ruff—of Spanish origin—called a 'whisk', that was, however, worn more by men. It was usually much smaller in outline, and was made of starched lace tightly stretched on a light wire frame that fitted closely all round the wearer's neck, with a centre, overlapping opening in front for putting it on. The back and sides were rounded, framing the head, but the front was straight and jutted out some 3 inches or 4 inches from the neck, and it was almost as wide as the shoulders (*see* Fig. 81).

To make an underpropper (*see* Fig. 81), one needs a long piece of

Fig. 81. Various types of ruffs: (a & b) the 'cartwheel' ruff; (c) the 'underpropper' or 'supportasse' in position; (d) construction of an 'underpropper'; (e) the 'whisk' ruff; (f) section of a 'whisk' ruff, showing the wire construction; (g) the 'fan' ruff; (h) a 'three-fold' collar ruff; (i) example of one ruff worn above another (in this case only very lightly starched); (j) The 'Dutch old master' type of ruff—another example of one ruff worn above the other, and both heavily starched; (k) the trefoil 'fan' ruff; (l) the 'wing' ruff—both k & l were very popular with Elizabeth I.

strong wire, one end of which is bent to form a shape to fit comfortably round the wearer's neck and shoulders, with the two breast-supports extending down about 6 inches on either side in front (in the case of a woman's low-neck dress, these supports might have to be a little longer).

The rest of the wire is then bent and shaped to form five rounded, pointed or oblong 'petal-like' supports, narrow at the base and widening slightly towards the top, and with a small space between each of them. The height of these uprights, of course, will depend upon the extent of the ruff to be supported.

The end of the wire will now have come round to the point from which the first end started, and in this way the whole framework can be made from the one piece. The spaces between the uprights should be bound down to the main shoulder curve, either with thin wire or by thread, and the whole structure should be bound round with ribbon or tape of the same colour as the ruff—or to match with the principal shade in the dress. Alternatively, the wire can be gilded.

ELIZABETHAN MEN

In so many costume dramas—and especially in the plays of Shakespeare—a man is called upon to appear in his shirt-sleeves. For instance, there is Orlando in *As You Like It* trying a 'fall' with Charles, the wrestler . . . though, of course, if one is the lucky possessor of as fine a physique as John Justin (who recently played this part for the Old Vic), one naturally strips to the waist. But even J.J. put on his shirt again before the love scene with Rosalind!

Other examples would be Antonio in *The Merchant of Venice* (Court scene) or Hamlet (Closet scene). Enough to indicate that an undershirt is often an essential part of the Elizabethan man's costume . . . and so we may as well begin by describing it.

Such a shirt would be white, just below the waist in length, with a plain turn-over collar attached to the pleated neck-band, and cuffs at the wrists. It is, however, scarcely worth while troubling to make one when what is known in the theatre as a 'ballet shirt' will adequately meet the case.

Over this shirt some men wore a plain, unstiffened waistcoat, not unlike what is worn today, except that the material was the same back and front and the neck was much higher cut . . . and occasionally there were sleeves.

It is said that the famous Earl of Essex wore a scarlet waistcoat when he was beheaded.

Over the waistcoat came the doublet, of which there were two styles in general use. The first of these was the Italian, a plain, straightforward garment following the lines of the body, with a low, upstanding collar that fastened in a V in front.

It should be made from a fairly heavy material . . . dyed flannel or Bolton sheeting or canvas . . . and it is all the better for being lined and slightly padded to emphasize the sweep of that manly chest! Hessian or burlap are too loose in the weave, but, with a lining added, these are excellent materials for making the more informal costumes of rustics and servants.

Doublets usually buttoned up the front, but for the stage (quick changes and things like that), a zip fastened down the back can save a lot of time, and the apparent front opening can be 'faked' by a row of page-boy gilt buttons.

The waist at the back and round the sides came just above the hips, and then fell in a rather exaggerated point in front, and there was often a 2-inch- or 3-inch-wide plain 'flap' (occasionally frilled) attached round the base and made of the same material as the upper part. A belt was always worn, and it is not difficult to imagine the uses to which it could be put in a trouser-pocketless world! Herein a man could tuck his handkerchief (sometimes called a 'muckinder'!), his gloves (stiff or soft gauntlets, with the backs of the hands embroidered or bejewelled), a letter from his mistress (which didn't mean then what it might mean today!) or his purse . . . one of those long, knitted silk bags with a horizontal slit, and a couple of small moveable rings that slid up and down and kept the coins in place at either end. How often in costume plays one has seen such a purse tossed with a lordly gesture to some underling (in payment for a dirty bit of work at the cross-roads): "Here, sirrah. There's for thy pains!"

From this same belt was slung the sword or a dagger, and occasionally a pouch that did service for a pocket. Sometimes there was an embroidered baldrick, or a gay sash worn diagonally across the body, under the left arm, and tied in a bow on the right shoulder.

With this type of doublet, a plain turn-down collar was worn, with a simple turn-back cuff. With the more elaborate styles, however, both collar and cuffs would be deeper, and finished off with a lace edging. There is a coarse kind of lace called 'torchon' that looks very handsome and rich, but it usually needs starching to get the best effect. Ruffles at the sleeves (cuffs) were only worn with neck-ruffs.

The second type of doublet was of the kind affected by the dandies of the period—those 'playboys of the northern world' of whom Sir Andrew Aguecheek in *Twelfth Night* is a fair example—and it was stiffened, stuffed and bombasted into a shape known as 'peascod-bellied', or 'shotten-bellied', which made the upper half of a man's torso look pigeon-breasted, with the lower part looking like our popular portrayal of Mr. Punch, in which his nose and his tummy follow the same curve. The surprising thing is to find so many of the heroes of that day—men like Drake, Raleigh, Hawkins and the rest—subscribing to this fashion!

The sleeves were often made of a different material and pattern from the body (horizontal bands, vertical stripes or criss-cross lozenges or squares, with a pearl sewn in the centre or at the intersecting points).

Usually the sleeves tapered from a wide, gathered shoulder to a tight wrist-band, in what we would today describe as a 'leg-of-mutton'. If they were very wide at the shoulder—which was the case with some of the more exaggerated styles—they were lined with buckram or padded out with wadding to hold the shape.

Some sleeves were designed in a series of 'puffs', and this effect was obtained by slashing the sleeve down its entire length from shoulder to cuff, then adding two or three ornamental 'arm-bands' (wide braid) above and below the elbow, and then pulling through the under-shirt. But this need not necessarily entail wearing a full shirt, as only the sleeves are concerned, and all that need be done is to attach a pair of separate sleeves to the under-vest (singlet) or to sew them inside the arm-holes of the doublet.

The doublet sleeves, however, were not always made in one with the body, but could be detachable, and in this case they were tied into the arm-holes with 'points' (metal-tipped cords or ribbons) sewn in corresponding pairs and then tied in bows, thus making it a lot easier to suggest variety with costume, and very useful where the wardrobe petty cash is slightly limited.

These points were not always visible, being hidden by a crescent-shaped 'wing' that slightly overhung the top of the arm-hole, though sometimes they were used as an attractive decoration. The wings were curved in shape, so as to fit round the top of the arm, and were cut from buckram, and then padded to give them 'weight', and covered with the same material as the doublet . . . just occasionally they might be in a contrasting colour.

Points can be made from white football bootlaces, which can then be dyed. Sir Thomas Seymour (who married Henry VIII's widow, Katherine Parr) is said to have written a farewell letter from the Tower—he was being beheaded in the morning—using one of his sleeve-points as a pen . . . dipped in his blood!

To make the ordinary (Italian) doublet, and to ensure a comfortable fit, it is a good plan to build it up on the basis of the actor's own waist-coat, using it as a lining . . . that is to say, if he's got one to spare in these days of the two-piece suit! Of course, both the waistcoat and the covering material will have to be reshaped to come up close under the throat, with the two front points remodelled into one. The doublet would be the same material, back and front . . . and don't forget the shoulder wings (*see* Fig. 82).

For the pea's-cod-bellied doublet, one needs a piece of buckram (slightly wider than the actor's chest and front of waist measurements), which will have to be shaped round the neck—on the shoulders—in front of the arm-holes, and at the under-arm seams (in fact, rather like making a breastplate). To obtain the desired projection, a slit must be made in the centre, top and bottom, and the superfluous width overlapped, and 'darts' will certainly have to be cut on the shoulders, under the arms and round the waist before one can be certain of an easy fit, and all the extra edges will have to be trimmed away before these 'darts' etc., are joined together.

The space between the lining (waistcoat) and the buckram shape must be padded out with cotton-wool or wadding—and before going any further, it is as well to give the actor a fitting, because if too much stuffing is used he may not be able to move about comfortably, or if there is not enough the buckram is liable to crackle!

When both designer and wearer are satisfied, the doublet can be covered with the outer material, using a dress-dummy . . . though, if he has the patience and the time to spare, it is much safer to continue working on the living model (*see* Fig. 82).

The doublet, with its attached (tied-in) sleeves, was either worn by itself or with the addition of an outer, waist-length jerkin of the type already described in another chapter, which was put on for comfort—or warmth. Sometimes a jerkin was made with sleeves, in which case they were *not* detachable, but instead were slit from shoulder to wrist-band, showing the doublet sleeve, so that if he wished, the wearer could slip his hand out of the cuff and let the jerkin sleeve hang down freely at the back, as was done with the bellows-sleeve. in the later fifteenth century.

A jerkin could be left open in front or just fastened at the top, or all the way down, with ornamental buttons, and, whether there were sleeves or not, wings or padded rolls (or two such rolls, one above the other) were always added at the shoulders. One style of jerkin that fell midway to the knees was thonged down the centre (leather bootlace) or it might be plain across the chest, being put on over the head and then laced up under each arm.

The shoulder roll can be made from a piece of wire bent to the curve of the top of the arm, and bound round with cotton-wool, and then covered with the jerkin material. Sometimes these rolls were decorated with bands of braid.

The parti-coloured hose of the first half of the sixteenth century and the short, pleated skirts of Henry VIII's reign had now entirely disappeared, and the covering of a man's legs was divided into upper and lower stocks—that is to say, a form of skin-tight upper breeches (called 'canions') that came down to the knee, with the lower leg covered by a stocking (nether-stock), which pulled up above the knees, and held there by being rolled round a garter. For stage purposes, of course, well pulled up tights give a smoother and less likely to wrinkle effect.

The tops of the legs were clothed in French 'round' or 'melon' hose, which varied in size from the shortest possible (sometimes no longer than a man's trunks, as worn today) to just a little way above the knee. This hose was usually padded, and at times to such an extent that it stuck out from the body as much as a foot all the way round, making walking a matter of some difficulty—and sitting down almost impossible!

One needed a trim leg to show off this style to full advantage, and, of course, with a Queen upon the throne each man tried to put his best foot forward. In the Terry Company we were always being called upon to wear tights, and the actor who played the part of Charles IX of France, in *Henry of Navarre* turned up at the dress rehearsal with such skinny shanks that something had to be done about them, and the wardrobe mistress provided him with leg-pads, which he put on like long pants under his tights . . . with the result that on the opening night he appeared with a gracefully curving pair of calves . . . of which he was inordinately proud!

In addition to the hose, there were also breeches that fastened just below the knee, with the stockings rolled up over the ends. These were known as 'Venetians', and varied from skin-tight to wide at the top and tapering down towards the knee, with the thighs smoothly padded, making the upper leg look a little like a plump, freshly-plucked capon!

In Elizabeth's time, if a man wasn't too confident, he kept up his stockings with ribbons tied round his leg, with big bows on the outer side of each knee—or he used the method known as 'cross-gartering', in which the ribbon was bound round from the front, below the knee, and crossed over at the back, and then brought forward above the knee, where it was tied in a bow, either in front or at the sides.

'Cross-gartering' at once calls to mind Malvolio, the puritanical steward in *Twelfth Night*, but most of the actors I've seen playing this part seem to imagine that the Elizabethan cross-gartering began somewhere around the ankles, and then continued up the leg to the knee (as far as I can remember, when Tree played this character, he bettered the instruction and carried the gartering still further up his leg, until it disappeared under his melon hose at the top—which, of course, was completely wrong). After all, the letter only said, 'Remember who commended thy yellow stockings'—nothing about tights—but then Tree did lots of naughty things with the play, though I wasn't aware of them at the time, and when I first saw him play Malvolio, he certainly made me laugh until I was nearly sick!

The only time I've seen cross-gartering properly tied was when Henry Ainley played Malvolio at the Savoy Theatre. But then Granville Barker was too painstaking a producer to make a mistake over a little thing like that. The amusing part, however, is that, having seen the play first at His Majesty's, I thought Tree must be right and Granville Barker wrong. But one lives and learns.

The melon hose was generally 'strapped' on the outside, which means that the top material was cut in a series of 2-inch or 3-inch vertical bands, trimmed with braid, and with the under-lining (over the padding) showing through between them. A far simpler way to suggest the same effect would be to add the strips (straps) all the way round, instead of cutting the material, and to fix them at the waist and to the inside edge of the leg-opening, with elastic to help in keeping the hose well pulled up. The hose, however, was not always padded, and then the lining was made full and loose, so that it puffed out between the straps, or 'panes', as they were sometimes called.

A longer type of hose, that came from Italy, was made of velvet, very loose and unpadded, with a tight band above each knee, over which the material was 'bloused', so that it hung down in folds to just below the knee, and looked rather like a short skirt (*see* Fig. 82).

Fig. 82. (a & c) Simple types of 'shoulder wings'; (b) the 'double roll' type of 'shoulder wing'; (d) the 'pea's-cod bellied' type of tunic (Elizabethan); (e) Example of 'upper stock' (canions) and 'lower stock' (nether stock); (f) the loose Italian style of 'melon' or 'trunk-hose'; (g) an exaggerated type of 'melon' or 'round' hose (French); (h) the correct method for 'cross-gartering', and (i) the 'cross-gartering', seen from the back.

There were various styles with capes and cloaks. Some were short—hip-length—and worn diagonally across the shoulders, and some of them had a high-collar and arm-holes or hanging sleeves. The long cloaks were draped, and not all of them had collars, which got in the way of the wider ruffs, but a few were fitted with hoods or cowls.

The flat black beret type of hat, which had been so popular with Edward VI, became known under Elizabeth as the 'statute' cap, and anyone over six years old was forced to wear 'one cap, knit and dressed in England' unless he happened to possess over 20 marks a year in lands . . . or had seen service in the church—which was one way to encourage trade for English cappers!

One of the most pleasing of the new hats had an upstanding crown made of gathered velvet, pleated into a stiff, narrow brim, with a band of metallic braid, or a gold cord, or a border of little gilt rosettes running round the base, and a feather plume at the side, held by a jewelled brooch. It was worn at a rakish angle, high on one side and down over the other eye. There were also the stiff felt Spanish hats, with a narrow brim and a low 'stove-pipe' crown . . . or, alternatively, with a wide, sweeping brim and a high crown.

Men's hats were as much a part of their indoor as outdoor dress, and they were very seldom doffed . . . except in the presence of the Queen.

Up to the end of the sixteenth century, shoes were still heelless, but the soles (cork) were often considerably thickened under the heel, thinning down towards the toe, which virtually acted as a heel. Such shoes were called 'moyles', and were made of leather, velvet and light-coloured satin, and very occasionally one might still find slashings over the toe-piece. Most of these shoes fitted well over the instep, similar to the slipper-shoes we wear today, and, indeed, these could be used (though not the patent-leather kind), and the best 'disguise' for making them look 'in period' would be to fasten a large rosette on top of each shoe.

To make this decoration, take a long strip of pink or white 2-inch- or 3-inch-wide ribbon (the kind with the 'postage-stamp' perforated edging looks prettiest . . . and if you can't buy any easily, it can be cut by hand) and gather the ribbon along one side, and pull it up tightly, and sew it securely. Then open out the ribbon as widely as possible, and fix a large safety-pin at the back so that it can be attached to the shoe. It is possible that more than one pin may be necessary to prevent the rosette from wobbling!

High brown or black soft leather boots, with tops that could be turned up or down at the knee, were also worn, and were held up by means of two straps fastened inside the front of each boot, with the other ends attached to a belt under the doublet.

For party occasions, these boots were sometimes in grey or even white, with decorated tops. For the stage, they can be made from felt, with a pattern painted round the top or a design picked out (with one of those leather-punching thingummies) and the inside edges touched up with gold paint.

In Elizabeth's reign, rings, brooches, chains, etc., were worn by both men and women in great and indiscriminate profusion . . . even a man wore ear-rings, and it was no unusual sight to see a pear-shaped pearl drop—though, admittedly, only hanging from one of his ears! A still more curious practice maintained amongst sailors (and some soldiers), which was for a thin black cord to be threaded through the ear-lobe and then tied in a knot in front! To expect him to follow this vagary of fashion might be asking a bit much of any actor, but the effect can be 'faked' by putting a loop of cord right round the ear, masking it as much as possible with the hair.

Most of the younger men wore their hair cut short—very much as we do today, though, perhaps, just a little fuller behind—and brushed straight back, without a parting. Sometimes, however, the hair stood high over the forehead, and then curved away in a wave from the brow.

It was not until the reign of James I that the typically seventeenth-century curls began to be seen. Nothing very exciting, either, at first—indeed, no more than a ringlet or two or a solitary 'love-lock' falling over one shoulder!

Moustaches and neatly clipped beards—pointed or square—were almost universally worn, even by quite young men . . . I say 'almost', because one will always come across those who prefer to be clean-shaven, whatever the prevailing fashion.

ELIZABETHAN WOMEN

The bodice and skirt were now made as two separate garments—nor were they always designed in the same material—and both bodice and skirt were often split open down the front to show an under-gown of a still different pattern.

Sometimes a skirt and a sleeveless bodice were both closed all the way down the front, with the under-garment visible only at the sleeves . . . or the front of the bodice only might be open, having no sleeves, half sleeves or long sleeves. Or it might be the skirt . . . and by these means it would be possible for a designer to offer three different act changes without having to provide three different costumes.

The bodice, whether open or closed was tightly stretched across the breast, with the typical long waist of the period, frequently ending in a point in front . . . which by the reign of James I became so exaggerated that in some cases it reached nearly to the knees!

To our modern girls—accustomed to wearing no more 'support' than a 'bra' and a two-way stretch—the means employed to produce the fashionable tight body would seem like the worst tortures of the Spanish Inquisition, with corsets made from strips of hard wood—and, in some cases, entirely of metal—which cannot have afforded much incentive for a boy's arm to steal around a girl's waist!

The pointed-bodice effect was sometimes emphasized by a triangular or shield-shaped 'piece' (heavily ornamented with embroidery and jewels) that differed in pattern and design from the rest of the dress. The straight top of this 'stomacher', as it was called, was attached level with the edge of the low-cut neck-line, with the point coming down and resting on the skirt. A 'stomacher' is made from a piece of stiffened buckram—which may be painted or otherwise decorated—and added to the costume by hooks and eyes.

The stiff quality so necessary with Elizabethan costumes can largely be suggested by heavy canvas linings, and the bodice should in addition be boned in front, at the sides (under arms) and at the back. Owing to the weight of the dress, strong hooks are invariably necessary, sewn round the inside edge of the bodice—two in front, two at the back, and one under each arm, with corresponding eyes on the waistband of the skirt. Without these, there is always the danger of body and skirt parting company!

Sleeves were similar in shape to the men's—that is leg-of-mutton—with the typical shoulder wings or rolls masking the 'points'. Some sleeves were arranged in a series of puffs by ribbons being tied closely together down the length of the arms from shoulder to cuff. Alternatively, there might be only one fairly large puff near the shoulder, with the rest of the sleeve tight to the wrist, finished off with a plain turned-back cuff, or maybe trimmed with lace or by a wrist ruffle.

A rather charming effect could be obtained from a costume made from black velvet, closed all the way down the front, and without showing either stomacher or under-skirt, and with a surface design in gold thread. The outer-sleeve might be split from shoulder to wrist—lined in white silk—and continuing in a long, pendent point to the floor. If the high neck was topped by a small, circular ruff, with ruffles at the wrists of the white-and-gold patterned under-sleeve, the overall effect would be worthy of the Queen herself, who, after the Massacre of St. Bartholomew's Eve in 1572 to show her grave displeasure at the base betrayal of the Huguenots, dressed herself and her whole Court in unrelieved black to receive the French Ambassador, who—feeling himself in disgrace, and hoping to make a good impression—had dressed himself from head to toe in white satin!

For the first time in English history, women now wore hoops as a means of holding out their dresses. In the early days, the skirt was still bell-shaped, but, though this effect had previously been obtained by pleating the heavily lined material and attaching it into a waistband, by the new method it was spread smoothly over a shaped petticoat, round which were sewn three or four horizontal slots at regular intervals to the inner lining, into which the graduated wire hoops were fitted, with the widest at the hem and the narrowest round the arching hips.

Such a hooped skirt was known as a farthingale (though there were other forms of spelling, one of which was 'verdingale') and, despite its Spanish origin, it quickly became popular in England as well as in other countries.

For the stage, the most practical way in which to present this smooth, bell-shaped silhouette is for the skirt to be 'gored', with a circumference round the hem of at least 9 feet—and possibly more—and to use a separate 'hoop-frame', as fully described in a later chapter, dealing with the Victorian crinoline of the 1860s.

A heavy canvas under-skirt, similar in size and cut, should be worn between the frame and the outer skirt, with a narrower petticoat, made from any convenient material, between the frame and the wearer's legs.

Later in the period, a rival farthingale was introduced from France, in which the maximum width was across the hips, with a front measurement of often as much as 36 inches, with 1 foot 6 inches to 1 foot 8 inches from back to front.

There are two ways in which this can be achieved. First, with an encircling padded bolster, attached to hang from the waist, over which the fully pleated skirt is draped. But do not go away with the idea that all you need to do is to run upstairs, and fetch the bolster from the spare-room bed . . . it wouldn't be anything like solid enough, and one will have to be made specially. This can be done by shaping (bending) a length of wire to go round the hips (the finished shape will be narrow from back to front and wider at each side), leaving it open (unjoined) at the back, and turning over each of the sharp ends to make a little loop, the reason for which will become clear in a minute.

The wire is then padded round with layers of cotton-wool wadding until it fits snugly round the hips. The roll is then covered with canvas, and hung from the waist by means of several strong tapes attached to a belt, which has a couple of hooks and eyes for fastening it round the body. A tape is tied into each of those end-of-wire loops for tying the open ends of the bolster together after it has been put on—and for this reason the wire must be sufficiently pliable.

The length of the skirt should equal the distance from the waist to the hem over the bolster—and this will vary, of course, according to the height of the wearer . . . but, to be correct, the hem of the dress should just touch the floor.

The skirt is made from straight ('ungored') lengths, with the whole of the fullness pleated into a waist-band. If the material is soft-textured, the least width round the hem would be 8 yards. Two under-petticoats should be worn—a narrow, shortish one under the bolster, and the other—about 2 inches shorter than the skirt—coming between the bolster and the dress, and to save on the material it can be made with a plain 'yoke', extending from the waist to just beyond the bolster, with the pleated petticoat attached round the edge.

The second type of farthingale was much flatter at the top—almost like a shelf—and to make this one needs a piece of strong, pliable steel wire of the correct length, and the way to estimate this is to cut out a brown-paper templet (shape), which would seldom be wider than 36 inches or more than 20 inches deep, circular at the sides and almost straight in front and at the back. By measuring round the circumference of this figure, one can get at the length of wire required—allowing an extra inch, at least, for overlapping the ends of the wire when joining, and if you can get it welded it is safer than soldering.

To make the wire conform to the right shape can be a tricky business, and the most reasonable way seems to be to place the paper templet on a wooden surface and outline it with a double row of nails knocked in closely opposite each other, and about a couple of inches or so apart, and then to thread the wire between the nails and shape the outline in this manner. The ends can then be joined together.

Cut a piece of strong canvas about ¾ inch wider than the paper templet all the way round, and then with strong thread sew this firmly round the wire frame.

In the exact centre of this canvas from all points, draw out a figure in charcoal that corresponds with the exact waist measurements of the wearer, and then sew a 2-inch- or 3-inch-wide length of strong webbing round this shape, so that it stands upright, and allow sufficient overlap for closing it round the waist with hooks and eyes. Cut out the tightly stretched canvas from *inside* the charcoal outline, slitting it in a star, and lifting the points and sewing them—at top and bottom—to the inside surface of the upright belt webbing, and neatly trimming off any odd ends. Finally, cut a line from the belt opening (which is at the back) so that it nearly—but not quite—meets the outer frame, and bind the two edges. This is done to make it easier for putting on the framework.

Two petticoats are needed, as outlined above, the top one with a length from the outer rim of the frame to about 2 inches above the wearer's instep and some 21 feet wide, which is gathered and pleated and then sewn round the edge of the farthingale frame. The skirt itself should be some 2 or 3 feet wider, and in length just touching the floor —not longer, for fear of tripping—and this, too, can be pleated to the edge of the frame. The flat top of the farthingale is then covered over by what was known as a 'waist ruff', made from the same material as the dress, and fan-pleated into the waist belt, and extending about 1½ inches to 2 inches beyond the outer edge, and neatly tacked into equal-sized pleats all the way round. There must, of course, be an opening at the back of this 'waist ruff', with an overlapping flap that can be pinned or press-studded across when the dress is put on. This type of 'cartwheel farthingale' is very becoming to wear . . . and can be a lot of fun! (*see* Fig. 83).

Fashionable women's shoes were made of rich brocade or velvet ornamented with pearls, and all sorts of means were used to add on

Fig. 83. Two types of Elizabethan farthingale: (a) 'the Spanish' (1560-1570); (b) 'the French' cartwheel (1600); (c) support for the cartwheel skirt; (d) skeleton diagram for 'hooped petticoat' (used with Fig. a); (e) diagram of the 'bolster' type of support (in section); (f) another view of the 'bolster'—it is tied together at the back.

extra inches in height, such as cork pedestals (from 2 inches to 7 inches or 8 inches high!) fixed under both heel and toe, which served the further purpose of protecting the wearer from the dirt and mud of the streets. One presumes that Elizabeth was not wearing shoes of this kind on the occasion when Raleigh so gallantly threw down his cloak for her to walk over. This incident is supposed to have occurred on Deptford Steps, and you can see the spot as you go down to Greenwich by river 'bus. It was at Deptford, too, that the Queen knighted Drake aboard *The Golden Hind*, and probably both these events took place on the same day.

These built-up shoes were called 'chopines', and were of Italian origin. Hamlet refers to them in the scene where he greets the arrival of the strolling players, as he laughingly addresses one of the boys, whom he has seen before, playing a woman's part. 'Your ladyship,' he cries, 'is nearer to Heaven than when I saw you last by the altitude of a chopine.' I have seen *Hamlet* a great many times, but I must confess it was not until I began research for this book that I discovered what that word meant!

Real heels were first introduced during the reign of James I. Not that they could by any stretch of the imagination be called 'high' . . . but women immediately adopted them with extraordinary eagerness.

The old prejudices against women showing their hair had now disappeared, and in compliment to Elizabeth—who is rarely depicted wearing a hat—many women went bareheaded—especially indoors. When they did wear head-coverings (out of doors), they copied the men's tall stove-pipe crowned felt hats with broad brims. Some of the older women wore them over tight, white under-coifs, which made them look just like the Welsh girls at a National Eisteddfod!

There were also small, narrow-brimmed velvet caps, with a bunched-up crown surrounded by a jewelled band holding a feathered plume. These caps were worn perched on top of the head or at a jaunty angle to one side. Of the one-time, almost universally worn crescents, only a very small version was still sometimes to be seen, and set very much further back on the head than in Queen Mary's time.

The most popular headdress, however, was the heart-shaped, winged cap, which dipped to a point in the centre of the forehead and then curved away in two semicircles over the temples, showing the smoothly brushed hair underneath. Such a cap could be made from various materials, from bejewelled velvet to lace-edged white batiste (a kind of cambric, named after the original maker, Baptiste of Cambray).

To design one of these caps is quite simple, and all one needs is a circular wire frame that fits round the head about 2 inches or so back from the front hair-line and round the nape of the neck at the back, with the centre over the forehead bent to form the 'peak' point. A circular piece is then cut from whatever material is being used, large enough to fit comfortably over the head like a cap, and pleated neatly round the rim of the wire frame. Next two crescent-shaped 'wings' are cut out, each mounted on a little wire support at the back (or inside if these pieces are cut double), and then attached to the foundation cap, with two of the crescent points meeting at the peak in front and the other two fixed round at the side of the head. An edging of lace or pearls, etc., is added, with a waist-length panel of some soft, dark material hanging down at the back (*see* Fig. 84).

The 'wings' can be made wide-spreading or close to the head, and in some models there are even two wings on each side, one above the other, and the finished cap may be worn either well forward on the forehead or further back on the head, and sometimes it was even worn over a tight, white under-cap.

Legend connects this type of headdress with the unhappy Mary Queen of Scots, so that it has become popularly known as the 'Marie Stuart' bonnet . . . but, in point of fact, it was a style that was by no means peculiar to her.

During the first few years of the period, women still parted their hair in the middle, but soon the style altered, and the hair was brushed straight back, arching over the temples. A much-admired feature was a little tuft of hair growing in the centre of the forehead, and called a 'widow's peak' . . . though it was not necessarily confined to those ladies who had lost their husbands! This same fashion had rather a vogue in England a few years ago, though, if I remember rightly (?), we called it a 'cow's-lick'! On the stage, of course, it is easy enough to paint in such a tuft of hair with a grease-paint liner.

As time went on, women dressed their hair in a high, front roll, brushed over a pad support, and the use of false hair—or even entire

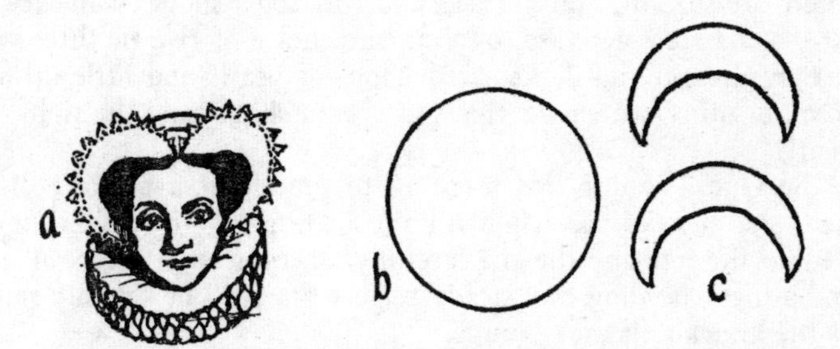

Fig. 84. (a) The 'heart-shaped' cap, worn with 'figure 8' ruff; (b & c) diagram of the component parts—a lace, or other type of edging (for instance white cord) may be added as desired.

transformations—became fashionable (red being the popular colour . . . in courtesy to Elizabeth), and certainly there is little doubt that 'our Liz's' hair was a wig!

For a moment let us become invisible and transport ourselves back in time, to visit the Queen's dressing-room and watch the great Elizabeth as she sits erect before her mirror.

On the table before her lie several cotton-wool pads, with which she has been applying chalk and rouge to her face in an endeavour to fill in the wrinkles . . . for, try as she will, even a Queen cannot hold time at bay for ever.

Elizabeth was born in September, 1533, and as the years rolled on it became her dearest wish to reach the age of seventy . . . which no previous English monarch had been able to do . . . but she died at Richmond Palace in March, 1603, six months too soon!

The last time I played at the Richmond Theatre the Palace stood empty and 'for sale' on the other side of the Green. I wish I had been rich enough to buy it!

The room in which we find ourselves is heavy with the scent of musk—her favourite perfume—for Elizabeth cannot abide bad smells! At her Coronation she had bitterly complained that the sacred anointing oil was rancid . . . words that 365 years later Bernard Shaw 'pinched' and gave to the 'Dauphin' in the Cathedral scene of his play, *Saint Joan*!

It is a bizarre reflection that gazes back at her, with its small, heavy-lidded, black eyes shining from the painted, mask-like face, with its hooked nose and long, expressionless mouth . . . and the great pearl drops in her ears contrasting strangely with her almost bald head!

Let us listen as one of her ladies repeats a piece of court gossip, which puts the Queen in a good temper, so that the thin lips parts in a smile, showing us her completely black teeth—a result (so it was said) from over-indulgence in sugar!

Over her embroidered shift Elizabeth is wearing a rich dressing-gown, and there are stockings on her legs and cork-soled shoes on her feet. A favoured maid steps forward, offering the choice of two or three wigs, each ready dressed and decked with loops of pearls and little artificial red roses, or other ornaments that glitter and shine amid the tight, red-gold curls.

As the Queen is due this morning to preside at a meeting of her Council, she chooses the wig with the little gold crown precariously perched on the top, and the girl carefully places it upon her head . . . a tricky business, needing cool steady fingers that will be soundly rapped across the knuckles if they bungle.

Elizabeth then rises and lets the wrap fall from her shoulders, and her corset is fitted to her body and tightly laced down the back, after which the enormous farthingale frame is tied round her waist. Now again there is a choice: Which under-dress will she wear? After a moment's thought, she selects a low-cut, sleeveless bodice, with an embroidered front (stomacher) and a similarly decorated petticoat. When these have been comfortably adjusted, the outer bodice and heavy over-dress—both open down the front, to display the rich under-garment—are put on, with the low-cut bodice leaving a wide expanse of bosom uncovered, as was the custom in England for an unmarried woman.

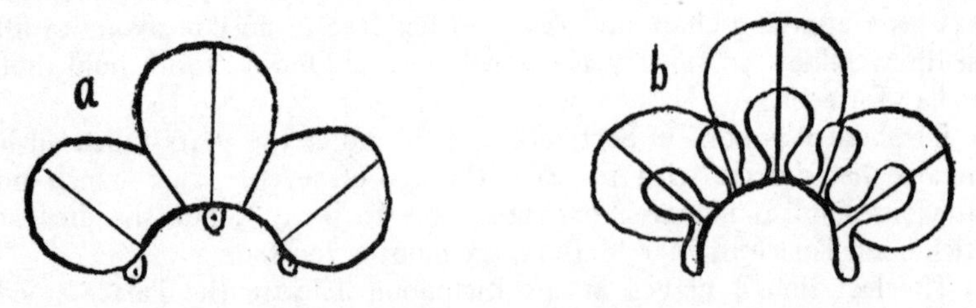

Fig. 85. (a) Diagram of the trefoil Elizabethan ruff, and (b) the ruff supported by the 'underpropper' or 'supportasse'.

There are great, long, stuffed sleeves hanging like wings from the back of her shoulders down to the floor, with the real sleeves (matching the under-gown) tied into the vacant arm-holes with 'points'. Her girdle, with its pendant pomander (filled with musk) and fan and oval looking-glass attached, is now knotted round her waist, and ropes of enormous pearls wound round her ageing throat. Then comes the underpropper —or *supportasse*—and, last of all, the huge fan-shaped ruff (*see* Fig. 85).

What would little Mr. Higgins, the tailor of St. James's, who created this type of ruff (and called it a 'piccadillie') have said had he known that in the future this same name would describe the most famous district in the world? 'Odds boddikins?' . . . 'Gadzooks?' . . . One wonders.

CHAPTER 10

Elizabethan Clowns

So many of Shakespeare's plays call for a clown, a fool, or a jester, but often these so-called buffoons are little more than plain country bumpkins, introduced for comic relief . . . that is to say, their foolery was no part of their profession (as it was with Feste, in *Twelfth Night*, Touchstone in *As You Like It* or the fool in *King Lear*), so that they were probably dressed more or less like the other characters in the play, except that their clothes might be rougher and not so well cut.

Launcelot Gobbo, in *The Merchant of Venice*, for instance—one of Shakespeare's most likeable clowns—leaves Shylock's service to join Bassanio, who, as he says, 'gives rare new liveries'. Therefore, from being poorly dressed in homespun doublet, short trunks and wrinkled stockings (although set in Italy, for some reason or other the *Merchant of Venice* is usually costumed in undisguised 'Elizabethan'), he must blossom out later in the play, wearing his new livery 'more guarded than his fellows' (which, by the way, does *not* mean 'more sober', as some people mistakenly imagine, but more elaborate . . . 'guarded' in Shakespearean parlance meaning 'braided').

A page or personal servant often wore his master's coat of arms as a badge on his upper right sleeve, and Launcelot might very well do that once he gets to Belmont.

Touchstone and Feste are typical jesters, and so Touchstone would wear a short-skirted, fourteenth-century, parti-coloured tunic, buttoned down the front, with a scalloped hem and elbow-length sleeves widening into long pointed pendants over tight under-sleeves. And each scalloped point would be tipped with a little brass bell.

His tights would also be parti-coloured, held up under each knee with a garter of little tinkling bells. He would wear heelless, long, pointed-toed, soft leather or cloth ankle shoes, with a long tongue hanging over in front and a tab at the back. A narrow, coloured leather belt went round the waist, with a pouch hanging from it, always at the ready to receive largesse . . . and as most of Shakespeare's clowns could sing, they didn't 'do' so badly in that direction!

Finally, the cap-and-bells hood that proclaims his trade. This was really our old friend, the chaperon, with the addition of pointed asses' ears and a peak on the forehead, or a wobbly cock's comb on the top of his head, or possibly two stuffed 'horns' standing out one at each side of his head, with bells added wherever possible.

Touchstone would carry a 'fool's head' (folly) or 'bauble', and this can be made from papiermâché or plastic wood modelled on to a wooden ball foundation, mounted on a short stick tied with coloured ribbons.

The Fool in *King Lear* would be dressed in a similar costume, but made from a rougher material and probably not parti-coloured, the reason for this being that he has some very pathetic sequences with the old King later in the tale, and one must play for sympathy in these scenes. He can, however, be provided with a bladder (balloon) on a stick, with one or two dried peas inside to make it rattle.

Feste can be much less conventionally dressed, and, as played by Hayden-Coffin in the Granville Barker production of *Twelth Night*, he wore a black-and-white-striped jerkin, with long, tight sleeves and similarly striped tights under short black breeches, with bunches of coloured ribbons at each knee. He had a simple, white, turn-over collar at his neck and turn-back cuffs at the wrists, and wore a stiff, felt, high-crowned, narrow-brimmed hat with a bunch of black cock's tail feathers falling at the back; soft heelless black shoes completed the costume.

Norman Wilkinson designed the costumes (and scenery), but, naturally, there is no obligation to follow either pattern or colour scheme, and I have only described them as something that I once saw.

PART IV

CHAPTER 11

The First Half of the Eighteenth Century (1700-50)

The early years of the eighteenth century brought no very substantial changes in the dress of either men or women, who during the greater part of Queen Anne's reign continued to cling to the rather heavy, stuffy fashions introduced by that indivisible royal partnership, William and Mary (1688-1702), with everyone striving to look prim, proper and prosperous, and as much as possible like a Dutch Old Master come to life!

MEN

Men now wore a knee-length coat, rather narrow in the body for the first few years, but after 1720 with the skirt-tails gradually flaring out.

These coats were designed high at the neck, but without upstanding collars, and a characteristic feature was the double row of parallel 'braided bars' down the front edges, one side with buttons and the other with button-holes . . . but, as the coat was very seldom fastened—except by one top button, and sometimes by another at the waist—for the stage, these button-holes need only be suggested and not actually cut.

The sleeves were fitted with wide, doubled-back cuffs, which were sometimes left open at the back, and there were three or four vertical braided bars and buttons, by which the cuffs were supposed to be fastened back against the arm. The sleeves themselves were not long enough to cover the wrists, and the deep lace ruffles of the under-shirt sleeves were always visible, hanging down below the coat-cuffs and covering the hands. These ruffles, by the way, need not necessarily be part of a shirt, but can be sewn inside the coat-cuff . . . unless, of course, the coat has to be removed, as in a duel scene, in which case the shirt should be very fully cut, especially in the sleeves.

These eighteenth-century coats can be made from either velvet, velveteen, fine ribbed corduroy or plain woollen material, that can be dyed in deep rich colours . . . a claret red was especially popular . . . or one can use patterned brocade (furnishing department) with a large, repeated design, though, of course, this can always be stencilled on afterwards in gold, silver or black on the coloured ground (*see* Fig. 86).

The pockets of these coats were usually placed waist-high, one on each side and were provided with wide 'flaps', decorated with a pattern motif that was repeated on the cuffs and sometimes down the front edges of the coat. A handkerchief with a deep lace border hung carelessly from the right-hand pocket, with probably a snuffbox reposing in the other. If an ordinary modern white handkerchief has a wide lace border added and is then steeped overnight in strong cold tea (no milk) it will give it that 'old ivory' appearance, and this is a tip worth remembering in connection with jabots and neck and wrist frills and ruffles. On the other hand, the lace edging of the handkerchiefs was sometimes coloured, and red or blue borders would be quite in order.

Snuffboxes were generally very ornamental affairs, and were made in a variety of different materials, such as gold, silver and enamels, and, in addition, they were often set with brilliants. Tortoise-shell, inlaid with mother-o'-pearl, was very much sought after, while other boxes were made with looking-glass sides, or with the mirror let into the inside of the lid. Some snuffboxes were as large as 3 inches square, and as likely as not filled with Vigo snuff.

The long waistcoats of the previous century, worn under the coats, now became a little shorter, though never less than by a few inches above the hem of the coat, and were fastened down the front with a long row of small, round metal (gilt) buttons, of which the bottom half-dozen or so were left undone. For stage purposes, it is often quicker to design these garments with a practical opening down the back, tied across with tapes—two at the top and one at the waist should be sufficient—so that the front 'opening' is really a false one (*see* Fig. 86).

These waistcoats were usually made of a different material and colour from the coats, and were often designed in a flowered brocade (if the coat was in one plain colour). There were also two pockets, set a little lower than those in the outer coat, but, as they were hardly ever used, it is enough in a stage costume just to sew a pocket flap (only) on either side, and a good period touch would be to add a gold metallic braid fringe—a couple or so inches long—to the bottom edge of the waistcoat (*see* Fig. 86).

Most men carried a dress sword (rather like a rapier, and much lighter in weight than a military sword) which hung from a leather sword-belt, worn under both coat and waistcoat, so that in making these garments 'slits' must be included, through which the top of the scabbard protrudes.

Swords, and the sword-belts that go with them, are items that I am afraid must be hired from a costumier.

When returning a drawn sword to its sheath, the correct procedure is to place the first finger and thumb of the left hand on the top (mouth) of the scabbard, and with them to guide the sword point 'home'. It absolutely ruins the smartness of the effect if a man looks down to see what he is doing, and the next time you watch an actor draw his sword in a play, watch him carefully when he returns it to its sheath, and you will know at once if he is experienced in costume work. You would never, for instance, catch John Gielgud or Laurence Olivier looking down!

Amber and ebony canes, hung from the wrist by a long tasselled cord, were often carried in addition to the sword, and throughout the period men carried muffs! In a play, however, it is generally the fop or the exquisite who has one on his arm, as it helps to establish his character, which might be less clear to the audience if all the men carried them. Gloves with an embroidered design on the back of the hand were always worn when out of doors, but less on account of smartness than as a protection against dirt!

Around a man's neck, he often wore a jabot—sometimes no more than a folded piece of cambric with a lace border, tied so that one end hung over the other in front—rather as the modern young man arranges his silk scarf. For special occasions, this cravat might be held in place by a jewelled brooch, though this was not a universal custom . . . but it looks nice (*see* Fig. 86).

Breeches were usually made from black velvet, though coloured (or black) satin was also fashionable with the courtier or the dandy. Cut fairly wide at the top, they narrowed neatly to just above the knee, and were fastened below it with a row of two or three small gilt buttons or a buckle.

Blue or red woollen stockings were pulled up *over* the breeches and *above* the knee, where they were gartered, with any surplus stocking turned down again, but still covering the knee. Sometimes, on court occasions, the stockings were of heavy, light-coloured silk, and then they might be worn pulled up *under* the breeches. Double garters—not unlike the Elizabethan cross-gartering—were occasionally seen *below* the knee.

During the Restoration (1660-83) breeches became more like loose plus-fours, with scalloped, turned-up ends, held at the outside of the knees with ribboned bows. At one time they became so wide that they were called 'petticoat breeches'!

For the first part of the period shoes were black, with long, square-shaped toe pieces, high, upstanding 'tongues', buckles and fairly high red heels. Later the toes became more rounded, though they were still long. The tongues became shorter and the buckles larger. In Restoration times a large floppy bow or a rosette was worn in place of the buckle (which was usually square), while the heels became more normal in height.

Most of the hats were three-cornered (tricorne), with one of the points coming to the front, and they were just as often worn inside the house as when out in the street. When removing his hat and bowing to a lady, a man usually held it against his chest—over his heart!—with the fingers of his right hand lightly placed upon the crown (*see* Fig. 86).

A tricorne can be made from a woman's wide-brimmed, black felt hat with the brim turned up on three sides, so as to slightly overlap the crown. To get the right effect, dampen the brim, and then wind it round three 'rollers'. When dry, the centres of each of these turn-over pieces can be lightly stitched to the crown to hold them in position. A narrow border of gold gimp can be added all the way round the top edges, or a pattern can be stencilled on with gold paint. Sometimes a fringe of white ostrich feathers (which can be bought by the yard at many milliners) is sewn round the inside edges of the turned-back flaps.

From 1715 onwards wigs became flatter and less ornate than they had been in the previous period, and the full peruke of the House of Orange, with its masses of curls that fell upon the shoulders, was now only rarely worn . . . and then only by such learned folk as doctors or professors . . . the 'full-bottomed' wig worn by our present-day court judges remain as a witness to those times.

The front hair of these wigs was now drawn towards the back of the head, with the sides arranged in horizontal rows of little sausage curls, or with the hair brushed forward and then frizzed, either of which styles partly or completely covered the ears, forming a frame for the universally clean-shaven face.

These curls were formed by tightly winding the hair round warm clay tubes, which were then pulled out sideways, leaving a firm little roll, which could be patted into place and, if necessary, held by a pin.

Many of the wigs were plentifully powdered in white or grey, though, of course, some of them were worn in natural colours, while others were made in white or grey, to look as if they had been powdered.

When a wig was being powdered on the head, m'lud or m'lady sat in front of the mirror, daintily shielding the face with a glass or stiff paper 'cone'—not unlike a dunce's cap in shape—while his man, or her maid, tossed the powder over the hair.

The back-hair curls were sometimes allowed to hang free, with a large black silk bow tied at the nape of the neck . . . a style known as the 'tie' wig . . . or the whole of the loose hair at the back was confined in a square-shaped black silk bag, with the top drawn up tightly and then fastened with the bow. A more military arrangement was to plait the back hair and tie a large black bow at the top and a smaller one on the end (sometimes there were two such plaits). This style was called the 'Ramilles' wig, and was originated by the soldiers who fought in that battle (1706) and had twisted their hair in this manner. Lastly, there was the 'pigtail', in which the hair was tightly bound round with a black ribbon so that the queue stood out stiffly at the back, with only

Fig. 86. (a) Man's costume around 1760-65; (b) Back and front of the long waistcoat; (c) design for the pattern for a brocaded coat; (d) design for a waistcoat-pattern; (e) the fold-over jabot; (f) diagram for the tricorne (or chapeau bras . . . because it was carried under the arm, when not on the head); (g) the kevenhuller hat (1740) which had a high peak in front—this hat, which was a more decorative form of the tricorne, usually had a band of gold braid along the top edge; (h) a hat known as 'the incroyable' (1795) which was of French origin; (i) another hat favoured by the dandy of the period.

the ends of the hair showing, and looking like an inverted shaving-brush.

Such were the means men employed for 'keeping the hair out of the way', and the more obvious remedy of allowing their own hair to grow, and then to cut it and wear it short, doesn't seem to have occurred to them!

Under the wig the head was usually bald, so that when the wig had been sent away to be curled, or when, at the end of a long day our fine gentleman—resplendent in his elegantly brocaded dressing-gown—merely laid it aside to sit alone with his wife, he wore a turban! This may have made him feel no end of a Turk . . . though I very much doubt whether his missus allowed him to behave like one! (*see* Fig. 87).

Fig. 87. (a) Unpowdered wig, 1715-1725; (b) the turban—worn as négligé, to cover the shaven head, when the wig was laid aside; (c) wig of the 1780's; (d) example of the 'pigeon's wing' wig, with bow and 'wig-bag' (1720-40); (e) wig of the George III period (1786); (f) wig, with pigtail, and side curl (1750).

WOMEN

At the beginning of the eighteenth century the Dutch influence exercised on women's fashions during the reign of William and Mary remained strong and unchanged. The death of Queen Anne, however, started the sartorial supremacy of women over their men-folk . . . an ascendancy which—after Beau Brummel in 1800 took a sobering interest in men's clothes—was to become so complete.

From 1714—and for the next 100 years—it became a 'woman's world', with the wigs, the delicately tinted complexions, the paint and the powder and the patches, the long, slim waists and the wide, panniered skirts, the silk stockings and satin shoes and red spindle heels, the flowers and the ribbons and the laces. And yet, despite the frivolity and affectation, there was still a certain bucolic simplicity (that has always been a saving grace in the English character) that supplied a much-needed sense of proportion!

The first important change in women's costume came with the reappearance of the bell-hoop in 1710, which ever since Elizabeth's reign had had a habit of recurring at irregular intervals . . . and, judging from the reflection in fashion's mirror, it looks as if we might be in for a minor come-back today.

In the eighteenth century the effect was produced by wearing a petticoat stiffened from waist to hem with several horizontal hoops of whalebone, which in those days must have been quite an expensive item, and—if you remember—in Gay's *The Beggar's Opera* a lively trade was carried on in stealing and selling hoops by some of the less respectable characters.

Some women, however, did not wear the hoop at all, but attempted to present the same effect with numerous petticoats. In the chapter on Victoriana, I have outlined a simple frame, which, although designed for use by the ladies of some 130 years later, will give exactly the same result as required here, and which is—for the stage—extremely light and comfortable to wear.

In the late 1730s the bell skirt went out of fashion in favour of the pannier, which became generally worn for the next fifty years or so. The aim of the pannier was to present a slim, profile silhouette and an exaggerated front width, with the skirt worn over a wire frame.

This pannier frame is made in this manner: Construct an ellipse out of strong iron wire of such dimension as you require, but not exceeding an overall frontal width of 3 feet 6 inches or a depth of 12 inches from front to back, because this is about as much as any girl can gracefully manage.

If the wire is not very firm, it may be found necessary to use it double, and any join(s) must be firmly soldered, with the whole shape bound round with tape. Make a waistband (webbing) that can be fastened with a strong hook and eye at the back, and attach the frame to it by means of evenely-spaced tapes or webbing strips, so that it hangs at a slightly forward angle—that is, lower in front and higher at the back, but not exceedingly so—and secure all the joining points as strongly as possible.

A pannier frame can also be made from strong wicker or cane, which is a good deal lighter in weight, with the ends joined by fastening a wire through holes drilled in the wood. It is then bound in the same way with tape and attached to the belt.

If it is possible to construct the two outer ends of the ellipse, so that they hinge *upwards*—as was the custom—it would be very useful, because then whoever wears the pannier dress can lift these ends, as, for instance, when she enters through a doorway or arch. Otherwise, the poor girl may have to come on sideways—like a crab.

The length of the skirts in this period was not always constant, but generally they fell to the floor at the front and sides (with a slight train at the back—and do not forget to allow extra length in any case at the back, owing to the tilted angle of the frame), or were just long enough to touch the instep. For evening and dance dresses, however, the hem in front might be as high as the ankle.

Many of the skirts were 'split open' down the front, to show a decorated under-skirt or petticoat, made of muslin or some similar fine material and as wide as the over-skirt—even though only the centre (visible) portion need be ornamented. But make sure that it is completely masked at the outer edges. The open-fronted outer-skirt is entirely optional—both open and closed were worn—and the closed skirt is certainly easier to design . . . but the open one looks more interesting (*see* Fig. 88).

If the pannier frame is of the maximum size, then, of course, a greater width of material is required for both the skirt and the petticoat. One way of saving on the material is to 'cover in' the top on either side with two 'saddle' pieces, and then to gather the dress material fully and attach it to the outer edge of the frame. This method could be applied to both the closed and split type of pannier skirt (*see* Fig. 88).

Another skirt, not strictly a panniered dress so much as a dress with panniers, was designed with an additional length of material—of a different texture, colour and pattern from the skirt—which was draped with a good deal of fullness round the back and sides, and caught up with the outer edges tucked under, and arranged in a series of diminishing loops or puffs, which can be padded underneath to help keep their rounded shape.

The bodice should be made of the same material, and sometimes a long, narrow panel was attached at the back under the pannier-puffs, and falling to the ground like a sort of train. In some ways this dress foreshadowed the 1870 bustle (*see* Fig. 88).

Another garment that should be mentioned is the *robe á la Française*, which was a sort of combined bodice and robe which became fashionable in 1720, and lasted for a number of years.

At first it was rather like an informal dressing-gown, and, as can be seen from the illustration, its chief feature was the way in which a width of the material was gathered at the back of the neck into a box-pleat, widening out to its full width at the hem. The armholes were wide and loose and without sleeves, so that the under-bodice sleeves came through. This robe was usually left open down to the floor in front (sometimes only to the waist), showing the decorated under-skirt.

Round about 1730 this gown was remodelled to fit more snugly and tightly under the arms, and sometimes it met across the front and had its own sleeves. The back pleat that had hung loosely, was now sewn down to the under-bodice as far as the waist, with the decorated under-skirt showing below (*see* Fig. 89).

This style of garment is fully illustrated by William Hogarth (1697-1764) in the National Gallery in his famous series of pictures, 'The

Fig. 88. (a) Diagram of the pannier frame; (c) the hinged ends of the frame; (b) waistband and tapes for supporting the frame to the wearer; (d) the split skirt and under-skirt; (e) diagram of 'saddle-piece'; (f) the 'puffed' over-skirt—the sort of costume for 'Little Bo-Peep'; (g) back-view of the above; (h) another arrangement of the 'puffed' over-skirt, with train.

Rake's Progress' and 'Marriage *à la* Mode', the latter depicting the unhappy adventures of a certain Countess from her marriage until her early death.

Hogarth had an uncanny flair for satirical detail and it is said of him that so accustomed did he become in looking for the frailer side of human nature that in the end he completely lost the magic touch for portraying the beautiful. This set of pictures is specially useful to a costume-designer dealing with this period, and one can look at them over and over again . . . and always find something new !

The eighteenth century bodices, whether they were made separately or as part of the costume as a whole, were all slim, tight and with a decidedly pointed front (and sometimes back as well), an effect that was emphasized by the long, vertical Vs in the surface trimming. And if an outer-gown was worn over an under-bodice, it was often single- or double-laced over the front.

Neck-lines were either square or round and fairly low-cut, but with the outline broken by a lace or coloured tulle frill—or perhaps a border of small artificial flowers. Sometimes the effect was further softened by a small linen ruff around the neck—in the Elizabethan style—or by a circlet of flowers, with the bare bosom below. For informal occasions, a gauzy fichu might be draped round the neck and over the shoulders, while rather charming (and easily made!) was a transparent, gauzy collar-cum-cape that had a tiny ruffle round the top and a frilly edge round the hem, which, when worn could be very flattering to the neck and shoulders of a slightly older woman! (*see* Fig. 90).

During this period most of the sleeves were still elbow-length and loosely ruffled or caught up in puffs, falling in a lacy, white cascade—as they had done in the seventeenth century. Other sleeves had wide, elbow-length, turn-back cuffs . . . inspired by those on men's coats . . . and only a few were wrist-length, with a small cuff and/or ruffle (*see* Fig. 91).

In addition to the high, red-painted heels, some of them were covered in brocade to match the upper shoe, and a distinctive feature of the period, with its cobbled streets, was the 'clog', which fitted into the

Figs. 89, 90 & 91. (a & b) Two examples of the early Robe á la Française (1720-30); (c) a later development of this garment (1730-50); (d, e & f) some neck-lines; (g, h, i, j & k) examples of sleeves—(k) is almost back to the Elizabethan!

space under the arch of the shoe, giving an effect extremely like our modern wedge-sole . . . and, incidentally, made walking very much easier.

These clogs were kept in position by being tied over the instep, and were useful as a protection for the feet, not only from the mud, but from all sorts of unmentionable refuse (solid and liquid) that was indiscriminately emptied into the streets—often, if one can believe the cartoons of the time, from upper windows—which must have made going for a walk quite a hazard! There is a story told of a certain Lady Wortley Montague, who, when a friend remarked upon the dirty state of her hands, replied that this was nothing . . . he should see her feet! Bath-tubs were rare in 1700!

Not many opportunities occur for wearing clogs in a play, but should an occasion arise—or one be contrived—it is a period touch that might give the critic from the local rag something to think about . . . that is, if he happened to notice!

Elegantly-painted fans, designed on silk by famous artists of the day, were carried (and fluttered to good effect) by both prude and coquette, and long gloves were worn, both indoors and out, though this was more from necessity than as a costume accessory (perhaps Lady Montague had mislaid hers). If a young man chanced to meet a lady of his acquaintance delicately picking her way in the street, as like as not she might be carrying a 'pomander', which was a hollow filigree ball, that opened on a hinge and contained a small sponge saturated with perfume —probably musk or civet . . . and in the eighteenth century, with its dirt and its smells, it must often have been a decided solace! This custom, however, was not new, and pomanders (hanging from a chain on the wrist) were in common use in the fifteenth century . . . and later. Cardinal Wolsey used one, cleverly disguised to look like an orange. A pomander can be made from the gilded outer casing of a tennis ball, with holes cut out with a razor blade, with a piece of chain or cord attached for hanging it from the wrist (*see* Fig. 92).

Other accessories were the muff and a parasol, the latter carried open over his mistress's head by a little blackamoor who was as much of a necessity for a lady of fashion as was her pet monkey. Little black boys, I admit, are not easy 'props' to come by, especially for amateurs—nor, for that matter, is a live monkey—and a stuffed one only looks like what it is! Doris Keane, in *Romance*, used to carry on a little marmoset, which, although it was 'stage-trained', got up to all sorts of unexpected tricks, and was therefore a great success . . . with the audience. Sarah Bernhardt also had a marmoset which one day turned round and bit her . . . and I'm sorry to say the 'Divine (?) Sarah' was so enraged that she held the poor creature on the fire with a pair of tongs. Let's hope Miss Keane was on better terms with hers.

When being borne in her sedan chair at night, preceded by a link-boy with flaring torch, Madame would hold a mask in front of her face that hid her charms from the curious stares of the passer-by . . . and also prevented her from being recognized as she hurried to the playhouse . . . or to an assignation.

In the early years of the century, a woman still dressed her hair—or her wig—built up in the somewhat exaggerated single or double 'peak' on top of her head, in which she followed the masculine style that became popular during the reign of William and Mary . . . though a double peak—on the stage—is better suited to a (comic) character part (*see* Fig. 93).

With the accession of the first Hanoverian George in 1714, a much lower and more natural style came into vogue, with the hair drawn back from the forehead and sides, and gently caught at the nape of the

Fig. 92. A pomander. The design can be painted direct on to the surface of a rubber ball, or it can be carefully cut out. The effect aimed at is to make it look as if it were made from metal (filigree).

neck, to fall in loose ringlets down the back or over one shoulder, with the hair powdered or left in a natural colour. Small wreaths or bunches of artificial flowers, intertwined with strings of pearls, helped to soften the effect, enhancing naturally good features and helped to make the most of poor ones.

They were, however, a rum lot in the 1700s, and the 'popular face' was one that looked 'round and well-fed' . . . and where necessary this effect was 'assisted' by means of pads worn inside the cheeks (rather like the cotton-wool swabs a dentist puts into one's mouth when he's doing an intricate stopping). These pads were called 'plumpers', and it seems likely that we get our modern phrase, 'Talking with a plum in the mouth', from those days.

The seventeenth-century cap, with its high, upstanding starched lawn or lace frontpiece . . . called a 'fontange' or, rather curiously, a 'commode'

. . . was now completely outmoded (oh dear! That sounds like a very poor attempt at a pun—but it wasn't meant to be), and a small type of cap—often no more than a scrap of pleated lace worn flat on top of the head—became popular for indoor wear.

In the days before the 'servant problem'—when a girl didn't think it beneath her dignity to wear a cap—house- and parlour-maids wore something very similar, and you can still see a sort of compromise between the cap and the old fontange on the heads of waitresses in some restaurants.

The mob-cap also made its appearance early in the century, and was often worn under a wide-brimmed, Leghorn straw hat, tied under the chin with a broad silk ribbon . . . thus becoming the forerunner of the Victorian poke-bonnet. Some of the mob-caps had lappets that could also be tied under the chin (*see* Fig. 93).

To make a mob-cap cut out from a piece of white linen or scenic canvas a circle with a 12 inch radius, and hem it round. Then lightly mark out an inner circle with a 9 inch radius, and sew a socket round it with tape, and then thread a ribbon through it, pulling it up so that the 'cap' fits easily over the wearer's head, and tie the two ends of the ribbon in a bow.

It is useful to make a rough pattern first in some odd scrap of stuff—or even with paper—and the measurements, of course, would depend

Fig. 93. (a) The 'double-peak' wig; (b) diagram for making a mob-cap; (c) diagram for mob-cap with 'lappets'—the hat ribbons are so arranged that they hold the lace-edged lappets as a 'frame' for the face; (d & e) diagrams for making the hood.

upon how large or how small you want the cap and the width of the surrounding frill, and when estimating them have the hair or wig dressed as it will be worn for the part being played.

Hoods—separate or joined to a cloak, and made of silk or wool—were the usual out-of-doors headdress at night . . . unless m'lady was going somewhere special, when she might wear a black mantilla over her head, pinned closely under her chin, framing her face like a lacy Balaclava, on top of which she perched a man's tricorne hat!

To make the hood is not difficult. Take a piece of silk or flannelette in a dark plain colour about 18 inches wide and 36 inches long, and then a second piece, for the lining, in a contrasting colour, but cut it 40 inches long. Sew the two pieces together, and neatly turn up that extra 2 inches so as to give a coloured border at either side. Fold the whole piece in half, and tightly gather up and sew one of the sides to form the back of the hood and give the front a goodish backwards fold to show the lining, and to ensure that the wearer's face will be clearly seen . . . because, although it might not have been the case in real life, it is essential to see it on the stage! (*see* Fig. 93).

To make a wig (crêpe hair or animal wool—excellent for eighteenth-century white wigs, and it can be bought in packets from most Chemists), always try to model it on a wooden wig-block of the right size . . . failing which, I suppose, there's nothing for it but to build it up on the wearer's head!

CHAPTER 12

The Second Half of the Eighteenth Century (1750-1800)

This period has sometimes been called the 'Romantic Age' . . . with Garrick and Mrs. Siddons enriching the traditions of the theatre, Gainsborough and Reynolds leading the world of English art, and Chippendale, Sheraton and Hepplewhite putting beautiful furniture into beautiful houses, designed by the brothers Adam.

Yet there was an extremely seamy side to the picturesque beauty and romanticism of the later eighteenth century, in which lunatics were flogged at Bedlam and, as late as 1784, a woman could be publicly burnt at Newgate!

MEN

The general trend in men's costumes in the later seventeen-hundreds was towards greater neatness and simplicity, and after 1760, for instance, only the old-fashioned—or the unfashionable—continued to wear the full-skirted coats and long waistcoats . . . and of these Sir Peter Teazle (*The School for Scandal*), Sir Anthony Absolute (*The Rivals*) and Mr. Hardcastle (*She Stoops to Conquer*) are good examples.

The new traditional coats provided a more slender silhouette, and though in some features they resembled the earlier garments, they were closer-fitting, and could be buttoned right down the front if m'lord desired . . . which, as it happened, he hardly ever did! The handkerchief and snuffbox were still found in the pockets, but the pocket-flaps were now much smaller.

In 1770 the first cut-away-type coat came in, with the front gradually sloping away towards the square-cut tails at the back. One innovation was that the coat no longer met across the chest, and another was the addition of an upstanding collar, which, however, by 1780 had developed into the more familiar 'turn-down' shape that has continued to be worn until the present day, though in the eighteenth century the coat had no front lapels (*see* Fig. 94).

At the beginning of the period the waistcoat had not greatly changed, and was still nearly as long as the coat, though it was not considered fashionable to fasten it (button up) in front any lower than the waist. After 1760, however, waistcoats began to get shorter and shorter, and though a few of them were still made of brocade, many others were plain and unpatterned. A novel feature with some of these short waistcoats was that they were double-breasted, with a small turn-down lapel at the top and two points below, very much in the style of some modern ones.

By 1790 the coat itself had become double-breasted and square-cut across the front, showing the two points of the waistcoat underneath, and with the tails hanging down only at the back . . . in fact, if not the father, at any rate a recognizable ancestor of our modern evening tail-coat.

At the neck there was a jabot, but the lace border was no longer as broad and, indeed, was often omitted altogether. A jabot is very easy to make. First cut from a piece of linen or white canvas a panel of 8 inches wide, and of the required length to fit comfortably round the throat. This strip is then pleated horizontally in overlapping folds, which are ironed and then lightly sewn down until the strip has been reduced in width to 3 inches. This should then be backed with some stiffer material, so that it will sit round the neck comfortably. Add four tapes—one at each of the corners, for tying it at the back, with the loose ends of the tapes tucked out of sight.

Now cut another piece of the same material, about 12 inches long and 8 inches wide, and fold it vertically—again with the upper pleat overlapping the lower one—until the panel has been reduced to 4 inches in width. Iron down these pleats, but do not sew them, except at one end, to hold them in formation. Stitch this end on to the *back* of the neck-band about ½ inch down from the top edge in the centre, so that it can fall over and hang down in front. A wide border of lace can be added at the bottom if desired, and if a jewelled brooch is worn, when pinning in place give the hanging-down strip just the suggestion of a 'lift', so that the material bunches a little round the brooch (*see* Fig. 94).

The sleeves of the coats had now become longer and with only a narrow turn-back cuff and no more than 2 inches of lace ruffle showing at the wrists . . . though I've noticed that if an actor has the chance to wear a sleeve-ruffle, he doesn't much care to have it curtailled!

After 1780 the cuff itself was often omitted altogether, and three buttons were placed at the lower end of the closed sleeve towards the back, just as is the custom with us today . . . except that Mr. Smart Guy often insists on five!

The ends of the breeches now always covered the tops of the heavy white silk stockings (servants, etc., would wear worsted), and were fastened below the knee with a row of three or four small buttons and/or a strap and buckle.

Naturally, none of these slight changes is completely arbitrary, and the overlapping within a year or two, either way, would not be at all a serious matter—especially in the theatre, where a designer should choose the best of each adjacent period when making up his costume plot.

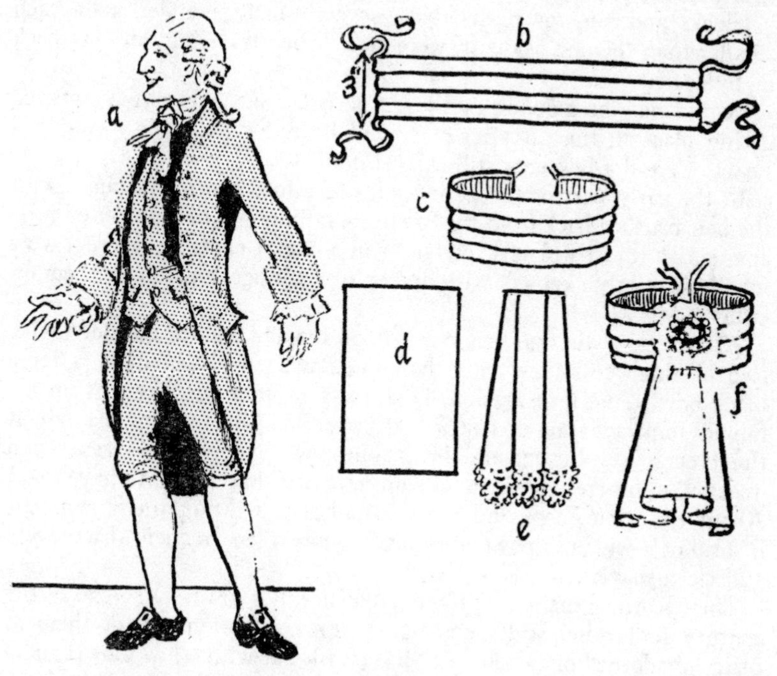

Fig. 94. (a) The early 'cut-away' coat, around 1780; (b, c, d, e & f) diagram of the jabot.

As before, the material used for making the breeches was usually black velvet or satin, but occasionally the breeches matched the coat and waistcoat, if unpatterned. As the waistcoats became shorter (1760), the breeches, which had largely been covered before, now took on a new importance, some of them being made of doeskin, which fashion demanded should be worn as tight as comfort—and decency—would permit . . . a combination that is still demonstrated every day by those magnificent *tableaux vivants*, the Horse Guards in Whitehall.

These trousers were fitted out with a couple of fob-pockets, and watches (so big sometimes that they earned the name of 'turnips') were attached to a fob-seal and worn with the watch in the pocket and the seal hanging outside. Some men, not content with one watch, wore two, one in each pocket. Nowadays the wearing of a second watch is the low comedian's 'prop', whereby he professes to be able to tell you the time in London . . . when 'it's Tuesday in 'Uddersfield'!

The heels on men's shoes were now much lower, the tongues shorter, and the buckles smaller. Top boots were also worn, covering the knees in front, and cut away behind them, at the back, with long, white woollen over-stockings put on as a protection for the silk hose underneath. Later, gaiters were sometimes used in place of boots.

Cloaks and long overcoats, with several small shoulder-capes, each smaller than the one below it, were worn when travelling on horseback or by coach.

Swords now became less and less a part of a man's everyday apparel, giving place to the carrying of a knob-headed cane, with a cord and tassel . . . and a few men still carried muffs!

In the early part of the period wigs remained much the same, with the hair brushed back from the forehead, falling in a tied cluster of curls at the back (or in a plait or pigtail or in a bag). Generally, the ears were wholly or partly exposed, with one or two sausage curls above them on either side.

After 1780 a wig that was very full on top and wide at the sides, with two or three corkscrew curls hanging down the back under a large black bow, came into fashion. Fred Terry wore a wig like this, in his famous impersonation in *The Scarlet Pimpernel*, that exciting play about the French Revolution, and he had it powdered in some scenes and 'natural' in others . . . which, of course, meant that he had to have two! About this time more and more men began wearing their own hair instead of a wig, and powdering became much less frequent. Faces were still clean-shaven.

The tricorne remained as the popular hat, but towards the end of the century four other styles made their appearance, and all of them in plain, unadorned black felt: *(a)* a smallish hat with a low crown and a stiff, flat brim; *(b)* with the brim turned up at the back and the front (but higher at the back); *(c)* with the brim turned up equally on either side; and *(d)* with a narrow, stiff, flat brim and a steeple crown, rather like the hats worn by the Roundheads in Charles I's reign.

In so many of the plays set in this period we have 'inn scenes', with 'landlords, servants and local yokels'. Take, for example, the ale-house scene in *She Stoops to Conquer*. These worthies are usually dressed in coats and breeches similar in cut to those worn by the gentry, but made in a coarser material. The cuffs of the coats might be turned back to show a bit of the linen shirt (but no frill), with a plain jabot—perhaps no more than a strip of linen tied round the neck, with the ends hanging down. Stockings would be slightly wrinkled on the legs, and loose, wide-tongued shoes would be worn.

A white apron would outline Mine Host's ample middle, held in place by a leather belt. The yokels would wear smocks and coloured neckerchiefs, with gaiters on their legs and straw sticking out of their rough shoes. Hair would be carelessly tied behind, and of course, unpowdered.

Some period costumes are what is known as 'traditional' (which doesn't mean you've *got* to follow suit . . . only that most people find it easier to do so!). For instance, take Tony Lumpkin, in *She Stoops to Conquer*. Popular Tommy Steele has recently made his straight-acting début in this part at the Old Vic. Probably because Tony is referred to in the play as the Squire, he is always dressed in a tailed coat of hunting pink (red), with a yellow waistcoat with gilt buttons (several of them undone) and white breeches. He wears an untidy-looking jabot, knee-boots with the tops turned over, and carries a hunting crop. On his head is a small, black, peaked cap with a little black bow on top, which is pushed well back on his curly red hair . . . another tradition which demands that 'costume comedy' must always be played in a red 'scratch' wig.

At the beginning of this period the materials used for men's clothes were still rich: velvets and ribbed corduroy, with silk and satin in various light colours, some plain and some with a small flower pattern. Narrow, vertical stripes were very popular with the dandies, who, by the way, were now known as Macaronies and flourished like the green bay tree in the 1770s. Their *un*original ambition was to be thought 'different' (we've all heard that one before!), to which end they wore tailless coats, striped stockings and towering wigs, with ridiculous little tricorne hats perched at a precarious angle on top (*see* Fig. 95).

After 1780 silks became less popular, and broadcloth and fine wools in black, brown, or dyed dark green and dark blue, cherry, purple and other dark colours, were the vogue with the fashionable man.

Most of these materials can be found in the upholstery departments of the big shops, which will offer a far happier and more profitable hunting-ground than the dress-material counter.

WOMEN

While the fashion in men's clothes moved steadily towards simplicity, for women there began one of the worst periods of exaggeration, with panniers becoming wider than ever, and wigs built up to such fantastic heights that the lids of sedan chairs had to be made to hinge back, or Madame would have had to squat on the floor. As it was, when riding in her coach, she often had to pass the time on her knees—a position which because of sheer discomfort could hardly have been described as devotional!

Even the doors and arches in some private houses had to be heightened to accommodate M'Lady's head, which on occasion rose to a height of 3 feet and over by the time the top ornaments had been adjusted . . . conceits such as a basket of flowers or fruit or a galleon in full sail . . .

and the cartoons of the day, showing her maid dizzily swaying atop a ladder while putting the finishing touches to her mistress's coiffure, were only a little in excess of the truth!

All sorts of peculiar ingredients went towards stuffing and bolstering up these monumental structures, which—once they were well and truly balanced—were liberally plastered with pomade and then powdered . . . not always completely white or grey, but with the black, brown, red or golden hair showing through in streaks, an effect that was far more attractive, in fact, than this description may convey. A few years ago, you may remember, it was the fashion of brunettes to introduce a white streak into their hair, nor is it at all unusual nowadays to see young girls with black streaks in fair hair or golden streaks in black hair.

Of course, not all women—nor any of the women all of the time—went in for these eccentricities, but it would be fun to deck the head of, let us say, Mrs. Hardcastle in *She Stoops to Conquer* with something of this kind, the more so as in Act II she draws special attention to it, thereby offering an opportunity too good to be missed!

Mrs. Candour in *The School for Scandal* and Mrs. Malaprop in *The Rivals* are both comic relief, and therefore they can be burlesqued as much as one likes, and, as so many effects on the stage are dependent upon contrast, this can be provided by the simpler hair styles of the younger characters . . . Kate Hardcastle and her friend, Miss Neville, Maria, Julia and Lydia Languish, respectively.

Lady Teazle, being the heroine of *The School for Scandal*, must not, of course, be made a figure of fun, though I think it pretty likely she would dress her hair as high as she *dared* for Lady Sneerwell's party (Act II, Scene 2), especially after Sir Peter had been reminding her of the days when she 'combed it smooth over a roll'. She might, therefore, compromise with a cascade of ostrich plumes, apparently growing out of a circlet of roses, set on top of her wig.

Today we would make one of these outsize wigs from a light wire frame, covering it over with white butter-muslin to give it a foundation, and then sewing on long vertical strips of crêpe hair, after having first gently teased it out. To get the streaky pomade plus powder effect, the finished wig should be lightly painted over with a fairly thick solution of whitewash and size, using long, upward strokes of the brush (*see* Fig. 95).

Between 1760 and 1770 the inevitable reaction set in, and the excessive exaggerations of costumes and wigs were only retained in the more elaborate party gowns, and then mostly by the older women. After 1780 panniers went out of fashion altogether, and skirts fell straight down again in front, with any fullness concentrated at the back with thickly gathered petticoats.

If the over-dress was 'split' in front, the sides and back would be looped up, so that they fell in festoons over the petticoat, and this effect was achieved by sewing sets of tapes a few inches apart *under* the

Fig. 95. (a) A 'Macaroni'. By 1770, these towering wigs were at the height of their popularity. As it was impossible to wear an ordinary sized hat, absurdly small hats were worn, perched on top of the wig—a fashion that greatly enraged the more sober-minded critics. These hats could only be lifted in greeting by means of the knob of a cane . . . or the point of the sword! (b) A fashionable lady's 'monumental' wig; (c) the back-view of a high wig; (d) diagram showing the wire foundation support necessary in making one of these wigs for the stage.

material, and then tying them together and putting a large bow on the same spot on the top surface to give the impression that the draping was due to it. Another method would be to thread tapes through sockets sewn underneath, and to pull these tapes up tightly, on the same principle used for looping curtains. Such a dress was called a 'polonaise'.

Some of the over-skirts were merely turned back from the front, showing their (different colour) lining, with the two ends fixed together at the back. Or an even simpler arrangement was for the over-skirt to be cut in front with a pattern of receding scallops, without being turned up at all (*see* Fig. 96).

The under-petticoats were often quite elaborate affairs, with deep lace flounces and frills, or decorated with an appliquéd design in pleated ribbon or gold cord.

Bodices were still tight and shaped (boned) to a pointed front, often showing an under-bodice. In 1780 women suddenly discovered (or re-discovered?) muslin, which immediately became all the fashion, with round waists and wide blue silk sashes tied in a large bow at the back, with long trailing ends.

At the beginning of the period, sleeves were still elbow-length, with a frill that was narrow at the bend of the arm, and hung lower, to a point, behind the elbow, but by 1780 they became long and tight and down to the wrist, with a small turn-back cuff and a narrow white frill.

Neck-lines were square, high at the back and rather low-cut in front, and surrounded by a narrow frill, but after 1780 a very low-cut, round neck, that tended to slip off the shoulders—as in Restoration days—became popular. After 1790 the surrounding frill was often lengthened, falling like a small cape over the back.

The gauzy fichu had never gone out of fashion, and it was either loosely draped over the shoulders and tied in front or had the ends tucked into the front of the bodice. It was also crossed over the bosom—with a good deal of fullness to spare—covering the whole surface of the front of the bodice (*see* Fig. 97).

Shoes remained more or less unaltered from the previous period, but in some instances bows were substituted for buckles, and in addition to the clogs a sort of wooden patten, mounted on an iron ring, was worn, with the feet fitting into a leather loop that went over the instep (*see* Fig. 98).

By 1780 the coiffeurs—having done their worse—gave up height, and concentrated their attention on width and curliness, though, fortunately, not to the same extent, and once more the shape of women's heads became almost normal, with many of them wearing their own hair, and in its natural colour. This did not necessarily mean that a white head (wig) was not seen on special occasions, or that a woman did not sometimes add a dab of powder to her natural tresses.

There is a lovely portrait of 'The Parson's Daughter', by Romney, in the National Gallery that is typical of this new hair-style. The young girl's face is framed in a great mass of light, ginger-coloured curls, with a section of wide green silk ribbon twisted through it and showing in front, with a big bow tying the curls that hang down her shoulders at the back. She wears a plain, dark dress with a simple white fichu tucked into a buckled band, worn rather high on her slim figure.

The whole picture is painted practically in shades of black, brown and white, with the merest touch of a warm, glowing red—with the green of the ribbon repeated in the background as the only other colour variant. Jean Forbes-Robertson, who played the female lead, Helen, in *Berkeley Square*, modelled her hair (wig) on this painting.

Delicately tinted complexions that made the women look like little china Dresden shepherdesses were very typical of the whole of the eighteenth century, and it is interesting to note that when Laurence

Olivier and Vivien Leigh were playing in *The School for Scandal* for the Old Vic Company at the New Theatre a few years ago, that make-up wizard, Max Factor, created for them an individual pancake make-up that embodied a luminous quality that made it specially suitable for the 'patch and powder' period in which this play is set. It is quite simply named 'O-L.1', and, of course, anyone can buy it.

It has been an invariable custom with women throughout the ages to want to cover their heads—both indoors and out—and even nowadays, when it seems less necessary, you will sometimes see smart women sitting down to lunch . . . in their own homes. mark you . . . wearing a hat, for all the world as if they were in a restaurant!

Plain mob-caps, with lappets that tied under the chin, were still worn in the house, or with a flat straw hat set on top, when out of it. Servant-maids often bound their heads round with a strip of linen with a frilled edge, tying it into a bow in front. Kate Hardcastle might very well be seen wearing just such a 'cap' when Young Marlow mistakes her for a barmaid. In the play, according to the terms of an agreement with her father, Kate may wear what she likes in the mornings, so long as she puts on a housewife's dress, to please him, in the afternoons. Her costume would probably be a simple, square-necked, flower-patterned bodice with elbow-length sleeves, and turned-back over-skirt of the same material, revealing a plain petticoat underneath. She might also wear a small, frilly-edged apron.

She must not, however, look too much like the real maidservant, who also appears in the play, and whose dress would be considerably plainer, and possibly made from checked gingham, with which she would wear a large plain apron. But, one must stress the point that Kate's housewife costume is in direct contrast to the dress she wears when she first meets Marlow.

Both high and wide hair-styles, of course, require a specially large size in mob-caps, and usually for out of doors a kind of lacy hood, that tied in a bow under the chin was worn instead. But the most amusing novelty that was bred from the new fashions was the 'calash', which was a sort of silk hood, tied under the chin, with the domed shape supported by several three-quarter-round whalebone hoops, with the ends on each side hinged together, so that the hood could collapse together and be lowered onto the back of the shoulders just like the hood of a calèche (low wheeled carriage), from which this headdress took its name (*see* Fig. 99).

Of course, ordinary-sized hats were much too small to be practical with the high *coiffures*, yet some women tried them, tilting them rather tipsily over their noses, and as the hats of this period were often loaded with feathers, ribbons and flowers, a quaint sight they must have looked! Which is all the more reason why Mrs. Hardcastle in the Garden scene and Mrs. Malaprop in King's Mead Fields should be provided with hats like these to wear.

With the wide hairdressing of the 1780s we come to one of the most

Figs. 96, 97, 98 & 99. (a & b) Two examples of the Polonaise; (c & d) two neck-lines; (e & f) a shoe and a slipper; (g) shoe fitted into the patten or clog; (h) the 'calash' (caléche)—in the London Museum there is an example of a calash, covered with dried seaweed that was used as a rain-proof protection!

attractive and becoming of all hats, the Gainsborough, with its wide, tilted brim, high crown and waving plumes . . . but, of course, it needs a certain flair to carry it off, which, fortunately, both Mrs. Siddons and the Duchess of Devonshire were lucky enough to possess. The Duchess, by the way, appears in *Berkeley Square*, too . . . but *not* in the famous hat, which seems a pity!

In the closing years of the century, women appropriated and adapted the masculine steeple-crown hat, to which they added such feminine trimmings as ribbons and buckles, and sometimes even bunches of ostrich plumes.

CHAPTER 13

Farewell to Romanticism (1800-37)

After a couple of comparatively short reigns, George IV and William IV (nicknamed 'Silly Billy'), England settled down to sixty-four years of uninterrupted 'Victoriana'.

The beginning of the nineteenth century saw the passing of the romantic and picturesque in men's costumes . . . those brightly-coloured single- and double-breasted tail-coats, with their red linings, shiny buttons and gay flowered waistcoats, the tight knee-breeches and still tighter pantaloons, the stiff, upstanding collars and the white or black wrapped-round cravats, so high sometimes that they half-covered the chin, and the high-crowned black hats (*see* Fig. 100).

MEN

It should not be very difficult to 'fake' a costume of this period. For the coat, one could use a modern tail-coat . . . and hope no one holds up his hand to object to its being black! Turn-back cuffs, of course, will have to be added to the sleeves, with the collar built up a bit, and a strip of black velvet to give it that long, 'double-roll' effect round the neck, with a 'notch' on each side in front separating it from the short, rather high, black velvet revers.

A double row of six shiny buttons and the bright lining (sateen) will go a long way towards suggesting the right period and livening up a dark coat, especially if it is worn with the correct pantaloons, for which one could cut off the feet from a pair of light-coloured woollen tights, binding the ends, and, by attaching elastic bands to pass under the instep of the boots, they can be kept tightly stretched . . . or, if it is felt to be a bit wasteful to cut down tights, a similar effect can be got by using a man's long-legged under-pants, but something will have to be done about adjusting the front.

For tight knee-breeches, again either use tights or pants, with a narrow band of braid sewn below each knee (like a garter) and a vertical row of three little buttons above it on the outside of each leg. The lower portion will then look like stocking, with the calf and foot covered with black-buttoned gaiters and black, buckled shoes . . . or wellingtons for an outside scene.

From 1815 and for the next few years, a snugly-fitting, double-breasted tail-coat remained the fashion with men for both day and evening wear, and, except that it was possibly a little longer in the waist and more sober in colouring (dark blue or green, brown or black), it did not otherwise greatly differ from the earlier coat, and it was worn with light-toned drill, twill or corduroy trousers, cut fairly full at the top, but narrowing down towards the instep, where the ends were tightly strapped under the boot or shoe.

Between 1830 and 1840 the frock-coat made its appearance. This was usually single-breasted, with six buttons in a row, of which, however, only the bottom one, or the last two, were fastened. There was an upturned collar, but no lapels, and the 'skirts' were fairly full. Frock-coats were made from broadcloth in dark blue, green, plum, grey, and black and white. There was also a double-breasted pattern, with velvet collar and revers and a double row of buttons, but it was more like an overcoat, and most often worn by older men.

This was the period when the feminine silhouette (sloping shoulders, pointed tops to the sleeves, trim, pinched-in waists and flaring coat-tails) was the *beau ideal* of the young man of fashion, who—much as he might pretend to despise the means—was seldom above wearing a corset to achieve his ends!

Such coats could be adapted from a knee-length (or shortened) overcoat or a man's cloth dressing-gown or jacket with the lapels cut away (for the single-breasted pattern), and the waist remodelled to fit more tightly to the figure. To ensure the 'flared' effect, a couple of 'gores' may have to be inserted, one at each side of a central back-slit, above which two large, flat pearly buttons are added, just above the apex, as a finishing touch.

If it is found necessary to make the trousers as worn with these coats (light for young men, darker for older), any ordinary pyjama-trouser pattern can be used, but it would probably be easier to adapt a modern pair of trousers to fit the required style.

The tail-coat of the earlier period was still sometimes worn for evening occasions, but in this case the trousers were darker, tighter and shorter (about ankle-length), with a downward slit just below the calf on the outside of each leg, fastened with a row of three or four small buttons. Below these came white socks and black shoes with bows.

(*Note:* With all trousers, pantaloons or breeches, in addition to tightly stretching them from the base, some provision must be made for holding them up securely at the top, and this is especially important when (if) tights are being used. Braces and buttons are all very well, but it is a combination that few actors completely trust, as buttons have a maddening habit of coming loose at the wrong moments, so that it is far safer to employ the old theatre trick of tying pennies or halfpennies into the material, over which the eyes of the braces are fastened, instead of over a button. There is also the additional advantage that the coins can be readjusted to any required level at a moment's notice.)

The 'points' of the high collar should 'cup' the chin, and to ensure a comfortable fit it is often better first to cut out a paper pattern, from which the collar can be made, using a doubled piece of muslin or linen that can then be starched and ironed out flat . . . and do not forget to add stud-holes at back and front and to double-sew the neck-band for extra strength.

The cravat or stock (black, white or in colours) took several forms: *(a)* wrapped neatly round the high upstanding collar; *(b)* wound round, with the ends folded across in front and tucked out of sight; or *(c)* round the collar, with the ends tied in a bow under the chin in front. Poets—and those who fancied themselves as poets—affected the open and unstarched Byron collar, which was loosely held together with a silk scarf, passed round the neck and knotted into a large, floppy bow in front (*see* Fig. 100).

If the character being played has to appear in his shirt-sleeves, use a white, drip-dry, nylon tunic shirt. Of course, the sleeves will not be quite as 'full' as they ought to be, but with luck no one will notice that, and if the collar of the shirt happens to be pointed, it may be possible to starch it on its own, which will then save the trouble of having to make a separate one. Finally, sew a 6-inch-wide strip of lightly starched white cambric frill down the front (to show above the high-cut waistcoat when a coat is worn) and add a narrow frill round each wrist to come below the cuffs.

For the tall hat, use an ordinary black top-hat, which, though strictly not the right shape (it should be slightly higher and wider at the top than our modern hats), will certainly pass, especially if a broad band is added round the base, with a buckle in front, and the silk is carefully brushed the *wrong* way to give the hat that 'beaver' effect.

For going to the theatre, opera or a reception, in addition to his top-hat, a man might wear a black cloak with a white lining—or a white cloak with a black lining—with a wide velvet collar, and cords to fasten it at the throat in front.

Such a cloak can be designed as a three-quarters of a circle, gathered at the top into a fitted shoulder-piece, so that it hangs in pleated folds. Some cloaks (*circa* 1840) had a second smaller shoulder-cape that was attached under the collar and hung over the main cloak (*see* Fig. 101).

The snuffbox, which had gone out of fashion with the last of the Georges, had been replaced by the quizzing-glass (2½ inches by 1½ inches on a 6-inch stem), and no dandy appeared in public without one!

When he held it, with a characteristic pose at arm's length, and stared through it at some unwelcome visitor (ten to one, a creditor!) it was enough to make the poor creature wish the floor would open and swallow him down!

Most gentlemen wore a flower in the buttonhole, and gloves on every suitable—and unsuitable—occasion (and of equally unsuitable colours, such as chrome yellow and violet) and rather high top-hats with narrow curling brims (black, grey, fawn and sometimes white). A cap, however, was often worn at a sports-meeting . . . or when our young gentleman

Figs. 100 & 101. (a) Man of the Romantic Age (1810-1830); (b, c & d) examples of neck-wear—the top-hat, by the way, was the only headgear suitable to the man of fashion; (e) the 'Byron' collar; (f & g) examples of hair-styles; (h & i) the evening cloak—(i) shows the 'double' shoulder cape; (j) diagram for cutting a cape.

'slipped across the Channel' for a quiet little week-end in Gay Paree!

By 1800 wigs and the powdering of the hair by men had become a thing of the past, and their own hair was now cut short at the back and left long at the sides and on top, where it lay in little, curled ringlets or fell in a 'wind-swept' profusion over the forehead—very much as one sees it on some of those 'Roman Emperor' art school plaster casts.

If the hair was parted at all, it was slightly to one side rather than down the middle.

A wise producer will naturally forbid his actors to have their hair cut for several weeks before production date, so that, if necessary, their hair can be suitably curled . . . to which, of course, some of them will immediately object! Yet it need only be a temporary measure, with the 'curl' combing out quite easily in the morning, so that really there would be no occasion to make a fuss. Indeed, when they see how attractive it can make them look, some of them may even insist on keeping it in permanently!

Faces were clean-shaven, but towards the end of the 1820s some men began growing a miniature moustache, rather like what we in later times called a 'Charlie Chaplin', and fashionable young men of this period 'sported' just a hint of a 'side-board', which, when it developed some years later, became so popular in Victorian times. Crêpe hair can be used here, or, better still, the actor's own side hair, brushed forward on to his cheeks in what is commonly known as a 'dog's-ear'.

WOMEN

During the early years of the nineteenth century—probably as a revolt against the tight-lacing of the late 1700s—women had adopted the semi-classical styles of the First Empire (1804-14), and under this influence dresses touched the floor, but were seldom wider at the base than at the top. The waists were high, with the neck-line cut round or square, with short, puffed sleeves, to which sometimes a transparent, rather full 'second sleeve' was added that extended from the elbow to the wrist, where it was caught in with a tight little frill (*see* Fig. 102).

Any ordinary nightgown pattern could be used here as the basis for such a dress, dyed rose pink, sky blue, pale green, lavender or yellow, or left white, with the colour introduced by the ribboned trimmings round the waist, neck, sleeves and hem.

All women wore flat, low-sided slippers—black, white or delicately coloured satin, or occasionally kid—with pointed toes and little ribboned bows, and, of course, without heels. Cross-over ribbons were tied round the ankles in a similar manner to our modern 'practice' ballet shoes, and the legs were either bare or covered with flesh-coloured silk stockings.

Somewhere between 1815 and 1820 the lower and slimmer waist reappeared, and skirts became fuller, often measuring as much as 7 to 9 feet in width round the hem, which by 1830 had increased to some 4 to

5 yards in circumference. Designed to fit snugly round the waist, the fullness was achieved by the insertion of 'gores' and the wearing of quilted and stiffly starched petticoats . . . and the wider the skirts, the shorter they became! In fact, hardly ever before had they been so short, sometimes up as high as the calf. And neck-lines became correspondingly lower—some of them cut much deeper that the Lord Chamberlain would countenance today—and it is said of Queen Adelaide, William IV's spouse, that she forbade her ladies to attend dinner with the family *en décolletée*. The King, on the other hand—having spent ten years of his life in the Navy, and therefore more accustomed to open spaces—refused to receive them unless they were (perhaps not quite such a 'Silly Billy' after all).

For daytime dresses, the sleeves were still short or elbow-length, and puffed at the shoulder, with the transparent second sleeve added only for evenings. If full-length sleeves were worn, they were generally tight from shoulder to wrist.

After 1830 sleeves were only tight from shoulder to elbow, after which they ballooned out, and were caught in at the wrist with a small cuff. Any surface decoration on these dresses took the form of flat or ruched bands of coloured ribbons, or wreaths and festoons of artificial flowers, with frilled flounces in horizontal tiers. All trimming, however, was only applied *below* the knees, thereby helping to give the added appearance of width (*see* Fig. 102).

For 'afternoon calls', there was a loosely fitting cloth coat with full, wide, 'bishop'-type sleeves with narrow wrist-cuffs, and they were worn open in front, and were known as the 'pelisse'. Such a coat could be made from a red- or blue-cloth dressing-gown, with the sleeves widened with vertical insertions . . . and if there happened to be a deep collar and/or quilted lapels (as is sometimes the case), so much the better. (*see* Fig. 103).

With this costume a lady carried a large, square muff, made entirely of fur (use fur fabric) or of fur and pleated silk in alternate bands.

Sometimes a silk or muslin fur-trimmed 'mantelette' (a form of scarf, which was wide over the shoulders and narrowed to long points in front) was worn for out of doors, and there was also a short, double-tiered ermine shoulder-cape, called a 'pelerine', which—since the medieval class distinction of 'being in the ermine' no longer held—could be indulged in by any Miss or Mrs. who could afford to buy one . . . and a very realistic 'ermine' effect can be obtained by sewing little 2-inch-long 'tails' of black velveteen on to white fur fabric or white plush, leaving the unattached ends hanging loose (*see* Fig. 102).

Long, narrow silk scarves, with plain or embroidered ends were draped over the shoulders and arms of many of the indoor dresses.

White or pastel-shaded silk and kid gloves with decorated tops (lace mittens for a young girl) were another important part of a woman's ensemble, and they were worn short with long sleeves, and long with short sleeves—and so devoted were the Victorian ladies to their gloves that they even wore them during meals and for playing cards!

Fans, too, were typical of the period—of lace or feathered, or of painted silk . . . but please do not use paper! These fans 'spoke' a language all their own. One flutter to the right, for instance, conveying an entirely different message (from a lady to her swain) from two flutters to the left! Fans were also very useful for making the 'whispered aside', and many a poor girl's reputation was irretrievably lost behind them!

Jewellery was plentiful, and somewhat on the heavy side, with long, dangling ear-rings, twisted chains, necklaces, bracelets, and rings . . . often worn *outside* those gloves (which, of course, was nothing new, as they did it in the sixteenth century). Carved cameos, breast-watches, and large ebony crosses (without, however, any religious significance!) rose and fell on many a dowager's bosom . . .

During the last years of the eighteenth century, and the beginning of the nineteenth, the fashion in hairdressing was for simplicity . . . though, of course, a woman's ideas often differed from a man's in the interpretation of the word! For the most part, however, the hair was worn on the short side, and arranged in a fringe of loose curls on the forehead and at the nape of the neck, with the rest of it piled on top in a 'bun', which was held there with a ribbon, or sometimes was surrounded by a circlet of artificial flowers (*see* Fig. 104).

Wigs, therefore, were obviously no longer necessary, and even an actress with short hair will find it fairly easy to dress her head as described above, and any additional curls that may be needed can be worked in either with the aid of a 'switch' or with crêpe hair—after the 'kink' has been taken out of it. (This can be done by steaming it over a boiling kettle, or by first thoroughly dampening it with hot water and then tightly winding it round some cylindrical object. By the time it is dry, it *should* have become straight . . . but please don't write to me if it isn't!)

Between 1815 and 1820 women began to part their hair demurely down the centre, with ringlets hanging on either side, and, as often as not, a woman wore a lace cap . . . especially if she had reached what became known as 'a certain age', which (alas!) was a milestone for which a spinster qualified pretty early in those days, when any unmarried girl over twenty-five was classed as an 'old maid' and considered to be more or less permanently on the matrimonial shelf!

After 1820, however, the back hair began to be piled on top of the head again, and during the next ten years or so it mounted ever higher and higher, and was sometimes augmented with sheaves, loops, wings, top-knots and masses of bobbing sausage-roll curls entwined with ribbons and gauzy flowers and jewelled pins . . . a confection that a wag of the period playfully christened 'la giraffe'!

Such a *coiffeur* would be surmounted by an equally frivolous, high-crowned, wide-brimmed straw hat, decorated with a profusion of artificial garden and field flowers, ears of corn, stalks of barley and feathered plumes, with broad silk ribbons loosely dangling or tied under the chin . . . with a curtaining veil hung all round to hide the blushes (*see* Fig. 104).

Of course, many ladies remained loyal to the earlier hairdressing styles, and I have only described this more or less 'exception' to the rule because I feel sure that any actress—given half a chance—would jump at the opportunity of 'wearing' it! If her own hair did not quite meet the demands (and to hire a wig was not practical), a great deal could be done with crêpe hair, combined with ribbons and the other floral decorations. It would, of course, be considered 'bad theatre' for more than one (comedy) character to appear like this . . . but even for just that one it would be very well worth while to make the attempt.

Figs. 102, 103 & 104. (a) Costume showing the 'double' sleeve—the 'below-the-knee decoration and the 'pelerine'. The sunshade is also typical in shape for the period (1820-25). (b) The 'pelisse'. The long, narrow fur boa is interesting to note, with the 'tail' held in the jaws of a small animal's head! Such a boa might be 9 feet long. (c & d) Hair styles 1800-1830. (e) The exaggerated hair-dressing, satirically referred to as 'á la giraffe' (circa 1830). (f) The equally absurd hat and veil that went with this style of 'hair-do'. (g) A poke bonnet (1815-1825). (h) A form of 'cap', as worn indoors by matrons and spinsters, of whatever age.

There was a large variety in the choice of hats and bonnets with straw, silk and velvet toques and turbans for evening wear. An interesting point of distinction existed between a hat and a bonnet, whereby a hat was only a hat if the width of the brim was the same all the way round, while a bonnet was only a bonnet when the brim was wider in front than at the back!

'Poke' bonnets with deep crowns and wide open brims, were also much in vogue, and were sometimes worn over a frilled muslin or lace under-cap, or a frill might be sewn round the inner edge of the crown to produce a similar effect (*see* Fig. 104).

Wars have always had an influence on women's headgear, and that 'little spot of bother over the water' with Napoleon was no exception, and many of the hats took on a distinctly military air, with high, straight crowns and narrow brims modelled on the 'shako'. Any trimming came well to the front, with one excuse being as good as another for a woman to fasten ostrich feathers to a hat . . . or to pin them in her hair . . . and, by the way, the now-defunct custom for debutantes to wear nodding plumes on their heads when making their curtsy to royalty was a relic of those days.

PART V

CHAPTER 14

Victoriana
(1837-1901)

MEN (1837-70)

Subtle changes in men's clothes were taking place all the time, and by the middle of the century the pinched-in waist and the flaring coat-tails were no longer the height of fashion, and broad, manly shoulders (often padded . . . as they still are today) and slim hips became the masculine ideal.

The frock-coat was now the habitual wear for men, with its increasing popularity largely due to the influence of the Prince Consort, who was rather partial to wearing it. In America, where this type of coat was also worn, it was even called the Prince Albert (but we in England—being more phlegmatic—named a watch-chain after him . . . and a short one at that!).

The black broadcloth frock-coat and waistcoat of the 1850s and 1860s was worn with sober, dark (sometimes grey) trousers and a white shirt with a high, stiff collar, narrow black cravat and a tall, straight-sided top-hat (called a 'stove-pipe'—and looking like one!) and was, indeed, a far cry from the feminine elegance of the 1830s.

In such a garment a man attended both business and social functions . . . weddings (including his own) . . . funerals (and how those Victorians revelled in them!) and in the end, if he was a well-loved public figure —sometimes, even, if he wasn't—he would appear posthumously in stone or bronze, still wearing his frock-coat, as the centre-piece in some park or square! There is just such a statue standing upon a high pedestal in the middle of the road where I live in London, commemorating Cobden and his Corn Laws (1868).

But in the 1860s a decided movement had begun in the direction of greater comfort in men's clothes (the inception of the lounge suit?), though of course, bright colours were still definitely barred—even a 'fancy' waistcoat being frowned upon—with nothing gayer for a coat than dark blue, grey or black. A dark coat, however, might be worn with trousers of a lighter tone—tan, fawn, grey, or even patterned with a brown-and-white check or stripes—or perhaps by a plaid mixture in lilac and blue!

This slant towards the informality of the lounge suit does not mean that the frock-coat disappeared overnight, but only that it gradually retired further and further into the background of fashion, until it was finally 'killed' during the 1914-18 War. In the meantime, Mr. Barrett, of the Wimpole Street Barretts (1846) most certainly wore one; so did John Worthing in the 'mourning sequence' in Act II of *The Importance of Being Earnest* (1895) and, of course, Old Spettigue as, with coat-tails flying, he chased Charley's Aunt around the Cloisters of St. Olde's College, Oxford (1892).

Evening-dress coats and trousers did not greatly differ from those worn today. The trousers, perhaps, were a little narrower in the leg (and still strapped under the boot), with the coat lapels a trifle higher, but it was the black or white waistcoat, occasionally made of silk, with its wide, deep oval opening, that was the real pointer to the period.

A man's suit is always difficult to design and cut—especially for the amateur tailor—and so, if one cannot come across a genuine coat of the period, the next best thing is to remodel a modern garment . . . but, of course, the more old-fashioned it is to begin with, the better the result. Evening dress, therefore, will present less difficulties, as the difference between 'then' and 'now' is not too apparent. The waist, perhaps, may need a little shaping (by taking in the seams under the arms and at the back) and the lapels raised and ironed into a new 'high' position, with another button added. A point to remember with evening-dress lapels is that at this time they were not always silk-faced, which means that one can use any plain black suit, and by readjusting the side seams of the trousers from the knee downwards their width can be narrowed, and the legs shortened by cutting away the turn-ups . . . and, by the way, don't forget to iron *out* the 'crease'!

If there is any difficulty in finding the checks or stripes for the day-time trousers, these patterns can be painted on to a pair of grey flannel bags (first tailored to the required style), using aniline water dyes, while for the plaids, how about cutting up the old school travelling-rug?

In addition to the 'stove-pipe' hat—sometimes called a 'beaver'—there were less formal head-coverings, such as felt hats with a rather high crown and a narrow brim, or a flat, low crown and a wide brim, and known as a 'shovel-hat' and worn by elderly men and devout divines of the less conventional denominations, and, of course, the black or brown bowler. Only the other evening I saw a chap wearing a rich, chocolate-brown 'billy-cock', which was a change from the usual black . . . and very smart he looked. The cap, too, was still popular with sportsmen—

and good sports! And in the late 1860s the stiff straw hat—which after 1900 became known as a 'boater'—made its bow.

Shoes with spats and boots with elastic sides or with cloth tops that buttoned up at the sides were the regular footwear for men at the beginning of the period, and front lacing did not come in until the 1860s.

Young men tried to make their feet look long and slim, and wore pointed-toed shoes that were miles too tight for them, suffering agonies in consequence (and aren't they doing exactly the same thing today?). If ever the hackneyed phrase, 'My feet are killing me', was known at this time, it would far more often have been said by the fashion-conscious young man than by a woman!

Any actor with long, naturally curly hair will find this a distinct advantage when playing a part set in this sequence of 'Victoriana', and there were several ways in which it could be dressed, any one of which would go a long way towards suggesting the right atmosphere: *(a)* rising in a 'tuft' above the forehead (Arnold Bennett wore his hair in this fashion, and more recently Herbert Morrison); *(b)* brushed straight back over the top of the head, but left long at the sides, and over the ears; *(c)* brushed forward to hang in a cow's-lick over the forehead . . . many young men do their hair like this today; *(d)* parted in the centre and brushed forwards over the ears at the sides (*see* Fig. 105).

To assist him with these various styles and give his unruly locks the necessary 'polish', a man liberally anointed his head with Rowland's Macassar Oil, which was sold in bottles labelled 'light' (golden) and 'dark' (magenta!), and it was due to what a well-oiled head could do to the back of an armchair that antimacassars owe their origin!

Sideboards that had been closely trimmed in the early 1830s, worn longer and sometimes continued right round under the chin in a sort of fringe in the 1840s, now became longer and still bushier in the 1850s, until by the 1860s they had blossomed out into what were sarcastically called 'Piccadilly weepers' (in America they were known as 'Dundrearys') and were a sort of elongated side-whisker that sometimes—in extreme examples—fell to the upper chest! Meantime, though, the chin was still clean-shaven, some of the younger men grew small Cupid's bow moustaches! Ferdy, in *Trelawney of the Wells* (Pinero), set in the middle 1860s, would not only have worn the 'weepers' *and* a moustache, but would have had a monocle as well,

Older men wore a drooping walrus moustache (awkward when drinking soup!) and sometimes a thick, long beard. Nor was it unusual to see a policeman ('Peeler') with a bull's-eye lantern (oil!) strapped to the front of his belt as he went 'full-bearded' about his nightly business.

WOMEN (1837-70)

With the 1830s short dresses were going out of fashion, and during the 1840s and 1850s, the skirt was again touching the floor, whilst in the

1860s some street skirts were so long that they swept up the dust! Moreover, the longer they got the wider and fuller they became, until some of them measured from 10 to 15 yards in circumference or, if the material was thin, as much as from 20 to 25 yards!

At first the wide dresses held their shape by means of numerous under-petticoats. I remember, when the 'hobble skirt' was in fashion, seeing a joke in *London Opinion* in which a rather 'modern little girl' of 1910 or 1911 asks, "... But, Mummy, *what was* a petticoat?" Any mother of the middle 1850s could have told her, and I cannot myself resist describing what the fashionable woman of that period had to contend with in the way of under-garments.

First came the vest, chemise and corset, and then her long drawers, with frilly lace trimming, which, although they were sometimes to be seen below the dresses of young girls, were *not* supposed to be visible with older women. But for proof that they *did* wear them, and the amusing contretemps to be experienced at a gusty street corner, one has only to turn to the comic cartoons of the day.

Over the drawers, she put on anything from six to eight petticoats—and sometimes more—one at least of which would be of flannel, with another wadded, and probably stiffened with whalebone, while the last two or three would have flounces of muslin sewn round the base, in case the top skirt should be lifted by accident (or by *design* . . . for it was a well-known fact that a fleeting glimpse of a trim ankle at the psychological moment could drive a susceptible young man to 'popping the question'!).

In the late 1850s, however, some clever person invented the crinoline support, which, with its resilient horizontal wire hoops (kept in place by a series of vertical tapes), not only held the outer skirt in the fashionable 'bell' shape, but also made it unnecessary to wear more than one or two nether petticoats—which in hot weather must have been a great relief. And, furthermore, the whole frame weighed something less than a pound!

The materials needed for making a crinoline skirt frame are as follows:

(a) Steel spring-wire—sometimes known as 'clock-wire'—which can be bought from most ironmongers or direct from a steel merchant (10 lb. weight of wire would be sufficient to make a dozen complete hoop-frames). Alternatively, the hoops can be made from lengths of thin, pliable cane, and there is now on the market a nylon wire which is similar to whalebone.

(b) About 15 yards of 1½-inch- to 2-inch-wide white cotton tape.

(c) A strip of strong white webbing, 2 inches to 2½ inches wide, to go round the waist, making allowance for the slight overlap for fastening (with two large, strong hooks and eyes).

(d) A reel of stout white cotton or thread.

(e) A packet of strong needles . . . and a thimble!

Six hoops, of varying circumference, are needed for each whole frame, thus: 55 inches (top), 66 inches, 77 inches, 88 inches, 99 inches and 110 inches (base). But the top hoop may sometimes be omitted if the dress is not required to stand out too far over the hips.

If the steel wire is used, then the ends should overlap at least 1 inch, and they *must* be securely soldered at the joining points—nor can one safely depend upon any other method.

Each completed hoop must be covered with the tape, and if it is carefully folded in half and then laid round the wire, this 'socket' can be sewn on the machine. But tack it roughly first, or you will find it will take double the time. When done, the wire hoop should be neatly and completely enclosed in a tape pocket.

When each of the hoops has been covered in this manner, next make the webbing waist-band, to the lower edge of which must be attached *nine* equal lengths of tape, each 38 inches long (which will allow a spare 1 inch at top and bottom for sewing to the waist-band and the lowest hoop, leaving 36 inches for the actual depth of the frame).

The nine pieces of tape must be sewn on at equal distances apart round the belt, but to begin with *only pin* the other ends to the base hoop, again spacing them at equal distances apart . . . each of which, naturally, will be wider than round the belt. This is a job that it is almost impossible to do without assistance, or at any rate without the help of a dressmaker's dummy, and the greatest care must be taken with the measurements.

Having got the bottom hoop in position, the other five (or four) can be attached to the vertical tapes at distances apart of about 6 inches . . . but still only *pin* them in position, as there is bound to be a good deal of alteration and readjustment required before an even balance is obtained, no matter how careful one may be . . . and you will need a great deal of patience . . . and pins!

When you are quite satisfied that the hoops are all hanging evenly, they can then be sewn in position, stitching the vertical tapes at both the top and bottom points where they meet the horizontal hoop pockets. This, I am afraid, must be done by hand, and it is as well to use the cotton double, as the strain at the joining points is pretty great. But once the hoops are safely in position it will be found that the 'frame' is light and easy to wear, gracefully holding out the top-skirt. Another point: wear a strong cotton or linen petticoat on top of the frame, between it and the dress, and another between the frame and any under-petticoats that are worn.

While, of course, the length (depth) of a 'frame' can be shortened at any time (as, for instance, for a different actress) by adjusting the vertical tapes, once the hoops have been soldered together, the width cannot be changed.

The average circumference for a hooped skirt, when completed, is about 9 feet, but in the theatre this measurement would, of course, depend upon how many of these skirts are worn in any one scene at the same time. Also the extent of the acting area must be taken into consideration, including the off-stage space required for making entrances and exits.

In one of the Cochran revues at the old Pavilion Theatre in Piccadilly Circus, because the dressing-room accommodation was so limited and the stairs and passages back-stage so narrow, the dresses worn by the chorus in a 'crinoline scene' had to be lowered from the flies for the girls to get into them on stage (and out of them again). As the girls wore very little underneath, there was never a shortage of stage-hands to assist them!

It is as well to have several dress rehearsals, as a hoop skirt needs careful management from the actress wearing it, especially when sitting down and getting up, as there is always the danger of the front of the hoop suddenly lifting up over her head!

One of the characteristics of the mid-Victorian woman was her 'gliding walk'—almost as if her feet did not touch the floor at all! This can best be achieved by taking very quick, short, little steps without lifting the feet from the ground, and, of course, without making a sound, and, as Victorian slippers had no heels, the feet will slide quite easily. It may need a bit of practice, however, but once 'the walk' has been mastered it is extraordinarily effective.

The part of Wilson, Elizabeth Barrett's ever-faithful servant and friend, in the Hollywood film version of *The Barretts of Wimpole Street* (Rudolph Besier) was played by the English actress, Una O'Connor, who had this 'slide' to perfection, and it was a sheer joy to watch her as in her full black dress she positively 'floated' about the room, where her mistress (played by the lovely Norma Shearer) lay trying to make up her mind—Should she? Shouldn't she?—to run away with the handsome Robert Browning (Fredric March).

A good deal of the fullness in the sleeves had now disappeared, and for a few years they became tight from shoulder to wrist, finishing in a turned-back cuff. But with the middle 1850s the 'bell' sleeve returned, becoming wider and wider to the end of the period.

For evening dresses, however, the sleeves remained short and puffed, or, if they were long, they were made of lace or gauze . . . but just as often there were no sleeves at all, with the upper-arm being partly covered by the 'bertha', or fichu, at the top of the bodice, with the then fashionable 'bottle-shaped neck' rising about it (*see* Fig. 106).

During the 1840s the colours worn by fashionable women for their day dresses were the softer pastel shades of grey, lilac, blue, green and off-white, and a shot-silk mixture. For evening wear, the dresses were trimmed with festoons and wreaths and bunches of gauze, silk or velvet flowers. Later, in the 1850s and early 1860s, the deeper and more serviceable colour schemes came into vogue—dark blues, reds, greens and browns, and sometimes all of them combined together in a plaid or check, with black velvet being specially popular for evening dresses.

In 1858 an inventor named Sir H. W. Perkin discovered aniline dye

—royal blue, emerald green, magenta and cerise (very popular!), and immediately it became available for women's clothes it revolutionized the existing colour combinations, so that often the extremes of dark and light, or two or more of the brighter colours, were startlingly juxtapositioned in one costume, which (mercifully!) could be toned down by an overdraping of black or white net. So wide did the wearing of bright colours now become that even brides, under their tulle veils, were not always dressed in white!

It was no unusual sight in those days to see sailors with pierced ear-lobes (even if they didn't actually wear rings in their ears, though many of them did) and, as naval men have always been noted for their far-sightedness, a current superstition arose that it was this habit that

Fig. 106. The 'bertha' neck line. Such a dress might have been worn by 'La Dame aux Camélias' ('Camille').

warded off blindness, and as the new hair styles left women's ears exposed, a perfect mania for 'pierced ears for women' resulted, and quite young girls—and even babies—wore little plain gold rings through their ears . . . but whether or not their sight was improved is something about which I should not like to commit myself!

By the year 1840 the elaborate hair styles had gone out of fashion, and a high top-knot was once more placed at the back of the head, with the front hair parted down the middle and drawn back to show the forehead. Gradually this top-knot sank lower and lower, until by the mid-1850s it had reached the nape of the neck, where it was often enclosed in a black, or coloured, chignon (or hair-net), with the side hair arranged over the ears in little bunches of curls, which sometimes followed all the way round to the back, in place of the knot, while some older women dressed the side hair over 'pads' to give an effect of greater width (*see* Fig. 107).

For evening wear this chignon was often made of gold or silver thread, or of beaded strands, like a 'Juliet cap', or ornamented with artificial flowers and jewels, *à la* Renaissance. Such nets and jewels, beads, sequins and flowers, etc., can be found at most stores.

Rowland's Macassar Oil was also much used by women for dressing their hair, and I remember my grandmother, who had started life with rich dark tresses, always used it. Of course, she was white-haired by the time I caught up with her, but she still continued to use the 'dark' brand (magenta) which streaked her hair, making her look a little like Madame Defarge, after a good day at La Guillotine!

Occasionally part of the front hair at each side was tightly plaited, and worn as an open ring round the ears—a style much favoured by the young Queen Victoria (1837), as may be seen from her early portraits and on the seated statue outside Kensington Palace (sculptured many years later by her daughter). The youthful heroine in the play *Marigold* (Harker and Pryor) wore her hair like this in imitation of the Queen, whom she so much admired and wished to see (*see* Fig. 107).

Many young girls still wore their hair with the centre parting and a series of short ringlets all the way round the head, with a snood (a ribbon fillet) tied in a bow on the top or at the side over one ear. Some of the characters who might dress their hair like this would be Lady Babbie in Barrie's *The Little Minister* (1840), Jane Eyre (Charlotte Brontë) and Kathy in the earlier scenes of *Wuthering Heights* (Emily Brontë), both written in 1847. and Rose Sibley in Act I (in 1860) of *Milestones* (Arnold Bennett).

For going to evening parties and dances, young girls wore shaped silk or lace scarves over their hair—broad on the top of the head and narrowing down into loosely-hanging lappets. Their more mature chaperons swathed their heads in black or white lace mantillas . . . with knitted head-scarves or shawls for the really elderly.

Lace caps were still worn by the 'unmarriageable daughters', and other 'middle-aged matrons' in the region of twenty-five to thirty years old, and even young brides occasionally wore them! Widows—whatever their age—indulged themselves in black bonnets glittering with jet and submerged by thick black veils, bordered with crêpe.

Jet you may have to beg for . . . but there *are* many charming elderly ladies who have quantities of it stored away . . . if you are clever enough to persuade them to part with it! As a matter of fact, though, I think I have seen it for sale in the 'hat-trimming' section in some of the larger stores.

Hats were mostly made of straw trimmed with flowers and a veil, and often tied under the chin with a broad ribbon. Brims became wider, framing the face, and the crowns either high or shallow, according to the hair style. But with the bigger and lower chignons the hats became smaller and worn further back on the head—sometimes with no back brim at all.

Figs. 105 & 107. Hair styles (Men): (a) young man, circa 1830; (b) an older man, about the same date (I wonder what Professor Jimmy Edwards would think of this 'handle-bar'?); (c) the more military type of moustache, same period; (d) 'the Piccadilly weeper', as favoured by the dandies (1865).
Hair styles (Women): (e) the hair-style, circa 1820; (f, g & h) 'the ring-round-the-ear' fashion—the young Queen Victoria wore her hair like this at her Coronation in 1838; (i) hair style for a young woman at a party (1840); (j) the 'bun', enclosed in a chignon (1840)—Princess Margaret wore something like this at her wedding to Mr. Armstrong-Jones; (k) hair style and cap (1860).

I must just mention one characteristic hat worn by the sportswoman when riding to hounds. This was as near a thing to a man's top-hat as made no difference, and was wound round with a spotted veil which tightly enclosed her face and blew out at the back like a cloud of smoke!

When travelling, ladies often carried their caps or bonnets in small, circular boxes—just like those so many young girls carry today (hoping, so I am told, that they will be mistaken for society models), though I do not think that what they have inside is caps! These 'band-boxes', as they were called—and still are today—were so named because originally they were used by men for packing their 'bands' (or collars).

Most 'crinoline period' plays can be entirely costumed with cottons or silk substitutes, which often look far more effective under stage lighting than real silk . . . besides being not half as expensive. Tarlatan, too, in black, white and most other colours, will look every bit as ornamental as lace for flounces, frills, trimmings, etc., while you will remember that the effect of velvet (so popular at this time) can be 'faked' by unevenly stippling dyed flannel with anilines.

(1870–90)

MEN

A development from the frock-coat was the 'cut-away' or swallow-tail morning coat, made from black broadcloth, with the lapels (still high) bound round with braid, worn with rather narrow, light-toned (grey) trousers—no 'turn-ups'—a tall hat, and black boots. This costume soon became the fashionable wear for all special daytime occasions, such as garden parties, the Royal Enclosure, and Private View Day at the Academy.

A similar coat, but worn for less formal functions—like going to church with the family—was made from a rougher material and often in a lighter colour (*see* Fig. 108).

Morning dress is still *de rigeur* if you should happen to be invited by the Queen to take tea at Buckingham Palace, but the style nowadays is slightly different, and the smartly cut black coat is worn with grey and black striped trousers, a pearl-grey waistcoat, a black tie, black boots and a shiny silk hat . . . and if none of these things happen to be in your wardrobe, well, there is always Moss Bros.

The lounge suit, first seen in the 1850s, was now worn for most ordinary occasions. The long-waisted, sack-like coat had straight front points (rounded edges came in later) and rather short, tight sleeves, showing shirt cuffs, and the high lapels made it necessary to use three or four buttons to fasten up the coat.

There were no twin slits at the back, as with our modern hacking jackets—indeed, there was no slit at all! Tweed and blue serge (a material seldom seen amongst the mixtures and neat pin-stripes in a tailor's window today) were most commonly used for these informal 'three-piece' suits, that included a high-cut waistcoat (nothing fancy!) and fairly loosely fitting trousers.

During Queen Victoria's long reign, styles in trousers had plenty of time for continuous change. In the 1840s they were fuller at the top than at the foot (peg-tops). By the 1850s they were exactly the reverse (bell-bottoms). In the 1860s and 1870s they were rather tight and short (to the ankle), and by the 1880s they were both fuller and longer and touched the instep. Throughout the period—and especially around the 1860s—stripes, large checks and plaid patterns were very popular, and were even allowed with the black cut-away coats! Turn-ups were seldom seen, and creases never.

Collars now at last became lower, with many of them the turn-down and 'wing' style (giving poor Adam's apple a chance . . .) though they were still stiffly starched. Some of the older men still clung to the high, upright collars, and so deserved the discomfort they must have had to endure in consequence. Ties, too, began to display a greater variety, both in materials . . . and colour.

Evening dress clothes had hardly altered at all, though here and there one might still come across a tail-coat being worn in the daytime, which is a costume production note worth remembering.

These mid-Victorians rather prided themselves that they had invented the check tweed knickerbocker, thought actually it was only a revival ol the knee-breeches of the 1800s . . . in a different material! These breeches came to just below the knee, where they were fastened with a button or short strap and buckle, and were often worn with a belted Norfolk jacket, dark woollen stockings (but no fancy turn-down tops or flashes) and black high-buttoned boots, with white gaiter-like spats.

The black top-hat and black or brown bowler still held pride of place, but there was also a white version of the bowler for coaching parties, race-meetings, etc. (paint a black bowler with whitewash or Ceilingite.)

For official afternoon functions—launching a battleship or laying a foundation stone—men wore a light-toned, cloth-covered top-hat, and there is a brand of pastel drawing-paper that has a slight surface 'nap' which is sold by most art shops in greys—also in tans and fawns—and if the paper is cut and neatly fitted round an old top-hat it will give exactly the right effect . . . or, of course, one can start from scratch and make the whole hat out of cardboard, and then cover it as described above.

The Victorians believed that the way to keep a top-hat shiny and sleek was to anoint it with frequent applications of stout, which was all very well in cold weather, but became a positive fly-trap in the summer! In Frith's famous picture, 'Derby Day', several of the men are depicted with green veils draping their top-hats in an effort to keep the flies at bay!

Other hats were the felt (slouch), the shallow-crowned straw (first seen in the 1860s), the tam-o'-shanter (for a cold, brisk walk along Brighton front) and a check cloth affair, like an inverted pudding basin with an adjustable brim (for up or down) and, of course, common or garden caps, of which the most amusing was the 'fore-and-aft', which, as the name suggests, had a peak both front and back and 'ear-flaps' that were tied together on top of the head with a little black bow, so that they could be let down in chilly weather and tied under the chin . . . which, I must admit, sounds most chic! This sort of cap was very popular with cross-Channel trippers, and was thought by the French to be typical of *ze mad Anglais*!

By the 1870s shorter hair was on its way, but men had not quite finished with their hirsute experiments, and sometimes, when the hair was parted in the centre, the parting extended all the way from forehead to nape of neck, with the ends of the front hair heavily greased and twisted up into two little 'horns' over the temples. It could also be parted down the back of the head only, and then brushed forwards over the ears, and worn with a small version of the Piccadilly weeper, which, however, began steadily to go out of fashion around the late 1870s.

Faces were not yet completely clean-shaven, and the sideboard was still a popular adornment, and occasionally it broadened out at the base and extended over the lower cheek in what was called a 'mutton-chop' whisker . . . a style much favoured on the stage by the 'old family solicitor' and characters of that sort.

Beards were often worn alone—without a moustache—especially the 'under-the-chin' fringe beard. Other types were the pointed and the full, which were worn with moustaches by the older men, while some of the younger ones went in for a long, droopy moustache without a beard. By the end of the 1880s clean-shaven faces once more became the general fashion (*see* Fig. 108).

Fig. 108. (a) Young man in 'cut-away' coat (1888) and check trousers; (b) the frock coat of the same period; (c) comedy character hair and moustache (1888), suitable for a 'retired major'; (d) mutton chop side-whiskers (continuing under chin) 1880 period, suitable for 'old family retainer'; (e) the more 'romantic-poetic' hair style, popular in the '80s—here the 'mutton-chop' fringe continues round the chin; (f) the shorter variety of the 'Piccadilly weeper' side-whisker (in fashion from 1865-1885); (g) comedy bald head and full beard and moustache (1883).

WOMEN (1870-90)

During the previous twenty odd years, the circumference at the base of the crinoline had steadily become wider and wider until—much to the sly joy of the cartoonists—women looked for all the world like animated tea-cosies!

With the second half of the 1860s, however, the overall shape had gradually begun to change, with the fullness in front being pushed to the rear and concentrated into a 'bustle', and some six years later the charming hooped skirt (which the fashion designers had prophesied would last for ever) had completely disappeared!

While the bustle was still in its early stages, it was designed as part of the costume, in the same material, colour and pattern as the rest of the dress. 'Gores' were inserted to obtain the necessary fullness in front, with the rest of the skirt pulled backwards and gathered into wide folds that fell in a graceful cascade, ending in a small train, which was even worn in the streets (*see* Fig. 109).

Around 1875 the bustle went temporarily out of fashion, and it almost looked as if the slim silhouette seen at the beginning of the century might return. The fullness at the back became little more than a large bow, which 'sank' lower and lower down the figure until it came to rest just below the back of the knees, with a pleated fullness spreading from there to the floor. In some instances the bow even sank as far as the backs of the ankles, with the long ends trailing out like a sort of fish-tail, making the wearer look like Hans Andersen's Little Mermaid! It would be fun to dress at least one (c[illegible]edy) character in this style if the opportunity presented itself (*see* Fig. 109).

In the 1880s, however, the bustle suddenly returned to popular favour, and by 1885 it was at its height (worst!), so that even little girls wore them. But there was worse in store for little boys! Some years previously a Manchester-born woman had emigrated to the United States to seek her fortune, where in 1886, as Mrs. Frances Hodgson Burnett, she wrote *Little Lord Fauntleroy*, whose golden ringlets, lace collar and cuffs, black velvet knickerbocker suit, red sash and stockings and black shoes with silver buckles, became the garb in which countless misguided fond mammas—both in America and England—made countless unfortunate little boys wish they'd never been born!

That part of the dress that formed the later bustle now became entirely different from the rest of the costume, and was usually arranged in a 'swag' fold in front—rather like a looped-up apron—with the sides pulled up towards the waist, and then falling at the back . . . no longer in a gentle cascade, but in a veritable Niagara of frills, flounces and sashes (*see* Fig. 109).

Since the early days of the century what had gone on below a woman's waist-line had been nobody's business but her own. With the return of the tight corset (1870-80), her hips once more became a matter for serious consideration, with the result that less than 100 years after she had kicked off her spindle, red-heeled Georgian shoes and thrown her stays out of the window, it began to look as if her one desire was as closely as possible to resemble the Arabian camel!

And what a frightening contraption the Victorian lady's corset was! Made of steel and whalebone, it closely confined her ribs and tummy, curving outwards into a sweep over her hips. High in front, it pushed up her breast into an ample bosom, making her look like Mae West in *Diamond Lil*' . . . and if Nature had been niggardly with her gifts there was always the 'little woman round the corner', who could be depended upon to 'do' something materially about it. No frills, no trimmings adorned her bust; just a fine, smooth, unwrinkled parabola, as like as not buttoned down the front from neck to waist, and sometimes so tightly that it was impossible for Madam to do more than smile—even at the wittiest epigram—for fear of sending her buttons flying . . . as, years earlier, they had flown every time young master Copperfield reminded old Peggotty that 'Barkis was willin' '!

For daytime dresses the bustle was usually confined to a reasonable size, and kept more or less under control, with the waist-line coming to a sharp point in front, and a high neck and tight, long sleeves without much shoulder fullness.

For evening wear, however, no pains were spared to make women's clothes as elaborate as possible, and they were decorated with frills, flounces, ruchings, flowered garlands, wreaths, festoons, ribbons tied in enormous bows, and wide, fringed sash-ends that appeared from goodness only knew where . . . in other words, everything—*including* the kitchen stove! Such costumes had no sleeves to speak of, but just narrow, decorated bands that went over the shoulders, supporting the deep, round *décolletée*.

At first it may seem an insuperable proposition to create costumes like these for amateur productions, but they will not appear so frightening when one remembers that it is the '*effect* of bulk' rather than how it is attained that is important, and, provided one can find the materials, and sufficient of them, it does not very much matter if none of them matches or is 'of a piece' with anything else. But, of course, a costume such as that described above would only be worn by an ultra-fashionable hostess giving a ball or a reception, and the majority of women had to content themselves with the mean, rather than with the extreme!

So much 'fashion' naturally needed some form of support underneath, and for this purpose there was what was called a 'bustle frame'—something like the crinoline frame, only flat in front, with the rounded curve only at the back—and sometimes one can still find one of these old bustle frames in some obscure little second-hand clothes shop. And this, I feel, is the cue for some bright soul to pop up with the suggestion that surely the simplest way out of the difficulty would be to attach a sofa cushion or a pillow at the back, and leave it at that! And, naturally, that *is* what I am sure has often been done—at any rate on the stage—but it was just that I thought I should mention the correct procedure first!

It is important, however, to bear in mind that whatever kind of support is used for a bustle must be flexible and not too solid or static, and a better plan would be to use two or three ordinary mattress or arm-chair springs (don't laugh—I mean this) fastened to an under-belt, so that they hang down at the back of the waist, with the bustle material draped over them. But, don't forget to bind the metal spirals with tape, or there may be rather a peculiar sound when Madam sits down!

Before 1890, the bustle had had its day, but none the less it was still considered necessary to partially assist Nature by wearing *something* at the back, and this 'something' took the form of a small pad stuffed with horsehair and called (for pity's sake) a 'figure-improver' . . . and the nearest thing I can suggest is to hang a church hassock at the back, and it is even conveniently provided with a brass ring!

By 1870 the middle parting was no longer considered modish, and women began to brush their hair straight back, with the ears exposed, but leaving a softening fringe on the forehead. The heavy chignon of the middle 1860s was now moved up again and arranged as a bun, placed rather far back on the top of the head. For formal evening occasions a couple of corkscrew curls ('love-locks') often lay at the side of the neck.

The centre parting, however, soon came back, with the top-knot loosened into a mass of curls and ringlets, adorned with ribbons and flowers—even bunches of artificial grapes, complete with leaves and tendrils. Not that this fashion lasted very long either, and with the 1880s women's hair became much shorter and more closely confined to the shape of the head, with a tightly curled forehead fringe and any surplus hair made into a flat coil, which was pinned at the nape of the neck.

A style particularly associated with Queen Alexandra—who set the fashions in smart society while she was still Princess of Wales—was to build up the hair in a mass of tight, flat little curls, in shape and appearance rather like a domed astrakhan cap. Many ladies followed her royal example, amongst them Princess May of Teck (later H.M. Queen Mary), but whether she adopted this style in a spirit of loyalty to her mother-in-law or from personal preference, who can say? At any rate, both ladies retained the mode until their deaths . . . and despite our modern 'tulip' and 'urchin' cuts, there is still many a dowager in the Royal Borough of Kensington who has never wavered in her allegiance.

To make a wig in this style could easily be done by gently teasing out crêpe hair, which has just exactly the right curly effect needed, and arranging it over a dome-shaped foundation (wire) of the right colour (*see* Fig. 110).

With these high, close-fitting hair styles, the wearing of straw sailor hats became very popular, while some of the Royal Family—ever lovers of the sea—demonstrated that it was possible for a woman to wear a man's yachting cap and still look feminine! (*see* Fig. 110).

Towards the end of the period even greater simplicity became the fashion in hairdressing, with the bun on top and the rest of the hair drawn up all round the head—not too tightly and rather higher in front than at the back—which sometimes necessitated the wearing of

Figs. 109 & 110. (a) An early example of the bustle; (b) a more advanced style; (c) the bustle, as worn by little girls; (d) the 'fish-tail'; (e) the 'Queen Alexandra' hair style; (f) the yachting cap, as popularised by Royalty; (g) a bonnet, period 1888; (h) diagram of the 'boater' straw hat, as worn by both men and women.

a circular, sausage-roll pad, with the hair brushed over it and held in place with little, curved combs. The ears were still uncovered, but the fringe had disappeared, leaving just a couple or so hair tendrils curling in the centre of the forehead and 'escaping' at the nape of the neck . . . such innocent little wisps and yet—according to Mrs. Humphrey Ward —able to 'twine themselves around a strong man's heartstrings' (and we all know what happens then !).

While the hair was dressed in this manner, hats and bonnets were small and tilted forward over the forehead, with a draped veil hanging down behind. An impressive collection of flowers, foliage, ribbons, feathers and bows clustered round the brim, often as much under it as on top.

You may remember there was a definition that decided the difference between a hat and a bonnet. Well, there was also a rule that governed the actual wearing of a hat or a bonnet. Before a girl 'came out', she was only allowed to wear a hat, but once she had been 'launched' into society or was safely married (which wasn't always the same thing!) she could with perfect propriety don a bonnet when 'leaving cards' or going to church!

Many of the hats worn at this period can still be seen in some of the museums, and there is one that particularly caught my fancy, that had a brightly-hued bird attached to a flexible wire, whereby it continually appeared to hover over a nest (fixed to the brim) in which there were three or four realistic-looking eggs!

Married women still wore caps in the house, but the younger generation (including the spinsters) was beginning to rebel against them. Widows still mourned the dear departed in black bonnets edged with white, and weighed down with long crêpe veils.

During the late 1870s, Oscar Wilde founded the Cult of the Aesthetic, one of its objects being to shock the middle classes . . . in which he was completely successful.

At select little gatherings the *jeunesse dorée* (stifling a polite yawn) breathlessly applauded the latest aestheticism of that prince of aesthetes as, sheltering behind a green carnation, he whispered his fiendishly clever epigrams.

As usually happens with a new movement, there was no lack of proselytes among the highbrow and the artistic, and soulful young women—throwing discretion . . . and their dressmaker's advice . . . to the winds—draped themselves in what (to be kind) can only be called 'the aesthetic costume', which was a woollen or art canvas, sack-like dress, that hung loosely round the body without any waist-line (looking rather like a long smock or nightgown), hand-embroidered with large, aesthetic-looking bright yellow flowers on a peacock blue, moss green or Venetian red ground!

The male acolytes went in for long hair and tight waists, and had frills on their shirt-fronts, and as they walked through the Burlington Arcade or gracefully posed on a street corner, they carried a single lily in a milk-white hand . . . lost in horticultural contemplation!

Gilbert and Sullivan deliciously satirized these cultural devotees in 'The Poetic Hero' and the chorus of 'Love-sick Maidens' in *Patience* (1881).

By the mid-1880s the public had had enough of this nonsense, and Wilde—who had yet to make his name as an author and playwright—was forced to accept the editorship of *The Woman's World*! By 1895, however, with two of his plays running concurrently in the West End he stood supreme in the London theatre . . . with all the pride that is said to proceed a fall.

CHAPTER 15

The Naughty Nineties and the not so much better 1900s

I have often wondered why they called the nineties 'naughty', because during the last decade of the nineteenth century there dawned a new and exciting era in the fields of industry, education, politics, literature, art, music and—most important for those interested in the treatre—drama.

Just imagine living in England at a time when Oscar Wilde was writing those imperishable comedies (1892-5) and to be able to go to the theatre and laugh at the (then) unheard-of absurdity, in Pinero's farce, *The Amazons*, of a lady of title bringing up her three daughters to wear trousers!

(1890 – 1914)

MEN

There was no very great change in men's clothes from the 1880s to the 1890s. Perhaps their garments became more square-shouldered in outline and a little looser in construction . . . but, looking back from the easy informality of our present times, they appear dreadfully tight and uncomfortable.

Professional men (lawyers, doctors, schoolmasters, M.P.s, etc.) still clung to that badge of urban respectability, the frock-coat and top-hat, but otherwise the three-piece lounge suit (blue serge or tweed) still did service for most ordinary business or social occasions—even attending the funeral of a conveniently deceased aunt or grandmother (and how remarkable it was to find how many of these old ladies had expressed a wish to be interred near a popular race-course!).

For the quiet little picnic with his 'young lady', or on a summer day's outing 'upriver with the boys', a young man might wear his lounge suit coat with white flannel trousers, a white shirt (with stiff collar and a black tie) and sometimes a V-necked pullover—hitherto only seen on the playing fields—in place of his waistcoat. On his feet would be brown leather shoes with white suède tops, but still the inevitable black woollen socks (to wear silk savoured of something 'not quaite naice, deah boy' . . . like wanting a daily bath or living alone in a flat!).

The 'young blood', 'masher' or 'swell' might, however, risk wearing a coloured 'clock' (a thin, vertical silk line, embroidered in purple, yellow or sometimes in white, that started near the top of the sock and ended in an 'arrowhead' on the ankle), which he would nonchalantly display every time he hitched up his trouser knees, preparatory to sitting down.

The trousers were still a little on the short side and rather tight, but by 1910 they were not only wider, but had creases down both front and back, and a 'turn-up' . . . with the socks in wool, cotton—yes, *and* silk—in the gayest of colours and patterns. And this is how the juvenile heroes of musical comedy—and the chorus gents behind them—would be dressed in those almost indespensable 'garden party' and 'up the river at Henley' scenes.

For walkin' or cyclin', fishin' or golfin', the knickerbocker suit—which in the 1860s had been the privilege of the aristocrat—now became the symbol of the happy-go-lucky sportin' middle class, in direct contrast to the betrousered dignity of the duchess' drawing-room on her 'At Home' afternoon ('Evangeline, press the deah Rector to another muffin!').

Such a knickerbocker outfit could be adapted from any modern check suit, with the trouser legs cut short and shaped to fasten below the knee with buckle and strap. The cut-off material can then be used to make the Norfolk jacket belt, and the 'fore-and-aft' cap that was often worn with it. There was also the narrow-brimmed check hat, types of which can now be seen in many smart hatters' windows since Rex Harrison recently revived the fashion by wearing one in *My Fair Lady*.

Most of the everyday ties were of black knitted silk, the same narrow width all the way down, and they often became so tightly knotted that it was almost impossible to *un*tie them! And, by the way, you can get a similar tie today from most men's shops if you ask for a 'slim jim' . . . and thus the roundabout of fashion keeps turning.

Shoes were generally black—occasionally brown—and rather pointed, and were often worn with white or pale grey one-piece spats, held under the instep with a strap. There was also a patent leather boot with a white or buff kid, or cloth top that buttoned up on the side or was laced across the front—but not through eyelets, but round metal 'hooks'. I have seen boots like these offered for sale on the street-market stalls in the Portobello Road behind Notting Hill.

With the first breath of spring—and apparently in those days one could depend upon the order of the seasons, with no weather forecasts to mislead one!—out came the stiff, low-crowned, wide-brimmed straw hats . . . and what sport the frolic wind made with them, merrily bowling them down the street at several miles an hour . . . to end ignominiously under the wheels of a hansom cab! To circumvent the breathless indignity of giving them chase, some men attached a metal clip to the rim of the hat, fixed at one end of a thin black cord, fastening the other end through the button-hole of their coat—but, of course, that didn't stop the hat from blowing off!

Nowadays it seems that only schoolboys wear straw hats, but they can quite easily be made for the stage from stiff cardboard. Cut a 2½-inch-wide strip for the rise of the crown—length according to the circumference of the head—and an oval-shaped piece for the top. The width of the brim should be from 4½ inches to 5 inches—and don't forget to cut the typical 'dog-toothing' round the outer edge.

The three parts should be joined together on the inside with lengths of glued surgical bandage, which is stronger than paper, and when dry the whole hat is painted over with a very pale yellow, glossy enamel. A ribbed-silk hat-band must be added, in pink, blue or with a vari-coloured stripe, with a large flat bow on the left-hand side (*see* Fig. 110).

Algernon Montcrieff would wear just such a hat in Acts II and III of *The Importance of Being Earnest.*

Around 1910 the Panama hat was introduced from America. It was made of fine, soft straw, but as it was rather expensive—and looked vaguely 'foreign'—it was never widely worn in England.

In the 1890s few smart men attended a dinner or a dance or escorted a lady to the theatre in anything less than their 'full regimentals' (i.e., tails, white waistcoat and tie and collapsible opera-hat . . . and quite possibly a cloak). *Fin de siècle,* however, saw the last of the dandies, and Oscar Wilde gives us an amusing and instructive description of one of them in the character of young Lord Goring at the beginning of Act III of *An Ideal Husband*:

'*Enter Lord Goring in evening-dress, with a button-hole. He is wearing a silk hat and an Inverness cape. White-gloved, he carries a Louis Seize cane. His are all the delicate fopperies of fashion.*' (His opening speeches are to his Butler, Phipps.)

"Got my second button-hole for me, Phipps?" he asks, and the Butler presents him with a new one on a silver salver.

"I am the only person of the smallest importance in London at present who wears a button-hole," he continues, studying his reflection in the mirror.

"Don't think I quite like this button-hole, Phipps. Makes me look too old. For the future, a more trivial button-hole on Thursday evenings!"

Today concession to appearances is no longer considered so essential (more's the pity!), and on a warm night you will see men sitting in the stalls at the theatre in their shirt-sleeves, and reading the evening newspaper! Before the First World War, however, many of the London theatres barred patrons from the boxes, stalls and dress circle unless they were in evening dress.

With the arrival of the dinner-jacket suit (worn with patent leather pumps decorated with a large flat bow in black ribbed silk ribbon) evening dress became less formal. In America they called it a 'tuxedo'—they still do—but although in the U.S.A. the trousers are of black cloth, the coat today can be made from all sorts of materials and in a variety of colours—white being currently the most popular. But in the 'land of the free' the waiters wear similar white jackets, which sometimes gives rise to amusing situations, in which the waiter is mistaken for the guest. In England, where, of course, the waiters are far more immaculately betailed than the people who hire them, the position is slightly different, and it is often the host who finds himself being surreptitiously tipped by a gate-crashing guest!

The collars of the Victorian and early Edwardian men were one of the distinguishing features of their costume, and almost more than anything else they stamped a man in his period . . . certainly more than the cut of his clothes, which towards the close of the century hardly differed from those of our own day—especially in view of the modern trend (and not only with the men) towards the fashions and foibles of our great-grandparents.

These collars were *(a)* high and straight up under the chin, *(b)* the same as *(a)*, but with the points slightly bent forward, though not enough to qualify for our modern 'butterfly', and *(c)* double (turned-down) but still a good 3 inches high. Of these *(a)* was the most commonly worn, and summer or winter helped the Englishman to 'keep his chin up'—though they must have felt damned uncomfortable!

But even when, from about 1900, the turn-down collar began to be more widely worn, the neck always seemed too big or the collar too tight, and men went about with permanent 'green marks' where the front- and back-studs had pressed! Their only relief came when wearing the evening dress wing collar, which at last gave the Adam's apple a breather!

The collars, cuffs and fronts of their dress shirts—'boiled shirts', as they were called—were so heavily starched that they felt like armour-plating, and some men (to save on their laundry bills) wore separate fronts (known as 'dickies'), which had an awful trick of popping out from the waistcoat and hitting a man under the chin! Cuffs, too, could be worn unattached, and these 'separates' soon developed into a stock joke for comic stage butlers and the *nouveau riche*, and for the 'dickie' to break loose or a man to 'shoot his cuffs' could always be safely played for a laugh.

There is a shop at the corner of Old Compton Street and Frith Street, Soho, that specializes in 'dickies', loose cuffs and high collars, etc., or, of course, they can be cut out from strong bleached muslin or linen and then starched in the ordinary way, but be advised, and make a paper pattern first, especially with the collar, so as to be sure of size and fit (and don't forget to cut the stud-holes).

In the 1890s men began cutting their hair much shorter, and most of them parted it more to one side than down the middle, and, together with a clean-shaven face, this style was considered 'quite the thing' from the late 1890s onwards. There were a few of the ultra-smart set who experimented with brushing their hair straight back from the forehead without any parting, and this had become the fashion by the time I first took an interest in looking into a mirror!

A small moustache with 'waxed' turned-up ends—*à la* Kaiser Wilhelm—was sometimes worn, though the more conventional among men still favoured the bushy 'walrus'. 'Sideboards' were still to be seen occasionally on the very young, and 'mutton-chops' on the very much older. King Edward VII's neatly trimmed beard was very popular with society, and, of course, there was also the pointed chin-beard (called the 'Van Dyke') amongst the bohemian set frequenting the old Café Royal.

WOMEN (1890-1914)

The last decade of the nineteenth century was particularly noted for the beauty of its women, and probably the most notable and the most beautiful of them all was the actress Mrs. Langtry, the 'Jersey Lily'.

Shops were proud to be allowed to display her photograph in their windows, and people in Hyde Park used to jump up on those little green chairs to watch her driving past. The reputation of her beauty was international, though sometimes the tribute paid to it was a little unusual! For instance, in Egypt, the dragomen were in the habit of christening their favourite donkey 'The Lily Langtry'!

With the exit of the bustle, one might have thought that women would be content to return to the simpler, more comfortable way of dressing . . . but, not a bit of it . . . and the 1890s are mainly associated in memory with the built-out shoulders, enormous balloon sleeves, tiny waist, and pyramid-shaped skirt . . . in short, the 'hour-glass' figure.

Naturally, this was not the achievement of a passing moment, and for a time at any rate the skirts continued plain and undraped, 'gored' to give the straight-front line, and gathered over a small 'improver' at the back. Gradually, however, the base width of the skirt widened again, just as it had widened into the crinoline of the 1850s, until by the mid-1890s the skirt was back at a 9-yard-wide circumference (and with a long-trained evening gown even wider!). But, unlike the crinoline, the material from which it was made did not fall in soft, graceful folds, and the dress was chiefly characterized by its stiff outline, almost as if it had been 'cast' in metal.

To present this sculptured, 'organ-pipe' effect, both back and front of the skirt must be stiffly wadded and lined (with felt?), while the extra width needed to give the required outward sweep of the material means that it must be generously pleated into the waistband most of the way round (*see* Fig. 111).

Creating the right silhouette is very important—those wide shoulders, the ample bust, the 18-inch, wasp-like waist, the rounded hips and gently curving tummy—but what are you to do if you are dealing with a modern actress who doesn't happen to possess these late-Victorian attributes? Can you reasonably expect her to lace and corset herself so tightly that in the end she has not even enough breath left to bid you 'Good evening'? The smallness of the waist, however, can be suggested by a clever building up of her bust and hips with layers of cotton-wadding . . . adding a figure-improving pad at the back and—if she isn't too touchy—by tactfully padding her tummy in front . . . and leaving the rest to the petticoats!

In the latter half of the 1890s a change began to take place, and though the shoulders, bust, waist, hips and tummy remained unaltered, the skirt lost a lot of its carved stiffness and followed more closely the lines of the figure to the knees, spreading out from there in soft folds that fell to the ground (*see* Fig. 111).

With the late Victorians the shape and style of the sleeves changed almost yearly. To begin with (1890) the shoulders were high and pointed, with the sleeves long and tight to the wrist (elbow-length, with a little frilly edge, were only worn with evening dresses). By 1892 the tops had developed into shoulder-puffs, and this type of sleeve became known as the 'leg-of-mutton' (which it rather resembled), and by 1896 the fullness had so much increased in size as to make the tops of the sleeves look like veritable balloons—often 3 yards round!

A stiff lining was not always practical or a sufficient support to ensure the correct stance, and, as may be imagined, all sorts of dodges had to be employed to give the sleeves the desired wide effect. One way to present the earlier upstanding tops to the shoulders would be to cut out crescent shapes in thick felt, with a central width of from 4 inches to 6 inches and a point-to-point length measuring about twice the distance round the upper arm-hole, pleating them until they fitted neatly round the top of the arms, where they would be attached to an undergarment in an upright, fan-like position under the outer sleeve (*see* Fig. 111).

The largest sleeves of all could be supported by a separate lining that had been further reinforced with whalebone or wire hoops of varying circumference.

Another means that was used to suggest the typical broad-shoulder effect was a double puff at the tops of the sleeves, or by wearing a wide-caped collar on the blouse or jacket—or a series of such collars—and I have been assured by someone who remembers wearing them herself that many girls in the 1890s resorted to 'sleeve-bustles', to coin a word, made from a spiral of thin pliable wire arranged in three or four widening coils (*see* Fig. 111).

Fig. 111. (a) The 'hour-glass' figure, fashionable around 1890-1896; (b) the less-sculptured and more graceful dress of the latter half of the 'Naughty Nineties'; (c) another example of the huge sleeves—sleeves such as these might well need the assistance of 'supports' to hold their shape; (d) the ruched felt shoulder support; (e) example of a 'sleeve-bustle'; the wire hoops are separated by four tapes, and the frame is made much on the same principle as the Chinese lantern.

The Victorian miss laid great store on the correct 'set' of her sleeves, but making love to her must sometimes have presented something of a problem—a flattened sleeve can be so revealing!

One of the main features of the dresses of this period was the number of flounces and furbelows that were neatly packed in under the hem (attached in tight layers to the edges of the petticoats), which seethed and swished like foam on a shingled shore as my lady sailed across the parquet flooring . . . or gathered up the dust in the city streets!

A good deal of art and artistry was needed to temptingly display these cascades of frill and frou-frou—as, for instance, when playing lawn-tennis . . . holding the racquet in one hand, and the skirt-train with the other—without giving so much as a glimpse of that forbidden ankle. . . . Oh, well, perhaps just a fleeting flash during the mixed doubles, to throw one's opponent's mind off his service!

But tennis and croquet were not the only games that occupied women's leisure moments, and it was during the 1890s that the 'new woman' was born. Self-reliant and self-sufficient, you will meet her in the early plays of Ibsen and Shaw, clamouring for freedom and equality of the sexes—with 'jobs for the girls' and 'Votes for Women'.

They took possession of offices, shops, businesses and factories, they smashed windows, and slashed Old Masters, and chained themselves to the railings outside the House of Commons... but though they ceased to be ladies, they never quite managed to be gentlemen!

Lillah McCarthy, a popular actress of the day, even invaded the Cabinet Room at No. 10, and with a stick of red grease-paint she scrawled 'Votes for Women' across Mr. Asquith's clean white blotting-pad . . . somewhat to his surprise, as he had invited her to lunch!

Sartorially, one of the most startling developments of women's demand for enfranchisement was the bicycle . . . and bloomers! (*see* Fig. 112). A few of the more 'womanly women' somehow managed to mount the saddle in full skirts, rather than risk exposing their nether limbs to public ridicule, holding up their trains and manipulating the handlebars at one and the same time. Yet, despite the comic cartoons of the day (vide *Punch*), bloomers had quite as much material in them as any skirt —and, in some cases, a good deal more!

Riding in the Row was another extremely popular exercise with some women—and far more dignified than the bicycle! In England, at any rate, women still rode side-saddle, though I have a photograph of an intrepid aunt of mine taken in the 1890s, that shows her sitting astride her mount, fearlessly cantering across Salisbury Plain.

Riding habits were short and tight, and put on over breeches and top boots, and worn with a corded-cotton stock. Gone was the topper and the flying veil of the 1870s and 1880s, and instead a flattish little black bowler was perched on the head, held on by hatpins or an elastic band under the bun at the back. But there was a small black face-veil, with large black 'spots', that was fixed round the base of the crown and pinned

Fig. 112. Lady in cycling 'bloomers', 1895. This nether garment was an invention of a Mrs. Bloomer, of New York, who introduced it as an example of 'rational dress for the enlightened woman'! The fashion, however, never caught on in England . . . except as a costume for cycling.

'"Is this the way to Wareham?"
She asked in voice refined.
"Bless me if I know, Mum,
I never wore that kind!"'

at the back, with the bottom front edge pulled forward and twisted into a little knot by the first finger and thumb, and then tucked in under the chin so that the veil fitted closely round the face. These spots before the eyes were supposed to enhance the beauty of the complexion . . . but they were very bad for the sight! Sometimes, instead of the spots, there was just one woven pattern on one side that rested upon the cheek, but it never became popular . . . it looked too much like a tattoo!

With the dawn of the Edwardian Era (1901-10) women's figures suddenly underwent a drastic change, due to the introduction of the 'straight-fronted' corset. Its close, vertical lines of strong whalebone (sometimes steel) which ran from top to base, while allowing for a lower bust, at the same time flattened the tummy and tightly compressed the hips.

Four suspenders hung down—two in front and two at the back—and to these the tops of the stockings were attached . . . thus dealing a death-blow to the 'garter', that relic of his 'conquests' which was treasured by so many a young man as knights of old prized their ladye's 'favour'. The Victorian Lancelot, however, did not wear it on his sleeve or round his hat . . . except, perhaps, on Boat Race Night! . . .

The 'vital statistics' in 1901 were around 38-inch bust, 26-inch waist, 42-45-inch hips, as against the 36 inches, 18 inches, 39 inches of the 1890s. But the most significant result of this corset was the new feminine 'stance', which became known as the 'kangaroo bend'—prominent, overhanging bust, flat, receding tummy and amply rounded behind . . . and those unfortunate meagre-chested, flat-bottomed girls (whose 'boyish' figures were to become all the rage during the years after the First World War) had to replenish Nature's deficiencies as best they could!

The collars of most day dresses of this period were high, with a silk or velvet neck-band (and in the early 1900s they were often 'boned' to keep them upright) with a largish bow or puff of stiff tulle decorating the back of the neck. Sometimes the top edge was finished off with a narrow, fluted frill, not unlike the ruffles worn by ladies in the sixteenth century.

The 'off-the-shoulder' evening dresses of the 1880s were now no longer possible, owing to the new high-shouldered sleeves, but some women made up for this (Paula in *The Second Mrs. Tanqueray* would undoubtedly have been one of them!) by wearing an extremely low-cut V, or heart-shaped *décolletée.*

The 'New Woman', of course, had no time for this sort of nonsense, and often wore a starched upright collar and black tie—just like a man—and I should 'dress' Miss Prism in *The Importance of Being Earnest* in this style, together with sizeable leg-of-mutton sleeves to her striped cotton blouse, worn with a plain, 'sensible' skirt, trailing to the ground. Act II of this play takes place in 'The Garden of the Manor House, Woolton', and she probably would have her straw 'boater' somewhere handy, and put it on for her walk 'as far as the schools and back' with Canon Chasuble.

Dresses were not usually provided with pockets, and many women wore a small silk or silver-link mesh bag, hanging at the side by a chain with a hook fastened into the waistband. In such a bag Lady Bracknell (in Act I of the same play) would have carried that all-important little book with its 'list of eligible, marriageable young men' . . . and if at any time you are producing this delightfully witty play, let me beg of you *not* to 'make-do' with a 3*d*. paper-back note-book—as I have seen done—because it should at least be leather-bound with, if possible, a metal clasp, with a socket for a little silver pencil at the back.

Around 1906-7 handbags in all shapes and sizes and materials became fashionable, and were large enough to carry all those mysterious articles without which so many women feel completely lost. Yet, whatever else they might have contained, any suspicion of 'make-up' as we understand the word today was strictly taboo. Only 'that kind of woman' . . . oh, and actresses! . . . wore paint in public, and it was then accepted as being more or less the badge of her profession—whichever one she'd chosen! The only 'aid' a girl was *permitted* to use was a *papier poudré* book, the leaves of which were impregnated with various shades of face powder, and with one of these—but only when she was quite, quite certain no one was looking!—she could try to do something about a shiny nose!

Jewellery during this period became less heavy and ornate, and small gold watches were often suspended from long chains, wound twice round the neck and hanging down to the waist, with the watch tucked into the belt or put into a 'watch-pocket' on the left breast. A watch might also hang from a gold or jewelled brooch, shaped like a ribboned bow and pinned below the shoulder. Wrist-watches did not come in until about 1911; at first they were very ungainly affairs, with the dials no smaller than a man's ordinary pocket watch.

Sometimes, instead of the watch at the end of the chain, there would be a small, round metal coin-purse, that opened with a spring. Of course, England was still on the Gold Standard then, and these containers were specially designed to carry sovereigns and half-sovereigns . . . and to wear and make use of such a purse in a play, set in the years immediately preceding the First World War, would provide a good production touch. They can often be found on sale in those antique jewellery shops in Church Street, Kensington.

Necklaces with heart-shaped lockets (containing a daguerreotype of her beloved or perhaps a lock of his hair), and bracelets with a workable padlock and key, were much in favour with young girls around the beginning of the present century.

Hairpins with imitation jewelled tops or combs with filigree flowers or butterflies attached to them were much worn with evening dresses, and were placed as high on top of the head as possible, in an attempt to make the wearer look taller! Dog-collars, too, made from several rows of pearls and diamonds—or paste brilliants—were a fashion that owed their early popularity to Queen Alexandra while she was still Princess of Wales. Today we call them 'chokers', but they looked most regal on a long, slender throat . . . and they also had their uses when the neck muscles were beginning to sag.

I have always imagined Lady Bracknell as wearing long, dingle-dangle ear-rings, but as a matter of fact the wearing of ear-rings had ceased to be so fashionable in the late 1890s and early 1900s, and, of course, nowadays, when it is so easy for a woman to screw them on, the custom for piercing the ear-lobes has practically died out (doctors used to charge a shilling for performing this service). For stage purposes, in any case, elaborate-type ear-rings are often suspended by means of strong cotton loops that go round the ears.

Real flowers—especially violets, that could then be bought for 1*d.* and 2*d.* a bunch—were an important accessory to both day and evening clothes, and I remember often seeing my mother tuck a bunch into her waist-belt, which is where they were most generally worn.

Stockings were still black—even when worn with white tennis shoes —and were woven in cotton, lisle or wool . . . and silk was still thought to be a sign of guilty splendour.

In novels and plays of those days many references are made to women's 'boots'. Usually they were black, and buttoned up the front or at the side, though some of them were laced. Black shoes were worn, too, but mostly by the more 'sensible' type of girl, and both boots and shoes had heels.

It was not until around 1911 that fancy shoes, low-cut and heeled and made in various materials and colours, came in for both day and evening occasions, and though black stockings—some with a patterned lace insertion over the instep—were still considered chic, some silk ones were worn in colours to match the shoes.

At the beginning of the period, the rather small, neatly dressed head of the later 1880s was still fashionable, but gradually the shape widened, becoming fuller, with the hair brushed straight back, and the sides brought up and combined with the rest of the hair into a bun on top— sometimes called the 'Psyche knot', after the Greek nymph whom Eros loved. The whole or at any rate the greater part of the ears was thus left uncovered, and a number of side and back combs, as well as a great many hairpins, were needed to keep the stray locks in place.

There was however, nothing arbitrary about this, and many women wisely followed the style that suited them best. Julia Neilson, for instance, wore her hair with a large bun placed halfway up the back of her head, with a row of little corkscrew curls nestling under it in the nape of her neck. She also kept a few wispy strands of hair shading her forehead. This style of hairdressing started a fashion that was widely imitated, as is so often the case when actresses lead the way, and my mother, who had been told she strongly resembled Miss Neilson, and therefore copied her whenever she could, dressed her own hair like this during the short period she was herself on the stage (*see* Fig. 113).

In the early 1900s many women wore their hair in a large 'bang' or 'pompadour' extending high above—and often out beyond—their fore-heads. The rest of the hair was then drawn back and twisted into a figure-8-shaped bun and worn low at the back . . . and a girl had to be very young, and have a very long neck, to do full justice to her profile under these conditions, and often the effect could be heightened by tying a narrow black velvet band round the throat (*see* Fig. 113).

In about 1903 it became fashionable for the front hair line to 'dip' down over one eye—a style that Marie Tempest made peculiarly her own, no matter what part she might be playing—and to achieve this effect the hair had to be 'dressed' over a sort of semicircular, sausage-roll pad, made from very fine wire mesh and thinly covered with artificial hair (of the right shade), which was light and airy to wear and could, moreover, be bent into whatever shape was required (*see* Fig. 113).

Camille Clifford, the original 'Gibson Girl' (so named after the character created by the American artist, Charles Dana Gibson), wore her luxuriant chestnut brown hair in this style in *The Belle of Mayfair*, but in her case, with the addition of a couple of extra 'rolls', piled one on top of the other (*see* Fig. 113).

At the beginning of the 1890s hats were small, with narrow brims, and set rather far back on the head. Small toques, too, were fashionable (another 'royal' lead) and were worn to fit fair and square over that knot on top of the head. By 1895, as the hair styles were beginning to get wider, toques increased in size, and the brims of the hats became broader and slanted more over the forehead. The height of most hats, too, was further increased by the monumental trimmings, flowers, ribbons, laces, bows, chiffon puffs and feathers—not just a quill or even a wing, but often the whole stuffed bird, which offers a grand opportunity not to be missed when designing a hat for Lady Bracknell or some similar character.

The 'New Woman', of course, often wore a man's plain felt trilby hat (which got its name from the drawings by another artist, George du Maurier in his novel, *Trilby*). With the severe, hard-brimmed straw boater, she might, rather incongruously, add a flower to the spotted veil.

With the elaborate 'pompadour' styles of hairdressing of the 1900s, many of the hats had ridiculously low crowns, with wide, frilly-edged brims that looked like huge, reversed meat-dishes that could never fit comfortably on any head . . . nor, indeed, were they intended to! They just sat flat on top of the hair, often extending several inches beyond it in front . . . or, if the hair was dressed more towards the back of the head, then jutting out behind (*see* Fig. 113).

These large hats often had a veil, either arranged to tightly frame in the face or to hang over the edge of the brim like a curtain that could be pulled up by both the hands and thrown back. This type of veil offered all sorts of possibilities for stage business—especially in those popular old Lyceum melodramas:

> *Enter a lady dressed entirely in black, with her hat draped in a thick, dark veil.*

Sir Hector: '. . . And who the devil are you?'

Lady (throwing back her veil): 'YOUR WIFE'!

The Curtain descends.

By 1907 the vogue for the large picture hat was at its height, and probably the largest and the best known of them all was *The Merry Widow* hat worn by lovely Lily Elsie.

Around 1908, however, a French hairdresser named Marcel introduced his famous 'wave', with the almost instant result that heads once more became small and trim, with the hair looking like a recently ploughed

Fig. 113. (a) The 'Julia Neilson' hair style; (b) the 'bang'; (c) the 'Marie Tempest' hair style; (d) the 'Gibson Girl'; (e) the 'Pompadour' and the sort of hat that went with it; (f) the 'pudding-basin' hat.

field! Naturally, hats shrank in proportion, and by the outbreak of the First World War had become rather like inverted pudding-basins, which hid three parts of a woman's face and made it sometimes a little difficult to recognize the girl you'd asked to meet you for tea outside Swan and Edgar's! (*see* Fig. 113).

PART VI

CHAPTER 16

Pantomime

Pantomiming (miming) is the oldest form of dramatic expression, but—as so often happens where research leads one back into the dawn of history—there are several opinions as to the origin and meaning of the word.

To our English minds it is sometimes confused (though quite wrongly) with the ancient Greek Pantomimus, a masked dancer, whose art consisted in telling his story by means of rhythmic movement entirely in dumb show (600-480 B.C.).

'Pantomime', however, is of Latin extraction, and means 'a player of all the parts'. In Imperial Rome (31 B.C.-A.D. 323) it described the performance of an actor who interpreted the tale, either solo or with the aid of a chorus. The plots were usually of a classical nature—in other words, 'the amours of the gods'—and, with the help of a 'three-faced' mask, the same player could portray Venus and her lover, Mars, with the jealous husband, Vulcan, surprising the guilty couple sporting in the long grass, greatly to the embarrassment of his wife and to the Olympian merriment of the lesser gods, slyly peeping through the bushes!

In this way, quite literally, the actor 'played all the parts', and in those days he had to be pretty spry at his job to keep the interest of an audience alive (and, incidentally, himself . . . if Nero happened to be out in front!).

Christmas pantomime as we know it in England is, of course, of much more recent date, harking back to the beginning of the eighteenth century, and had its origin in the *Commedia dell' Arte*, the dances of the Arlequins and the performances of the ragged, wandering players of the Paris fairs.

The plots at first were still classical, but around the 1800s the public began to tire of mythology, and dramatized fairy stories and nursery rhymes became the fashion instead, at first, only as short curtain-raisers to the main programme that followed, but later, as more elaborate scenery was used and more actors were introduced (with women sometimes playing the heroes!), they became of such length as to constitute the principal attraction, and the dances of the Arlequins (with Harlequin, Columbine and Pantaloon) dwindled into a more or less plotless epilogue known as the Harlequinade.

In the Harlequinade it was customary for Harlequin and Columbine to appear as eloping lovers, pursued by her husband (father or guardian), Pantaloon, and his blundering servant—at first Pierrot, but later Clown.

In the early years of the nineteenth century a good deal of horseplay was introduced, with the Clown becoming the chief character, shoplifting strings of sausages, with which Pantaloon, now his weak-witted accomplice, would be caught red-handed by the Policeman, the buttered slide for the angry Butcher to slip on, the pail of paste emptied over the Dandy's head, and the red-hot poker brandished by the Clown, and frequently laid to some purpose upon the unsuspecting trouser-seat, and the final 'spill and pelt' of vegetables, flung in street battle.

Joseph Grimaldi, as the Clown, became the most famous of the Drury Lane Harlequinaders, and even today clowns are called 'Joey' in affectionate memory of him.

The traditional costume for Harlequin is the close-fitting suit, patterned all over with bright-coloured (red, black, yellow and blue), diamond-shaped lozenges (derived from the patches on the rags worn originally in the *Commedia dell' Arte*), with a ruffle round his neck and wrists—and in some cases round his waist. Also retained from his early origin is Harlequin's tight, black velvet mask that covers the upper half of his face, and sometimes his head as well, like a cap . . . or, he can wear a triangular shaped white (or black) felt hat. His socks are white and his ballet shoes black.

Harlequin always carries a black or silver thin, flat, wooden lath or wand, which has the magic power to transfix anyone he slaps with it —until he chooses to release them by another tap.

The costume could be made by wearing tights and a close-fitting, round-necked, long-sleeved vest, on both of which the lozenge shapes could be painted with dyes, and a charming effect can be produced by outlining each pattern unit with a thin border in gold or silver paint. The frills would be of tarlatan, with perhaps a sequin or two here and there along the outer edge, and a silver waistband with a front buckle hides the join between vest and tights (*see* Fig. 114).

Columbine is usually dressed in conventional ballet costume, with a tight, white satin bodice—without sleeves or shoulder straps—and the most diminutive little skirt . . . actually no more than a stiffly-outstanding frill!

With this costume she wears a wreath of silver roses round her head, and white tights, with white satin ballet shoes.

During the eighteenth century Columbine was dressed in long

Regency skirts, with short, balloon-like puff sleeves and a very low-cut neck line (*see* Fig. 114).

The Clown of the Harlequinade was not dressed at all like the circus clown, but wore a tight-fitting, elbow-length-sleeved blouse over a long-sleeved under-vest. The body of this garment was white, and patterned in red spots or other designs (circles, triangles, lozenges, etc.), with the short sleeves in red and white stripes. With this he wore knee-length breeches, similarly striped, and white leggings (tights) with the designs

Fig. 114. (a) Modern Harlequin and Columbine: (b) a 'Regency' period 'Columbine'; (c) Harlequin with hat and wide ruffle; (d & e) types of the old-fashioned Pantaloon and Clown; (f) the more modern type of clown.

repeated up the inner and outer sides of the legs. His shoes were white leather, and there was a wide, buckled belt round his waist and frills round his neck and edging the short sleeves and breeches.

On his head he wore a bald wig, with a stiffened 'pigtail' standing upright in the middle, with a ring of white or red curly hair around the back and sides, ending in a beard with a long point. His eyebrows were very bushy, and he had a red, turned-up nose (false) and red patches on his otherwise dead-white face. His mouth was wide and red, and his laughing eyes outlined in black.

In some old prints Clown is depicted wearing a laughing half-mask, and in others he is shown wearing a loose, short-sleeved, red-and-white-patterned outer coat with long pointed tails ending in tassels (*see* Fig. 114).

Several explanations have been put forward to account for that backbone of the British pantomime, the female Principal Boy . . . one being that no man would care to sing the sort of songs usually provided or to behave in the manner that used to be expected from the traditional Principal Boy.

Another theory is that the custom originated from the Roman Feast of Saturnalia (which took place at a time approximately corresponding with our Christmas season), in which the masters became the slaves and the slaves became the masters, and the normal order of society was reversed, with a general interchange of costume by both sexes. This would account for male comedians playing the Dame roles—another topsy-turveydom well suited to the spirit of pantomime.

Augustus Harris, whose name was so closely associated with Drury Lane Theatre, demanded a 'ripe opulence' from his Principal Boys, of whom Queenie Leighton, with her egg-timer figure, Harriet Vernon and Nellie Stewart were three famous examples. There is an amusing story told of one aspirant to pantomime fame (as Dandini in *Cinderella*), whose feminine statistics did not quite fulfil Mr. Harris's ideas of what a 'Second Boy' should look like, and she was sent up to the wardrobe to augment her deficiences, reappearing a few minutes later the proud possessor of no mean bust! "Oh, God—*no*!", screamed Mr. Harris, tearing his hair. "That's the Principal Boy's *bottom*!"

Pantomime reached its heyday at Drury Lane between 1879 and 1896, with Dan Leno and Herbert Campbell in the leads, and Augustus Harris often engaged as many as 400 to 500 in the cast, including several well-known variety artists, and fathers and mothers (who would never have deigned to enter a music-hall) came, and brought the children . . . and thoroughly enjoyed the warm, vulgar, typically British fun!

Since those days there has been less insistence on 'curves', with such svelte Principal Boys as Phyllis Neilson-Terry (Prince Charming), Fay Compton (Robin Hood) and Mona Vivian, who created those loveable little gamins, Humpty, Hop and Robbie Crusoe, whose adventures from poverty to riches so endeared her in the hearts of young and old alike.

There had never before been anyone quite like her . . . nor will there be again since she retired.

But tastes change, and now it would seem that time-honoured custom for a female 'Boy' has been set aside by Harold Fielding, who in 1958, at the Coliseum Theatre, London, presented Bruce Trent as Prince Charming, in *Cinderella* (though the Ugly Sisters were still played by men), with Bob Monkhouse, as Aladdin at the same theatre in 1959, and last Christmas a revival of *Cinderella* at the Adelphi.

Pantomime offers the amateur a most elastic proposition, for a production that can be either elaborate and spectacular (such as *The Sleeping Beauty*, usually set and costumed in medieval times) or plain and straight-forward, based on one or more of the better-known nursery rhymes, round which he can build his own show to suit himself—and his pocket—*Simple Simon, Little Red Riding-hood* or *Goody Two-shoes*, the original story for which was written by Oliver Goldsmith!

All these delightful fairy-story characters can be dressed in old English country life costumes . . . Dolly Varden (*circa* 1870) for the girls short, flower-patterned skirts, with frilly little puffed sleeves and low, square-cut neck-lines, worn with low-crowned, wide-brimmed straw hats—rather like large soup-plates, tilted to one side—tied on under the chin with a broad silk ribbon. The short, little hooped dresses that so many girls are wearing today (with the addition of side-panniers in a different coloured or patterned material) would be just the thing to use.

Or there is the dainty Kate Greenaway (*circa* 1800), which was high-waisted, with short, puffed sleeves, and lace-edged pantalettes reaching to the ankles and peeping bewitchingly below the hem of the flower-spotted dress (longer than the Dolly Varden and without the panniers). A little mob-cap or, alternatively, a sun-bonnet and black or white lace mittens and white socks and black ballet shoes would complete the charming picture.

For the lads of the village, use bright cotton smocks—a bit shorter than the usual farmhouse variety, and hanging loosely or tucked into the tops of shorts or buckled knee-breeches—or dress them in deep, wide-collared shirts, dyed to some attractive colour scheme, open at the necks or tied with huge, floppy bows. Coloured waistcoats (left unbuttoned) could be worn with these shirts—or with white shirts—with bright-coloured stockings or buttoned gaiters and leather shoes (house slippers) with bows, buckles or pompoms.

If tights are needed, those gay-hued playtime stockings that are quite inexpensive and so much the vogue these days would be very suitable, or, if economy is the password, use men's long-legged woollen or cotton pants (dyed) with an elastic band under the foot and the top tightly braced up to prevent wrinkling. Caps, berets, and old felts, or straw beach-hats, set at rakish angles on their tousled heads, will give a finishing touch.

Amongst the more elaborate and ambitious pantomimes are *Cinderella* and *Aladdin*, both of which are gay and colourful, with good strong plots that need little building-up.

Cinderella is the heroine of an almost universal fairy story, and our English version is based upon Perrault's *Cindrillon (Little Cinders Girl)* and it is interesting to find that the traditional business of the crystal slipper which she drops on the Palace stairs is due entirely to a *mis*-translation of the original, in which the words *pantoufle en vair* (a *fur* slipper) are mistaken for *pantoufle en verre* . . . of glass!

It has been suggested that in the first place the story originated in a Nature myth, Cinderella being the dawn oppressed by the night clouds (the Ugly Sisters) and finally rescued by the sun (Prince Charming), which might make a charming subject for a ballet or mime.

Cinderella is usually played in early Georgian costume (1700-50), with flaring, full-skirted coats, longish, flower-patterned waistcoats, and knee-breeches, white stockings, and black-buckled shoes (for the men) and hooped dresses, with slim-fitting, long-waisted bodices (for the women). Such costumes may be a bit expensive to hire, and perhaps not quite so easy to make . . . though, of course, it *can* be done (*see* Fig. 115). There is, however, nothing to prevent one from transposing this charming tale into some other, and easier, costume period. Heaven knows they do it with Shakespeare, so why not with pantomime?

Another possible drawback to *Cinderella* is the crystal coach and ponies, but even this problem is not insuperable if one is willing to compromise, and the difficulty could be got round by substituting a sparkling, sequin-studded sedan-chair (which would be quite in period), building it round an ordinary 'bent-wood' with panels of cut-out hard-board. Two footmen can then easily life the chair by means of the side-poles and carry Cinders off to the Ball.

If white, powdered wigs are used, they can quite simply be made at home from 'animal wool', which—as has been stated—can be inexpensively bought in packets from the chemist's. It is beautifully soft and silky, and infinitely preferable for this purpose to crêpe hair, and the best way to use it is to attach (sew) it to the thin, white gauze foundation cap, and women can mask the front edge with an attractive little row of ringlet curls across the forehead, and men, of course, could do the same thing (even a male Prince Charming, I am sure, would raise no objections). Or if a narrow strip of the thin, gauze wig foundation is allowed to extend about ¼ inch beyond the front hair-line, it can be gummed down on to the forehead (using white hard spirit varnish from the ironmonger, which is generally found to be more reliable than the made-up bottles of spirit gum) and then carefully covered over with grease-paint to hide the join. This is the method employed with costume wigs in the film studios, and occasionally it can be spotted in a close-up! On the stage, however, it should be completely invisible from a short distance.

Fig. 115. (a) 'Prince Charming', in 'Cinderella'; (b) 'Cinderella', herself. It isn't every day one meets a Prince . . . even if 'he' is only a 'Principal Boy'. . . .; (c) diagrams for cutting the 'Prince's' coat. These are *not* drawn to any special scale, and are only intended to indicate the separate pieces required, and each would, of course, be cut double. I. Front panel of the coat. II. 'Gore' to give fullness. III. Side panel. IV. Back panel. V. Under portion of sleeve. VI. Upper section of sleeve. VII. The cuff. VIII. The pocket lapel.

Aladdin, dramatized by H. J. Byron in about 1860, is, of course, a tale of old China, and the costumes should not be difficult to design, being mostly variations of our old friend, 'the tunic', and with very little adjustment a pyjama suit can be adapted to represent almost any Chinese costume . . . and the Oriental make-up should do the rest.

The collar must be stiffened so that it stands upright, and the front fastening of the jacket arranged to cross over the chest from left to right, so that it appears to be done up near the right arm, with a coloured (sometimes also patterned) border strip added and repeated round the collar and edges of the sleeves. These can be either tight or wide—bell-shaped—an effect that can be got by opening the pyjama arm seams, and inserting a wide 'gore'.

The trousers should be made to narrow from the knees downwards, where they are caught in tightly round the ankles with a repeat of the coloured border band. But, for the sake of contrast and variety in the stage picture, a few of them should be left wide at the base . . . though, of course, the tapering ones look more attractive! White socks and black felt slippers, without heels, should be worn, with the characteristic white line all round just above the level of the sole. This, of course, can be sewn on with white tape.

Leichner foundation grease-paint No. 8B, highlighted with bright chrome yellow and shaded with a lake liner, No. 25 or No. 31, is the make-up for Chinese characters . . . or Max Factor Pan-stik No. 8A shaded with a No. 6 liner.

For half of the pantomime, Aladdin is a poor boy, and therefore his tunics can be plain and simple in unpatterned red, green or dark blue, with the trousers in a contrasting colour. But if Aladdin has a 'good pair of pins', I imagine 'she' would insist on dispensing with the trousers altogether . . . in favour of tights! (*see* Fig. 116).

On 'his' head he would wear one of those wide-brimmed, conical hats, tied under the chin with cords—the sort of thing you can buy at almost any seaside kiosk, and if you look you might even find one in that cupboard under the stairs (hat, not kiosk!). But in any case these conical hats are quite easy to make out of thin cardboard by cutting out a circle, and then cutting a quarter segment out of that, and joining the cut edges either by gluing, sewing, or pressing through those brass paper-fasteners. The hat is then painted with enamel or covered with some shiny material (*see* Fig. 116).

As Aladdin's fortunes improve, so his costumes should become more and more elaborate, with tassels added to the ends of the long, pendent sleeves, and lots of gold or silver embroidery and trimming on the tunic, with perhaps a fringe of little bobbles round the edge of the hat . . . or tiny, tinkling bells might be a novel idea.

Abanaza, the Wicked Uncle of the story, is generally represented as a Persian merchant, with the Jinnee of the Lamp, depicted as an Indian in turban and loin-cloth (and nothing else!), with his body painted green (Leichner grease-paint Nos. 334-6, or Max Factor Pan-cake or Pan-stik No. 1,742), with green sequins stuck one on each eyelid . . . and, of course, the taller and thinner he is the better!

In professional pantomimes, The Slave of the Ring is usually played by a scantily, though glitteringly, dressed girl, who performs an acrobatic solo dance in the Ballet of the Jewels in the cave scene. But, of course, there is no reason why the part should not be played by a man, who can also be a Persian or an Egyptian, but *not* a Chinese.

The Emperor and his daughter, the Princess Badroubadour (whom, of course, Aladdin marries) are Chinese, with the Emperor dressed as a conventional mandarin in a long robe (for which a colourful, richly decorated dressing-gown over silk pyjamas trousers could be worn), with a plain, black, round-shaped hat, something like a pill-box, only higher and wider round the top than at the base. This can be cut out from cardboard or buckram, and covered with shiny black sateen (*see* Fig. 116).

The Princess would also wear a longish rather tight tunic and tapering trousers underneath. Her sleek black hair would have a long forehead fringe (not too thick) and a centre parting running from the front of her forehead to the nape of her neck, the hair being pulled tightly to the sides and plaited into a flat ring over each ear, and a circlet of bright little flowers pinned on either side of her head. Such a wig can be made from either crêpe hair or black Silko, which can be bought in 1-oz. hanks and then sewn to a black gauze foundation cap (*see* Fig. 116).

The Courtiers (men) would be dressed like their Emperor, only less ornamentally so, and to introduce variety into their costumes some can wear shorter tunics and trousers. Court ladies would also wear longish tunics and trousers—some tight and others loose, and of different colours and patterns.

Aladdin's mother, Widow Twankey, must naturally exaggerate any comic potentials in her costume (she runs a Chinese laundry) except, possibly, in the Finale, when, sharing in her son's good luck, she can, if she likes, outshine them all.

The naming of this old lady, by the way, derives from the tea-clippers which at the time the story was written were racing homewards from the East, laden with cargoes of 'twankay'.

The usual chorus of villagers, etc., and other characters in the story pretty well follow the costume pattern already described, in as great a variety of bright colours as possible, with a few in black here and there to point the contrasts, but, of course, none of them at any time as elaborate as Aladdin in his best, who in the Finale must be completely gorgeous in his black silk tunic, plentifully besprinkled with diamanté, with cloth of gold or silver trousers—or sheer, leg-embracing black silk tights! His hat should now be ablaze with sequins, and he ought to wear black flat-soled slippers, gaily embroidered with jewels . . . I say 'ought' because every Aladdin I've ever seen comes tripping on for the Finale in the highest of high heels!

Robinson Crusoe is another popular favourite, which was first dramatized by Sheridan from the well-known story by Daniel Defoe.

In this pantomime we come up against the difficulty of the cannibals, who are generally fitted out with brown stockinette 'bodies and legs' (black for Man Friday). Far and away the best thing to do, of course, is

Fig. 116. (a) 'Aladdin' and his Princess; (b) suggested costume for 'Wishee-Washee'; (c) the Emperor; (d) simple costume for the Chorus; (e) diagram for making 'Aladdin's' conical hat.

to stain the bodies and faces with a solution of permanganate of potash (from any chemist: just melt the crystals in hot water and apply the liquid with a small, tight sponge, washing it off after the performance with soap and warm water).

But as the chorus gents are also required to appear as villagers, sailors, pirates and grandees in other scenes, they cannot very well commence the show with browned faces, and yet they won't have the time between appearances to do more than quickly smear over their faces and necks with brown grease-paint (Leichner Nos. 11 or 12 or Max Factor Nos. 1, 2 and 2,880 Pan-cake or Nos. 16 or 17 grease-paint). For speed, I think the Max Factor method may be preferable, because with their Pan-cake one can put one make-up on top of another, provided each is darker than the one before it. So that if the desert island cannibal scenes can be so arranged as to come at the end of the first half, there is plenty of time for making-up again during the interval for other appearances in the second half. The cannibals will need short, gaily-coloured raffia skirts and black, fuzzy-wuzzy (crêpe hair) wigs, and white gloves can be worn to save having to make up the hands.

Robbie's fur coat for the island scenes can be designed from a white skin hearth-rug (pinched when the landlady isn't looking) or, alternatively, quite a good effect can be produced with a mixture of white and off-white thick rug-wool, arranged in small, loose, overlapping loops tightly sewn on to a 'foundation body' . . . leaving a few short strands hanging down here and there at the lower edge.

If funds are very limited, one can often get away with using the fluffy side of ordinary white surgical lint if it is delicately strippled (sprayed) over with a very pale grey dye. Lint can be bought in quite wide pieces, and it has a definitely downy sheen which can be made to look reasonably like white fur . . . from a distance! But please remember that in the original *Robinson Crusoe* story his coat was made from white goat-skin, and resist the temptation to imitate leopard, tiger or mink . . . or any of the other popular furs! (*see* Fig. 117).

The fur hat is usually high and round and pointed at the top, with perhaps a bright cockade at the side . . . a few white hen's feathers, begged from the poulterer round the corner and then dyed green, with red tips, may save you the otherwise painful necessity of plucking the parrot!

Like Aladdin and most of the other heroes of pantomime, Robbie Crusoe must be fabulously dressed for the Finale, which, anyway, is little more than an excuse for the principals to march down a long flight of stairs and take a well-deserved bow. In *Robinson Crusoe* the cast includes Polly Perkins, Robbie's girl-friend, Will Atkins, the villian of the story, who tries to scuttle the ship and is therefore usually dressed as a pirate, and Mrs. Crusoe (Dame), who unaccountably accompanies her son to the desert island!

Pantomimes that depend for their plots upon animals can hardly be

Fig. 117. (a) 'Robinson Crusoe', an old time Principal Boy; (b) suggested make-up for 'Man Friday'—the necklace of 'teeth' is made from date stones that have been painted with white enamel; (c) a couple of hungry cannibals!

put on without the necessity of hiring the animal skins, and these can work out quite expensive. Such shows are: *Dick Whittington* (cat and rat), *Puss in Boots* (cat), *Beauty and the Beast* (bear), *Goldilocks* (*three* bears!), *Little Red Riding-hood* (wolf) and *Mother Goose* (bird) . . . even *Old Mother Hubbard* needs a dog, and Jack, in addition to his beanstalk, has a cow. Dick, being a historical character, should be dressed in his period (1350). Sir Richard Whittington, who really became 'thrice Lord Mayor of London', lies buried in that white-walled church just beyond London Bridge.

Mother Goose was specially written for Dan Leno at Drury Lane by J. Hickory Wood, and it was the first pantomime I ever saw—and what a spectacle it was! Devised in the true panto tradition of the Lane, there were transformation scenes, mammoth ballets, traps, lifts, 'graves' . . . and a Harlequinade to finish up with.

Completely incongruous, and played against a background of topical chorus numbers, 'patriotic scenes' and acrobatics, pantomime is a form of entertainment that has in our time added a new definition to the language, wherein a 'state of utter confusion' can be described as 'a proper pantomime'!

Tail-Piece

Before we say '*Au revoir*', let me just quickly remind you once more of the salient points in costume-designing and making:

(i) In a period costume intended for the stage it is *the general impression*, the easily and quickly recognized character—or characteristic—that is of far more importance than precise detail and slavish imitation of the original.

(ii) Make all your patterns and designs as bold and large as possible (small patterns are lost at a distance), and keep the colours as clear and uninvolved as you can. And another thing. Too many colours together, presented at one and the same time, defeat their own ends . . . and, what is more, they worry the eye of the beholder.

(iii) Never neglect to offer *contrast* in colour and design. And in creating a costume, don't let yourself be carried away by the beauty of your own work, but remember *practicality*, and don't forget the poor actor who has to wear it, and *move about* in it, sit down in it, lie down in it and perhaps even 'die' in it.

(iv) Remember the drastic tricks coloured lighting can play with the colours in materials, and where possible, when choosing them, try them out under the actual lighting combinations you will have to contend with.

(v) Finally, in designing a costume for a basic wardrobe bear in mind both its present use—and its future usefulness—and use strong, plain materials that will stand up to the wear and tear of repeated washing, cleaning and remodelling.

And so—with my blessing—for the present I must leave you.

Good dressmaking. . . .

Bibliography

Medieval Costume in England and France. By Mary G. Houston (A. & C. Black).

English Costume. By Dion Clayton Calthorp (A. & C. Black).

Historic Costume for the Stage. By Lucy Barton (A. & C. Black).

Costume Design and Making. By Mary Fernald and E. Shenton (A. & C. Black).

Historic Costume. By Nevil Truman (Isaac Pitman & Sons, Ltd.).

Royal Portraits (with an Introduction and Notes). By R. H. Wilenski (Faber & Faber).

Dressing the Play. By Norah Lambourne (A Studio Publication).

The British Museum Guide to Greek and Roman Life.

The Oxford Companion to the Theatre. Edited by Phyllis Hartnoll (Oxford University Press).

Fanfare for Elizabeth. By Edith Sitwell (Macmillan).

Greek Dress. By Ethel B. Abrahams (John Murray).

The Story of Prehistoric and Roman Britain. By C. W. Airne (Sankey, Hudson & Co.).

The Story of Medieval Britain. By C. W. Airne (Sankey, Hudson & Co.).

The Story of Tudor and Stuart Britain. By C. W. Airne (Sankey, Hudson & Co.).

The Story of Hanoverian and Modern Britain. By C. W. Airne (Sankey, Hudson & Co.).

The Bayeux Tapestry. By Eric Maclagan (King Penguin Books).

The Holy Bible.

The Apocrypha.

Index

F

G

H

P

T